The Wanderers

THE WANDERERS

The Saga of Three Women who Survived

Ingrid Rimland

Publishing House
St. Louis

To my father, exiled to Siberia in 1941

This is fiction, gleaned and condensed from the driftage of history.

Concordia Publishing House, St. Louis, Missouri
Copyright © 1977 Concordia Publishing House
MANUFACTURED IN THE UNITED STATES OF AMERICA

Library of Congress Cataloging in Publication Data

Rimland, Ingrid, 1936–
    The wanderers.

    I. Title.
PZ4.R5766Wan [PS3568.I39]   813'.5'4   77-24290
ISBN 0-570-03266-0

Book One
Katya
[1914—1941]

1

When Johann Klassen communicated with his God, he always did so in High German. He would have thought it sheer heresy to talk to his Lord in the Low German that his forefathers had brought to Russia more than a century ago when they had followed the beckoning of Catherine the Great. Even though twelve decades of close-knit living in the Ukraine had polished these diphthonged sounds into a smooth and comforting language, Low German was reserved for everyday use—to speak to Susanna, to admonish his children, to chat across the neighbor fence when the day's work was done and twilight lingered for hours in the pungent air. But High German was the language of his Creator—the language of the Bible, the hymnbook, the daily discipline calendar sheets with which to start the day— a mighty and impressive language that wielded power and determination and was as sharp and cutting and as upheaving as the blade of his plow which furrowed his land.

"For those who love God, all things shall turn out for the best," he now muttered to himself, a little awkwardly, yet savoring the affirmation of his faith, for he was a strong as well as a sensitive man, keenly aware of propriety. He was also, he knew, at this hour a man in need of divine reassurance, for Jasch Kovalsky, having returned from the market of Melitopol, had brought to his village the tale of Sarajevo's assassination.

"Sarajevo?" the settlers had asked, only mildly perturbed. "Imagine! To permit bullets to fly into the very middle of a bone-dry, sun-drenched harvest day . . . How dangerously negligent will worldly leaders be!"

"Sarajevo," Jasch, the bearer of ominous news, had repeated, and had added, in passing: "And German loyalties in Russian wars . . ."

The elder sighed from worry and relief at having found the words to touch the root of his concern. Jasch and his constant oracles of doom! Why take them seriously? But to be sure, tomorrow his sermon would have to deal once more with God's eternal benediction. It was an easy topic to cover, and fitting as well in times such as these, when divided loyalties confused the hearts of too many Mennonite youths. All this afternoon he had struggled with what he would say—how he would put across to his own hot-headed sons this certainty that was so firmly anchored in his heart.

Yes, he would remind them once again of God's unwavering support, which lay obviously and for all to see upon His people. Records were kept in his church's archives, telling posterity of those times when the benevolent Czarina herself had come and driven through the Mennonite villages in a buggy drawn by six black horses, and had smiled and waved to the children of those who had come in covered wagons from the Vistula Delta.

"This land I have set aside to be devoured by the German plow," she had explained to her stern-faced companions, spreading a map over her knees. "I dream of filling the entire landscape around the Black Sea with diligent, enduring German people."

His grandfather was among the first who had signed their names into the pages of the life of the *Gemeend*. He had taken care to pass this story on to his sons, who then in turn had told it to their children. Johann Klassen knew it well by heart; he had heard it many times himself when he had been a boy. Not always had their homeland been as lovely as today, when village after prosperous village lay spread out over the countryside, all but submerged in orchards bent with fruit. His parents had handed down the story of his people's hardest beginnings, when their eyes had first fallen upon the desolate plains of the Ukraine—a desert without tree or bush, dry and fissured, barren to the touch. More than one generation of Menno's numerous descendants had sunk into an early grave before the flatlands had yielded to the German farmers' calloused hands.

From the mother colonies the villages had radiated out into the farthest distances of Russia. One could still see the traces of this movement on the map. It must have been like the unfolding of a German *zwieback* dough—fermenting and growing and spreading and feeding on honesty and perseverance and one's unwavering trust in God. Where it spread, it hardened and stuck. The best and richest soil was soon in Mennonite hands—village after village receiving not only a German name but an orderly number as well, for order was highly revered.

The elder's thoughts turned briefly to the memories of those years when his people had continued to search for inexpensive virgin land, to satisfy the ever-present issue: what to do with the generations that pushed at the seams of the mother colonies? One child after another had filled the narrow sleeping rooms, and untold worries had come of that, for here and there—though not too often, to be sure!—a child of good old stock and solid parentage had been foolishly lured into the Russian cities and been sucked up by the Slavic blood and been lost to its people forever.

A firm resolution began to take shape in Johann Klassen's heart: "I will say it loudly, and I will not back down: 'Has not each one of us felt this responsibility to be the very center of our existence since the days our forefathers were called upon to draw life's riches from Russian acres? We could not have done what we have done, had we given in to pressure and sacrificed our *Vaterland's* bonds. It is an obligation our ancestors placed squarely into the very middle of our lives—to be a model and example to the ignorant Russian peasants who live hidden and furtively in low-roofed, mud-plastered huts among the edges of our settlements . . . '"

He sighed deeply from such concentrated thinking, feeling in the very marrow of his bones: "This is where it counts. This is where we really live; this is the core of our being. For more than a century we have kept our language immaculate so that we could lead an immaculate life. How could we ever relinquish such riches!"

From the steppe came the spicy scent of cut grass and chickweed. Traces of the sunset still colored the tips of the locust trees, and stillness held the air.

Jasch Kovalsky walked slowly through Waldheim, preoccupied in his own fashion. A Mennonite legend was on his mind—a tongue-in-cheek saying that the settlers themselves were fond of recounting when feeling secure in their folkish cohesion, cemented together by an unblemished conscience, hard work, the Bible in every home, the sky above and their bountiful soil beneath their feet. He had heard it from his mother many times when he had been a little boy:

"When the Good Lord created all denominations, there—in the very first row, spread-legged,—stood a thick-skulled, heavy man, striving for more than his share of attention. The wise Creator, mingling with his kin, tapped him gently on the shoulder: 'Move over a bit so that others have space ... ' The Mennonite, without checking who bothered him thus, had shrugged off the Lord's admonishing hand, replying with haughty irritation: 'Who's trying to push me around?'"

Jasch smiled a thin, tentative smile, thinking of his mother's special brand of bitterness. He had done his best for many years to put her out of his mind. Not that what happened to her in her youth had altogether been her fault, although a goodly portion of her misfortunes, he had to admit reluctantly, had certainly been brought about by her own trifling, frivolous heart.

"I was born poor; my parents died young," she had lamented many a time. "I was passed from hand to hand, from farm to farm, at the mercy of the *Gemeend,* never permitted to grow any roots." She was known to have been a foolish girl, too vain about her dark eyes, her shimmering blond hair, too eager to catch up on life's promises. In her yearning she forgot to compensate with virtue what she so clearly lacked in riches.

One of the traveling gypsies had done her in with little effort on his part and even less regret.

Jasch hated gypsies. He hated these creatures with more than a passion—he hated their flat, four-cornered faces, their widely-set cheekbones, their bland, beardless chins. He heartily agreed with the village elders that they were a plague upon the land, as obnoxious as the sparrows in the spring, appearing each year at the outskirts of the settlements, hoisting their blankets and lighting their fires and lying in wait with casual assurance to prophesy a rosy future to the giggling brides of the year. Young and brazen, so gossip had it, his mother was lured into a tent to catch a glimpse of what life held in store, and had emerged sentenced to years of disgrace behind sunflower plants and ever thicker-growing weed.

There had been rumors from the beginning, as rumors were always quick to flourish when female virtue was suspect. Only a woman like Susanna Klassen—herself beyond a flicker of reproach!—could still afford to turn a disbelieving ear to the gossip that grew in shape and substance by the day:

"The way she pleats her skirts about her waist . . . "

"Her footsoles are flat upon the ground . . . "

"And her eyelids are drooping from tears . . . "

"Nothing but gossip," Susanna had staunchly insisted, putting a matronly arm around the beleaguered girl.

But not even Susanna was really surprised when late in the year she found herself opening her door to an urgent knock from the outside. She had reached out for the girl and drawn her in from out of the rain, urging her to take off her clothes and to wrap herself in the warm sheepskin that hung on the wall by the fire. But the girl had backed away. Therefore Susanna had made her a cup of chicory coffee, strong and hot and black and bitter, and had had to be satisfied that the girl, after a while, would permit her to pull off her stockings to dry by the stove. By the time the evening prayers were to be said, her silent visitor, holding onto her coat despite the fact that the fire made perspiration pour off her face in strings of beady rivulets, had fallen into an exhausted sleep, and Susanna had said to her uneasy husband, pushing him firmly out of the kitchen:

"I will have to stay with her throughout the night."

Jasch never lived down the stark, humiliating realization that he was helped to life behind Aunt Susanna's cleanly swept, whitewashed oven.

13

Ohm Klassen, in Christian concern, had seen to it that the girl was given a little hut on his land. There she could fend for herself and the child, close to the eyes of the *Gemeend* so that her life might serve as a lesson to bird-witted hearts. In time, she had married Ivan, a Ukrainian in the employ of the elder Klassen's stables, although to the end of her days, she had always mumbled her maiden name to identify herself and her child.

In defiance—of what?—Jasch had taken the name of Kovalsky.

His parents, he remembered, behaved like a pair of stubborn mules. Their Sunday afternoon walks, reserved to vent their pent-up anger, were keenly scrutinized behind starched curtains along the village street, for in their frequent harsh arguments they would loudly call each other names in broadest daylight that others would not dare to think at night. The family had all but drowned in debt, for Ivan's two scurvied horses could barely pull the plow to furrow the tiny patch of sunflowers and potatoes behind their house. His mother had taken to washing and mending for Susanna's growing family, but her iron would smoke, her wash board would be rusty, the pulley of her well would squeak disgracefully from lack of oil.

The village women, with one voice, became more sharply disapproving of their fallen sister as the years went on. Why was it that here and there a button was constantly missing? Why did her skirt show a rip in the back? Why did the little skinny bastard tyke have to walk to school with broken, knotted laces in his shoes? Why this? Why that? Why in the name of common sense? Why was it she never learned to bake, the irresponsible Russian slut?

"Either her *zwieback* are raw and sticky in the middle, or the crust is charred black, or she forgets to close the windows so that the dough collapses from the draft . . . "

Her sins were many, indeed. Her slovenly life became such an irritant to Aunt Susanna's infallible sense of order that one morning—armed with three chunks of soap, a broom, a pail, a huge soft rag, and more than just plain resolution—she finally

14

determined to set matters straight. She later told her neighbors left and right that upon entering the darkened hut, what but a slightly tilted mirror was the very first thing she should see? And there was straw on the floor in her kitchen, carelessly piled in Russian fashion around the stove. And a calf was dozing by the fire. Yes, there was a bed, a table, and two chairs. The cupboards, she discovered, were strewn with the crumbs of the previous week. The windows on the inside, she informed her neighbors primly, were painted a very gaudy blue, but they were narrow and low to the earth—and blind at that, fly-blackened, greasy to the touch.

Slowly working backwards, she had swept cobwebs and dead spiders from under the bed, along with a forgotten Easter egg, although by now the year was far into September. On her way out, she had even cut back a handful of watermelon creepers that had grown over the steps, and had gone home and scrubbed her fingernails and sighed and shaken her head for days at the memory of what she had seen.

After this visit, for unexplained reasons, Jasch's mother had ceased to come to the Mennonite church. She wore an embroidered Ukrainian blouse the following Sunday as she readied herself to drive to Melitopol to acquire a tiny *Ikona*—a sweetly smiling figurine which she foolishly cherished for the rest of her days, decorating it with saintly pictures, candles, and embroidered pieces of cloth on which she continued to squander her kopecks the years before she died quite suddenly from an infection in her finger.

Jasch still kept the *Ikona* hidden in a drawer, knowing that to this day, it was a matter of deep personal grief to Aunt Susanna to realize that it was possible for someone at the very doorstep of the elder Klassen's church to fall addicted to Greek Orthodox incense and thus ignore the true Savior Jesus Christ—that it was possible despite his efforts to be caught by the glitter and gaudiness of Russian churches which made eyes hurt and hearts heavy from shallow-witted gloss.

Thus, Jasch grew up with a badly split soul.

15

It was Aunt Susanna who patiently taught him to pray in High German, but he heartily cussed in Russian when out of her sight. From the Ukrainian Ivan he learned how to spit a perfect circle of sunflower seeds around his chair by the oven so as to show indifference to one's meager life; but it was Ohm Klassen who undid such valuable teaching by a mere generous nod of his head permitting him to cleanse and tidy the horses for the day of the Lord so that not the tiniest speck of dust or chaff would cling to their manes and tails—for nothing but the piercing satisfaction of a menial job well accomplished.

Along with the twins, Jasch was permitted to read the German Bible in Klassens' summer room on Sunday afternoons, his hour to be invited as a regular guest to the whitest bread and cake, to hot aromatic coffee, to golden butter poured over juicy chicken legs chilled in the depths of the cellar. But early next day, he knew full well, he would have to knock on Aunt Susanna's kitchen door where she would wait with a wet, soapy towel, poised to scrutinize his ears for hidden dirt.

There were times when he would try, obliquely, to get revenge. He had his own defenses, to be sure. He was, for example, full to the brim with hair-raising stories of ghosts and of witches which could be cleverly used to frighten his playmate Katya out of her wits:

"The soot in the chimney has caught fire," he would say ominously.

"Three sparrows have fallen out of their nests."

"Our cow, this morning, was giving bloody milk."

"And I saw a yellow cat chase a big black dog around the corner . . ."

He was careful to tease and taunt, hint but never tell, feeling shivers of guilty satisfaction when he saw her grow stiff with excitement and fear and cling to his neck in childish fright. At night, he would replenish his imagination listening to Ivan's deep, ringing, beautiful voice as he sang his Ukrainian songs— songs that were mellow with sadness and deep as the night, full

16

of a poignant sorrow that told of the cruel misfortunes of the ones who always lost in their struggle.

The melodies would bring tears of self-pity to his eyes, and at times both he and Ivan would weep convulsively. Were they destined to lose out to the righteous and strong, who were consistently served life's riches? Sitting closely together, the man and the boy would spin stories, all with a moral tucked onto the end, all designed to make up for a harsh and bitter life, mysteriously permitting the little man his triumphant, victorious hour of revenge and equalization.

But there was also a crisp, clear morning when Jasch, a little boy of ten, scrubbed clean to the roots of his hair in honor of the New Year that shone brightly through the windows, marched up to Aunt Susanna's kitchen, threw open the door, and imitating Ukrainian custom, flung a handful of grain onto her cleanly swept floor, shouting with heartfelt conviction:

" . . . we are sowing and reaping and wishing you luck the coming year . . . "

And would stand crushed with misery from Katya's mock despair: "Now look what you have done!"

Thus, it was easy to see how all his life Jasch would have difficulty perceiving a path to a life free of tormenting conflicts. The distinction between right and wrong was not an easy, clear-cut matter regardless of how closely he listened to his heart.

It was said of him around the villages with something like patient regret:

"He could not grow up to be a wholesome man. Now he is forced to bend according to the winds . . . "

And bend he did, indeed!

His dual nature, it was held, was responsible for his yearning to follow the railroad tracks which were the threads to the world. Of late, he had developed into a capable merchant, expertly trading with tobacco, feather pillows, yarns, bristles, and brooms. He loved to go to Melitopol, for he was an avid gossip at heart. He loved to chat with the Russian women while they sat broadly at the sidewalks on blankets, offering their goods to customers hurrying by. Hands in his pockets, he would ask with casual assurance:

"And what's new in the Petersburg Palace?"

The women would make the sign of the cross when whispering the name in secrecy:

" . . . Rasputin is Satan in person . . . "

" . . . his mangy beard is full of lice. His boots leave stains on the carpets of our dynasty . . . "

" . . . he puts his hands upon the bled-out body of the child. His eyes can stop the bleeding . . . "

" . . . he has done it, time and again . . . "

" . . . and our Czarina, tearfully, kisses the hem of his foul-smelling shirt . . . "

Jasch would let himself be pushed here and there so that he could listen in close attention to what was said in the Russian streets.

" . . . a worthless vagabond is ruling us," people would say hatefully.

" . . . the Emperor is a helpless tool in the hands of this uncouth Siberian monk . . . "

" . . . the Emperor rules, but it is the *Nyemka*—the cold German woman . . . "

Massive flyers were distributed after dark: "The Land to the People. By Redistribution if Possible. By Revolution if Necessary." Stooped factory workers would gather on street corners and whisper. Jasch's imagination always ignited itself on such whisperings. He who had nothing to lose and much to gain was keenly receptive to that which was said in the streets of the cities.

Ferment was everywhere. In Moscow, small eruptions had already taken place—quickly quenched, to be sure, by ruthless force of weapons. But rich German stores had been plundered, and some industrialists were said to have been murdered in bestial fashion. Only last week, in the famous Red Square, a throng of people had cursed the Imperial Couple, had asked for the incarceration of the German Czarina, had howled for the

18

abdication of their Holy Czar, and had demanded the gallows for Rasputin.

_____

As Johann Klassen passed the mulberry hedge that divided his homestead from that of his neighbor to the right, he saw Gerhard Wall close the front gate behind him.

"Good evening, Gerhard," he called. "Katya will be out in a few minutes; I believe she is still helping her mother."

The young man's face softened in anticipation, for he loved his bride-to-be and had loved her deeply and steadfastly for as long as he could remember. Their betrothal had been announced from the pulpit the previous week, along with the message that those objecting to this union come forward now and have their say or keep their peace forever after.

The customary waiting time was drawing to a close. Three buggies had arrived already, filled to the brim with distant relatives who had heard of the coming event and had welcomed the opportunity to stand ready with wishes and prayers. The village midwife had paid her visit to take a measured, scrutinizing look at the blushing girl's hip structure to ascertain that future generations were assured. Speculation as to the splendor of the wedding day had kept the gossip channels humming.

Late fall was the time to be wed, when barns and attics and cellars were filled to the ceiling, when one could afford those leisurely drawn-out days of celebration dictated by custom and lore. It was but a mere few weeks until then; already wave after fragrant wave of saturated summer air was drifting over the homesteads. Soon, the fields would be swept with the melancholy songs of the migrant Ukrainian workers as the days pushed steadily ahead to a harvest richer and more generous each year. Whole villages would have to be invited, for with a kinship such as theirs, who would bother with but single names?

"Good evening, Ohm Klassen," answered Gerhard Wall. They walked along the street without a further word, as men who were at ease with each other.

"You will stay for supper?" the elder asked at length.

Gerhard Wall nodded, his eyes fastened upon the girl who now stepped out of the kitchen. He smiled slowly, and she turned her lovely face to his, and their eyes held for a moment. Then her little brother Benjamin was between them, reaching for both their hands, forming a lively link of kinship.

"Let's go sit on the garden bench," said Katya.

The father smiled. For the past fifteen years, they had sat on their bench; children at first, their sandy cheeks pressed against each other. Then time had brought a little distance between them, sudden and grievous and not to be explained. The elder Klassen had watched for a while, rather thoughtfully, reliving the torments of his own shy youth. One afternoon he felt compelled to call Gerhard Wall into the sanctity of his summer room to ask with a frown on his face:

"What goes on between you and my girl?"

There was a long pause in which they had looked at each other, drawing reassurance from each other's faces. Then they shook hands. No more was necessary between them, since they were men who lived meticulously by rules that were written nowhere but were widely understood.

Around the villages, it was said of Gerhard Wall: "An honest fellow through and through." When he had been a child of ten, he had been handed down a revelation that told him clearly that he was destined to become a worker in the vineyards of the Lord.

As Johann Klassen bent his heavy frame to enter the kitchen behind the house, the smell of freshly baked buns and cabbage soup swept into his face.

"I'm home, Mother," he said quietly, and briefly he nodded to his wife.

"Yes, Father," said the woman.

Silence engulfed them, as the flies buzzed outside against the meshed window screen, attracted by the aroma of the supper which the woman readied at the stove. The fire crackled, and

20

from outside came the sounds of the cattle returning for the night, and children's laughter, and Katya's soft, even voice as she sent Benjamin to wash his hands for supper.

Johann Klassen sat down by the table, contentedly watching his wife. The eagerness of young love outside reminded him how he had found Susanna more than two decades ago, when the awakening of his manhood had given him much grief during that one long, hot summer. He knew himself to be a man of careful, slow decisions, and girls at first had terrified him. During the hours alone in the fields, desires and wishes that troubled him greatly had set his blood afire until there was no peace and no reprieve, no matter where he turned.

"Leave me be, Satan," he had prayed on such occasions, for he was well versed in the Devil's untiring efforts to tempt God's prudent children. Then, as the summer went on, and September had set the chestnut trees aflame, he had finally asked in humility:

"Lord, if it be Thy will, let me find the right one."

This is how his eyes had fallen upon Susanna when she had come to visit from Chortitza. He had asked her shyly one evening, after everyone had gone to bed and had left the young people alone in the summer room:

"Susanna, will you be my wife? My heart aches for you."

And the girl had flushed deeply and had nodded her consent, for marriages were always tied according to the motto: "What's close is familiar—what do we know about a foreign life?"

Hesitatingly, he had walked over to her. For a moment, unsure and trembling, he had felt overcome to take her to his heart. But then he had clumsily put his heavy hand upon her flaxen hair and had fought a lump in his throat:

"I will ask your parents tomorrow."

A letter had come for him shortly thereafter—the first letter he had ever received. It had lain in the mailbox, tucked underneath the weekly *Voice of Peace*. He had barely dared to open it.

"Now I know how much we love each other," she had

21

painstakingly printed on lined paper that had been carefully torn out of a notebook. With a burning face, he had hidden it under his pillow, and with a heart so full it nearly burst, he immediately sent her a poem of similar content.

She had borne him five children, not counting the ones who had died young, and Tina, who was deaf and dumb and a heartache to her parents because God had decreed that she was not to speak.

He knew of people who wanted to bring modern ideas into the colonies. They pointed accusingly to the huge deaf-mute school in Tiegenhagen; they wrote long, scholarly essays on the inbreeding through centuries that had made the Mennonites one kith and kin. But Johann Klassen was troubled little why that should be a danger. Were they not like one intricately woven net, with kinship ties criss-crossing the colonies and reaching far into Siberia and Tashkent? And was there not comfort and strength in that?

How Susanna had grieved over Tina! She had gripped the edge of the table one morning and had clutched her heart and said hoarsely: "There is no light in her face." He, of course, had known by then. He watched her weep all morning to give her ample time. Finally, in late afternoon, he pushed his buggy out of the granary and put a soft blanket on the back seat for Susanna and the child to sit on, and went into the house and said:

"It is time, woman. It has to be done."

He had held the child briefly to his face, and then turned and steadied his wife. He had held himself very erect as he slowly proceeded along Waldheim's main street to Tiegenhagen, looking neither left nor right, knowing that out of every front door a friend or neighbor waved, with eyes that had clouded, too.

It was only after Hein was born, and shortly thereafter, the twins—strong, lusty boys who yelled and bounded and kicked—that Susanna's grief had lifted and quiet happiness had filled the homestead once again. "Peter and Paul, named after the Biblical Apostles," he had told his neighbors left and right. And after yet

22

another year, there was Katya. "Named after Catherine the Great, our strong-willed German-born Empress of more than a century ago . . . "

"Now it's enough," the village midwife had cautioned, and Johann Klassen had nodded his consent.

But then, after ten years, when he had long believed Susanna past child-bearing age, she had once more given birth to a son. His heart had rejoiced, because it was so obvious from the start that Benjamin—quiet, willing, obedient, and malleable—when grown would go to Germany to soak up the strength to be drawn from their distant *Vaterland,* and would return stout and secure to take over the spiritual reins from his father's uneducated, callused hands.

"There comes Jasch Kovalsky, Mother," he presently said to his wife, looking out of the window. "Put another set of dishes on the table."

"Another cup of coffee, Jasch?" Katya asked quickly.

With a smile, she pushed a generous slice of the layered cake onto her guest's empty plate, for soon, she knew, no attention would be paid to her and her hospitable skills. Her father, she could see, looked set for spiritual battle. The twins sitting across from her, looking like two pugnacious roosters, were all but bridling to meet tradition head-on. And Jasch, she observed beneath lowered lashes, was carefully biding his own good time, patiently waiting for his turn to put his oblique, upsetting thoughts into the very middle of a heated conversation. An evening to be savored for its stimulating sparks, she was sure!

"Thank you, Katyushka," Jasch now said formally, looking at her with longing, knowing full well that she was spoken for and that he must forget her if he could. "Half full, maybe? That's enough! That's more than enough!"

She kept her eyes lowered as she refilled his cup to the brim, ignoring a guest's protests and lamentation as one should always do. "Have another slice of the cherry cake, Jasch. Please? You can't shame me by eating so little. Why, you haven't even begun to eat, as far as I can see." She had waited all day for this hour around the supper table with Gerhard by her side, with a guest or two to be spoiled, with little brother Benny sleepy in her lap.

"Just for the sake of argument," Peter was already demanding loudly, "on whose side should we fight, should we be forced to fight?"

"We are pacifists," said Johann Klassen, scowling at his son. "We don't carry a gun. In wartime, we tend to the sick and the wounded."

"On the Russian side? Are we, therefore, Russians?" Paul quickly came to Peter's help.

"We are Germans, and you know it, you whelps," asserted their father with heartfelt conviction. "Why belabor this fact time and again? We are of German origin. And we are Christians. And that is the alpha and omega of our nationality." In emphasis he put down his cup so as to launch himself more comfortably into hs favorite lecture. "Virtue," he said heavily, "is composed of Germandom and Christianity . . . "

"The fact remains, "his son smiled, leaning forward, "that the language you speak is not German. It is a language—an unwritten language at that—that has had an anemic growth in the shelter of centuries of sectarian isolation. You know how it started, when our ancestors fled from the Netherlands to the Vistula Delta where there was freedom to live according to their inner voice. In the Prussian swamps, enforced by brutal persecution, began this strange fusion of language, blood, and belief . . . "

"It was God's grace and our German persistence that helped us resist the Catholic fire and sword. And the floods of the Vistula Delta. And the hardships here in the Ukraine. And the early raids by hostile Asiatic tribes. And the blindness and bigotry of power-drunk heads of state who tried in vain to tamper with our Lord's promise and our German contribution of peaceful, never-ending work!"

Why, this was a powerful passage indeed he had just

24

managed to deliver! He felt a little shaken from his sudden eloquence. He hoped it would not dissipate before next Sunday's sermon.

"High German," said his son, calmly, "is much revered, carefully nurtured, never abused. High German is our pride and our joy. But at home, among ourselves, we slip into Low German the way we slip into our comfortable clogs when it is time to milk the cows. And Low German, Father, ironically, is only partially of German origin . . . "

"What utter nonsense!" cried the elder, stung. "How little you know of our past! Why, it has its very roots in the Low German countries . . . " Perhaps there was a tiny grain of truth in what this fledgling asserted, but their Netherland ties were weak and forgotten, and their German roots sustained them as a people now on foreign Slavic soil.

"How could anyone doubt that High German was but a borrowed treasure? And the danger is there that one day we will be presented the bill for having taken advantage of a country's hospitality without once bothering to learn to say 'thank you' in the language the Russian *muzhik* can understand."

"I don't speak Russian," said Mother Susanna whose concrete mind grappled with the accusation. "But your father speaks it very well."

"That is not quite true, " mused Johann Klassen, smilingly, somewhat ruefully stroking his beard. "I have tried, to be sure. But I break my tongue on those heathen words. Why, every time I try to say *Dniepropetrovsk,* my tongue twists itself into a triple knot." He added hopefully: "But didn't I do very well when I spent six weeks in Melitopol five years ago with that Russian family when our wheat deal had to be cleared?"

"And didn't you come home every weekend to reassure Mother you hadn't yet been devoured?" countered Paul, cruelly holding his father's embarrassed eyes.

"Well . . . " The elder Klassen shuffled his feet in discomfort, and the twins nodded seriously at each other and scored a point of victory in their behalf.

"You know perfectly well," Johann Klassen defended his cherished belief, "that the early struggle for survival did not permit us to get acquainted with the Russians at our gates. Our fathers were so involved in eking out a living that there was no time to pause and look around, even if they had wanted to. We never did have a chance to learn a proper Russian, so there was no choice but to adhere to our German ways."

"Low German will not stretch far when it comes to understanding the world beyond our gates."

"How unfair can you be," said his father. "Wherever Germans settle, they build a school. We have hundreds of schools—good schools! And our teachers have always been strong and upright men, well versed in the teachings of the Bible and well aware of their obligation toward our young."

Paul's cheeks flushed in anger. "That is just the point I am trying to make. All too often, at least in the past, a teacher was a wandering minstrel who happened to drift by and claimed to know his letters. During summers, he often served as the village herdsman as well, and in the winter he was more concerned with using the rod as an incentive to scholarship than with scholarship itself. You have told me this yourself! A little reading and writing, arithmetic with whole numbers, perhaps a multiplication table tacked onto a prayer toward the end of the day—but lots and lots of Bible recitations! So help me—when I think of all the verses I was asked to memorize . . . " To his annoyance he felt the color rise in his cheeks for having spoken heresy in the presence of his father.

The elder leaned back with a sigh. He was, as he well knew, an unlearned man, although he stood in awe of books. In his summer room there was a shelf reserved exclusively for the two rows of books he had in time acquired. Books, in his home, were highly revered, if seldom read. Did he not own a book entitled *From Pole to Pole* along with a Bible-sized calendar called *Antarctic Diary?* He owned a book by Fritjof Nansen. *Indian Tales* stood next to *The Treasure of German Lyrics.* He had even read a novel in his youth, he now recalled, feeling his emotions strangely

26

warmed. Even now, when alone, he would sometimes take his boy Benjamin on his knees and share with him the magic of the printed word as he remembered it from prior readings.

"I have always tried to do my best," he said slowly. "As best I knew how. And now that it has become apparent that that is not enough . . . " He sighed. "Our ties to Germany are weak and insufficient. But my sons! Remember one rule that is clearly written in the Book: We have to render unto Caesar what belongs to him, and unto our Father what is His, no more and no less. As a people we are different and cannot mix with foreign blood without a price too vast to pay."

Jasch Kovalsky sat idly, turning his cup of coffee in his hands. In deep discomfort, Katya kept her eyes on her lap. The elder Johann Klassen, her own dearest father, was a good, kind, thoughtful man, but tact was not one of his fortes. She heard her mother add, gently:

"We do our best. Look here on the wall. We have the portrait of the Russian Czar right next to the picture of the German Emperor."

"Yes," Jasch now replied cynically. "It is tempting indeed to parade one's loyalties for everyone to see, is it not, Aunt Susanna?"

Katya felt resentment flush her cheeks. Jasch could speak his mind if he so chose, any time of the day or the night, and count on being welcome in their midst. She understood his festering wound and had tried to soothe it on many a previous occasion. But there was no need to be unkind and rude. She felt so strongly angered by Jasch's disrespectful remark she barely heard Gerhard's calm, peaceable voice as he tried to defuse the suddenly charged conversation:

" . . . the Russification measures of thirty years ago did bring some changes into our lives, not all of them for the worse. Russian became the language of the street. But never on our playgrounds, in our churches, in our homes. Thank God, it remains Low German in everyday use, and High German on sacred occasions."

27

"Yes," agreed Mother Susanna heartily. "It is easy to show vanity by speaking High German in everyday use. One can be accused of vanity so easily. And one would fall prey to the village gossip that way."

" . . . yet had it not been for the fact that we kept to ourselves . . . " Johann Klassen, by now, would not be stopped. He held a thread in his hand. He had a maxim by the tail. He took a deep breath and pushed his chair back with both of his hands. But before he could speak and settle this matter once and for all, Gerhard Wall once again interrupted him calmly:

"It is difficult for you to understand, Uncle Klassen, that the Russians do not see you as you are. You think that by being God-fearing, and honest and upright, all is well. It is for you, because you are the man you are, and I respect you greatly for what you are. But . . . "

"But what? When Catherine the Great sent her messengers to Germany, it was understood and signed and sealed that we would bring along our German heritage intact. In gratitude for this concession, we built daughter colonies that stretched as far as our frontiers would permit. We could not have done what we have done, had there been something wrong in our endeavors, and had God's grace not rested visibly upon the labor of our hands."

One had to be on guard indeed so as not to be tempted into self-righteousness before such riches as were theirs: well-fed horses and cattle, brass and silver on spring-suspended buggies, huge orchards stooped with fruit, pantries loaded to bursting with the products of the land. No depletion, he was sure, could ever make more than a dent in this fullness that continued to flow from German acres. With pride one could point to village after clean-raked village, built by a simple and diligent people who tilled their soil from dawn to dusk, and whose hands, the *Voice of Peace* repeatedly asserted, fed almost one-fourth of the Russian people.

"Ohm Klassen," said Jasch slowly, leaning forward. "I know that you work hard. But we all do. Aunt Susanna would not let a bread crumb go to waste, and I know that she owns only two dresses—a work dress and a gown in which to pray. However . . . "

Mother Susanna beamed broadly at such well-deserved praise, forgiving him instantly for his thoughtless remark. Frugality was at the very root of her upbringing, the principles of which she took great care in passing on to Katya now. Nothing was ever to be wasted in a household such as hers. After the elder had finished with the *Voice of Peace* on late Wednesday afternoons—for that was the hour when he turned pensive— little Benny was dispatched to take the paper to Penner's house, who in turn saw to it that Aunt Ens would get to read it in plenty of time before five o'clock on Saturday night. That was when she needed it back to spread it over her freshly baked *zwieback*. Afterwards, Katya would roll the grease-stained paper into a fly swatter to use while milking, and—having finished her chores in the barn—she would neatly unroll it again and start rubbing the lamp shade free of accumulated soot, a ritual to be performed with meticulous care on the steps of her home each Saturday night. The paper, now crumbled to pieces, was then put thoughtfully behind the oven so that her mother could start fire easily the following day. Such were the well-known, time-proven ways to accumulate one's wealth in one's coffers.

She heard Jasch Kovalsky assert, vehemently:

" . . . the gulf is widening! Millions and millions of peasants are chafing under the burdens of a landed nobility!"

"I have never . . . "

"You have benefited from a corrupt Czarist regime! And you will become a pawn between the poor Russian peasants and the Czarist-loyal aristocrats. You are neither, and neither one would stand on your side, should civil strife break out!"

Now was the time to shout, for one should shout indeed from righteous zeal!

"We did not come to steal the Russian land!" roared the elder Klassen, gripping the table with both of his hands. "We came to find reprieve from Anabaptist persecution, and we

29

settled in a land that had hitherto seen nothing but the hoofs of the Cossack horses. Thanks to our God and our prudence, it proved to be a land of golden opportunities, the fruits of which we are only now beginning to reap!"

"The *muzhik* grumbles!" cried Jasch in turn, dramatically.

"The *muzhik* has always grumbled! So what? We have a Father in Heaven! When more than a hundred years ago our ancestors found themselves in the same sore distress—when in their worry and fear they looked here and there and everywhere to find a path in accord with their conscience—it was Russia's great Czarina whom God had chosen as His tool to help the Mennonites in their bewilderment and fright. At the very hour when the Prussian King called them to the sword! Then, and not a day before, came the messenger from Russia and promised them as much land as they needed, and relief from taxation for many years, and spiritual freedom for as long as the sun will hang in the sky. If these commitments no longer hold true, our people will once again take to their pilgrim's staff. We have done it before!"

"There is talk about expatriation!"

Johann Klassen sat back and wiped his perspiring forehead, weak from the force of his emotions. "Fill my cup once again, Katyushka," he said to his silent daughter, trying to calm himself.

As far back as he could remember, there had been rumors that the Mennonites might be forced to share their wealth. But those stories had been around for a very long time. One grew used to them, even though now and then a meeting was called where somber-faced leaders would caution the settlers and would warn them of upheaving changes to come.

Jasch said ominously:

"Dark forces are stirring in your land. They are creeping up on you through decades of outward security."

And Peter leaned forward, too, holding his father's glance;

"What will become of our pacifism, should we be given no choice?" He lowered his eyes before his father's inflexibility.

30

But he added, and there was determination and fierceness in his voice: "I know that if my family were threatened, I'd be the first to fetch a gun."

"Oh, no!" cried Katya. "You wouldn't! And you couldn't! Our Lord Jesus Christ has decreed that those who reach for the sword shall fall by the sword."

"I am sorry." The youth briefly touched his sister's hand. "I did not mean to frighten you."

"We cannot choose, for we have been chosen by our Lord," said Johann Klassen with finality. "For those who believe, and follow the narrow, promising path, all things shall turn out for the best." And he looked at Jasch, saying to himself: "He isn't this, and he isn't that. He is a thorn in the flesh of our people, and a stranger to the Russians as well."

The day's work was like lead in his bones; suddenly, he felt very tired. Everything had been said that needed to be said in this matter. But then he softened, thinking his own voice too harsh in his ears:

"My hot-headed boys! When I listen to you, it seems to me that my old house is shaking. Yet it is all so simple. Why tear down the old and the proven to build something new? Our past has taught us many a lesson. Happiness cannot be had at the price of neglecting the faith." He looked at his twins. Then he said firmly: "I am confident that should our heavenly Father think it expedient to sort the oats from the chaff . . . "

There was a silence in the room. After a while, the elder cleared his throat. "Mother, put away the dishes. Good night, Jasch. Be sure to close the front gate. And be sure to come again. You know that our door is open, regardless of our disagreements in these matters. Gerhard, do you want to stay to say our thanks? It is late, so let us pray before we dim our lights."

"Good night, Jasch," said Mother Susanna, too, putting a brief, soft hand to Jasch's tense shoulder, for it distressed her greatly to see him so often distressed.

Katya swiftly helped her mother. The men pushed back their chairs and walked into the summer room. The Bible lay open by

31

the window. After a moment's hesitation, the elder turned to his sons:

"Since we are not permitted to take the sword to aid our chosen homeland, let us in loyalty use our weapon of prayer."

They knelt with bowed heads, engrossed in their thoughts. The two women, entering, quietly took their places behind the men.

" . . . *Und fuehre uns nicht in Versuchung, sondern erloese uns von dem Uebel. Denn Dein ist das Reich. Und die Kraft. Und die Herrlichkeit. In Ewigkeit. Amen.*" And lead us not into temptation, but deliver us from evil. For thine is the kingdom. And the power. And the glory. Forever. Amen.

Outside, all lights were extinguished by now. The large, sprawling homesteads lay nestled against the tensed body of the hushed Russian land.

The foreign Czarina was said to have publicly stated:

"I blush to have come from German stock."

Could anyone have stopped Armageddon?

The first year of war had been a desperate race for nature's abundance, for the hot summer air had simultaneously ripened the orchards and fields. Grains and fruit had dropped in lavish showers to the ground. As in past, untroubled times, the settlers had expected their diligent, seasonal workers to arrive in droves from Poltava—simple, unspoiled people, dressed gaudily in hand-woven cloth or inexpensive colorful dresses. Their humble possessions—a comb, some hair pins, perhaps a set of cards with which to play away their gains—tied into a handkerchief, were all that they would bring along, for what was needed at such times except two willing arms and a deep joy for the harvest's luxuriance, except a willingness to stay and help reap nature's riches?—until the first cold gusts of winter air would push them out of the settlements and back into their paltry huts.

However, only a trickle had arrived that fall—sullen rows of people, taciturn of gestures and very sparing of words. Not a single Ukrainian song had drifted over the fields.

Katya had not been married that year.

It did not really matter. She was young. She was strong. She was willing. Those were days meant for reaping! She had helped from dawn to dusk to straighten the large, wide trusses of straw—setting them, one by one, like miniature huts along the edges of the field. The twins had switched their horses by the hour, thinking it sheer desecration to stop longer than for a mere quick drink of cool water kept in a big-bellied barrel in the grass beneath the shady acorn tree. The storks, the swallows, and the starlings began to leave their gabled roofs. What was a year? The twins, at times, would bounce their little brother between them back and forth so that the child would scream in choking fright and sheer delight and at night fall like a dusty bundle into bed, the smell of hay and harvest still clinging to his hair and limbs.

Katya, in later years, would always recall this moment's emotions of fervent gratefulness for a year's work well accomplished, as she had kissed the sleeping child, in tired, glad appreciation for life's straight continuity, for life's unending bliss. What was a year's delay except deep happiness postponed? Of course she would wait, and gladly. In mellow anticipation of the day when she would speak her marriage vows, " . . . till death do us part," she thought of death sometimes, as young girls will, in somber sentimentality, as something that somehow could never happen to her. Souls were called home, of course, at the Lord's mysterious bidding, but always the old or the infants whom He wanted back for their untainted hearts, and the Kingdom was theirs for the asking.

On a map pinned up in Johann Klassen's barn, she could see how the front was creeping closer.

It was Gerhard's habit to study the Russian papers. His voice somewhat unsteady, he had told her last week that a number of German farmers living along the Volga had been exiled to the farthest corner of the land. To be capriciously taken from the

33

middle of an urgent harvest was cruel injustice indeed. Kind, good neighbors who had done no wrong and bothered no one, were forced to leave their homes behind and go into an unknown future. But they were, after all, only Lutherans. Good, believing Christians, to be sure, but careless in their dealings with the world, never too concerned about the encroachment from Russian side. Several of their villages had already been absorbed into neighboring Ukrainian settlements and had lost their strength and their essence.

Out of nowhere, random incidents began to trouble the Mennonite settlers. Insignificant things, to be sure, in the very beginning—no more annoying than a flea bite here and there. One could not put one's finger on the source. What could one say when old Ivan, stooped deeply to bind the corn, would stretch as the twins were passing, and would wistfully follow them with his eyes?

A rumor was started that Ivan had taken to locking his door at night.

"Did you hear about Klassen's Ivan?"

"I wonder what he has to fear?"

"Is he afraid someone will steal his samovar?"

"Or his old felt boots?"

"Or his Ikona?"

"Or his lice?"

This story caused uneasy mirth among the people of the village. A neighbor here and there would stop him in the street, slap his shoulder left and right, and ask slyly:

"Now, Ivan! What is this I hear about your lock and your keys? Now, why are your ears turning red?"

No one had ever locked his doors at night. Nothing could happen. They slept with open windows, with only a small milk bench leaned against the double door so that in case the tomcat wanted to stray at night it would not loosen the heavy chain that prevented the door from swaying back and forth in the night breeze and waking the little children.

"Next year, Katyushka?" the twins would tease their sister.

She managed a forced little smile. Who was it who once had proclaimed that the war would not last longer than three weeks at the most, for Germany had nothing to eat? A year of war had now passed. Before she knew it, a second would be gone.

The twins rode over their land to check on the watermelon patches. Weeks ago, the plants had started to throw their creepers to all sides. It was now no longer permissible to put a hoe or a foot on the fields so as not to disturb the growth of the creepers. In due time, the fruits could be harvested after this undisturbed period of absolute rest in the sun, having built up such pressure that by the merest touch of the tip of a knife, they would burst into crimson sweetness with a small, concise explosion.

Jasch had promised to guard the southern patch in the morning to keep away the roguish Ukrainian urchins who thought of stealing watermelons as their exclusive childish right. Jasch often took on odd jobs here and there. The twins could see him from afar. They also saw to their amazement and chagrin as they rode closer, that to their right Ivan was pulling his rickety cart—and did he not roll it straight across the juicy creepers, without regard for the fact that two grooves were already cut alongside the ditch for his convenience?

To their astonishment, the twins observed that Jasch stood languidly, not in the least attempting to reprimand the sinner for his indolence. Infuriated, they galloped closer, shaking their fists and yelling:

"Hey! *Muzhik!* What do you think you are doing? Don't you know that this is our patch? You can't just walk over our watermelons, you impudent boor!"

Ivan must have had a generous sip of vodka, though it was still early in the day. For when drunk, Ivan was known to discover within himself an unexpected flair for stubborn, full-mouthed resistance. His eyes would become glassy, his cheeks flash a purplish furious red. At such times, Ivan was not intimidated by the Devil's very tail. This faithful servant of theirs for more than two decades now turned on the twins like a hornet, raising a sassy fist in return, and shaking it threateningly in their direction:

" . . . are you going to forbid me to pull my own cart over my own countryside? Who do you think you are? *Nyemtsi!* Damn *Nyemtsi!* Haven't you stolen my land . . ." A torrent of curses followed, delivered expertly as only old Ivan could do when goaded by his poisonous potion, " . . . and now you want to tell me what to do?"

So much for Ivan! The twins, matter-of-factly, lifted the sputtering fool off his cart and deposited him not too gently in a mudhole nearby to teach him a sensitive lesson. But when they turned to Jasch for applause and approval, Jasch stalked off nonchalantly, as if what took place was not for his eyes to see or his ears to hear or his heart to ever remember.

Soon thereafter, the twins, along with the very last one of Waldheim's eligible, eager young men, were called to Melitopol one morning, to return at night in unison, in a somewhat frenzied, feverish state of mind, singing loudly in the streets, proudly parading the flaming Red Cross of Mercy on their broad, youthful shoulders.

The elder Johann Klassen had listened by the window, a leaden ballast on his heart. From where had come the mesmerizing power of a ruthless war's macabre splendor? As if details of warfare should matter to his boys brought up so carefully by gentle hands. It was hard for young hearts to be quiet when the world was all but aflame with patriotic fury. It was next to impossible, cried the twins, to be weaponless in a weapon-spiked world!

Once again, Gerhard Wall said to his betrothed:

"Next year, Katyushka. Next year for sure!"

Now his troubled observations radiated from the front:

" . . . the hate for all that is German permeates every facet of our lives. We are suspected of collaboration with the enemy, since we speak a fluent German and can talk directly to the prisoners of war. We have learned to avoid provoking the anger of the lowliest of Russian soldiers. As Christians and as

36

Mennonites, we try to keep our peace, though our blood boils and our hearts cry for revenge. Never once have we let our servants be subjected to the indignities and humiliations we now feel, day after day . . . "

High winds began to roar across the steppe, propelling a mass of dead, dry leaves along Waldheim's deserted streets. Katya stood by the window, her eyes on the tumble weeds. The sidewalk outside had turned into a soggy swamp. A vague, unarticulated dread took her sleep away. Ceaselessly, it seemed to her, the dogs would bark at night. It ate on her nerves.

"Why don't you let Ivan take you to Melitopol?" Johann Klassen tried to console his saddened child.

There had been times when she could walk into the store of her choice, and say her name, and be assured of courtesy. Greek, Jewish, and Armenian merchants vied for the privilege of serving her—of piling in front of a Mennonite bride the linens and fabrics she would want to buy to last her for life. Now, a silent Ivan at her side, she found locked doors, closed windows, drawn drapes wherever she went. It was impossible to ask for an explanation from averted faces. Shrugging shoulders sent her, feeling a weak rage in the pit of her stomach, into a well-known restaurant, where she sat for an hour and a half, ignored and deserted, without being served a single drop of tea. She finally found herself pushed into the street by Ivan's broad shoulders and lifted onto the buggy without as much as a word, but not before she had caught a glimpse of a sign in a store window that she had overlooked before:

"Germans and dogs not allowed on these premises."

"Let's go, Katyushka," Ivan had urged her on, swinging the whip across the horses' backs. His jaws moved furiously. Now and then, he let go of his spittle with an explosion.

"Oh, stop that, Ivan!" she cried.

He did not reply. He sat there, mumbling to himself.

She was hungry, exhausted, frightened, bewildered to tears. It was an eerie ride home. She all but fell into the arms of Jasch, who waited for them by the gate:

"Thank God you are home! Katya. Katyushka. Wait a minute . . ."

"What is it, Jasch? Let go of my arm."

" . . . Rasputin has been murdered! People in the streets of the cities are weeping with joy: 'The devil is finally dead.' Rumor has it that he was lured into a basement and given poisoned wine and cake. Others say that someone tried to shoot him, but that the bullets did not penetrate his body. One of his boots was found on the ice of the Neva River. The Czarina is said to be insane with grief. The people are in turmoil, and doom lies over Petersburg. The "Marsellaise" is shouted in the streets. Banners are carried bearing inscriptions: 'Down with the Government!' 'Down with the War!' 'Down with the *Nyemka* Czarina!'"

She shook him off, now running home through the darkening day. She opened the door to the kitchen. Her mother stood by the stove, tears streaming down her wrinkled face. Johann Klassen sat silently in his chair. Katya, often shy to show affection, felt compelled to put her arms around his head. Holding her fingertips to his temples, she bent over his shoulders so that she could read the note he held in his hands.

"It's from Gerhard," he whispered tonelessly, and buried his face in her palms.

"Father . . . Say something, dear."

He shook his head. She took the letter out of his cramped fingers, trying to decipher it, with difficulty, in the last fading light of the day:

" . . . soldiers, sent out to quench the riots, are running over to the opposition in order to fight against the Czarist-loyal troops. The Palace of Justice is aflame. The Winter Palace is trampled by dirty Russian boots. There is talk that ditches had to be carved in the Kremlin's cement to drain off the blood of the dead and the wounded . . ."

Katya turned to her father, feeling a malevolent fist against the very heart of her sheltered life:

"Father . . ."

The elder's voice gave way:

" . . . Katyushka! My dearest child! All prison doors are open. Assassins, by the thousands, are flooding our land . . . "

2

His name was Nestor Razin.

Only his youth had prevented the gallows. He would have been hanged, as two of his brothers were hanged, had it not been for his youth.

"Anarchy is the mother of all order . . . " he would write while still imprisoned in Butyrky, for did he not taste on his lips, more by the day, the piercing, potent force of rhetoric? " . . . The destructive spirit is the creative spirit . . . " For centuries, they had been bled by their czars. And now, was it not true, they were bled by their cities as well? Cities lived off the sweat and toil of a generous, gullible people. Towns were pulsating, cancerous growths. Alien settlements had sprung up all over the Russian land, sapping its strength, tormenting it to fury, driving its gentle souls berserk with pain. " . . . Cities and towns and settlements are there to be destroyed . . . I see it fitting and right that my brothers' dulled lives find a voice by way of my merciless deeds."

Many years later, after her own life had turned aged and brittle, Katya would sometimes be asked by people too young to have known the terror that came in the Antichrist's wake:

"Is it true that he was a very handsome man?"

Katya would always pause to search her heart:

"He had raven-black hair and large grey eyes. He was short and slight of build. But I don't remember his face. I don't remember his face at all."

He was a man of many faces: cunning, strong-willed, reckless to the point of self-destruction, deeply enamored of his anarchistic sentiments. His origin was humble. His father had been a bonded serf, a drunkard, and a petty thief. His mother was a simple peasant girl, much given to romantic leanings. Could she have known—illiterate soul—the ancient legend of a hero of like name whose valiant life was spilled in battle with foreign invaders at the very point where East met West? She could not have foreseen her son's claim to immortality when, as a grown man, he put his bloody heel upon the plains of the Ukraine. For as civil strife swung open the gates of Butyrky, Nestor Razin stalked into freedom a cruel and vengeful man, reeling on the very edge of insanity. Kicking open in furor the dungeon gates of the Ukraine, releasing a deadly flood of thugs who were sucked into his mob. His path to Poltava was lit by the fires of the prisons as he burned them to the ground.

"Never for a moment," he would later recall, "did I doubt that the people in the place where I was born would take me back as one of their own."

A shaken village clerk handed him a stack of secret files. Nestor spent two days in seclusion, arranging and rearranging names. Henceforth, no one could know for sure whether his name was listed as one of the traitors of the land, for Nestor kept hidden inside his boot the key to the infamous list.

It took all his persuasive talents to explain to the dull-witted peasants that, according to anarchist standards, order was now a thing of the past. Their hesitant eyes forced him to sharpen his message to a focusing point that even the slowest simpleton could well understand. "Seize land and wealth for redistribution. Do so by means of terror and force."

"All ownership rights," he would argue, "were founded on the law of the Romanoff Empire. Now the Romanoffs are dead. That makes those laws invalid. Does that not make sense?" Nothing had ever made more sense to the little man sensing his hour of revenge.

Folklore renamed his hometown Razingrad.

His followers pointed to him—the man who had lain in chains for nine years and had suffered the agonies of the oppressed. He walked along the street with face aglow, girls hanging on his arms like carelessly worn ornaments. Samovars would hum throughout the night so that he, speaking to the hushed audience, could tell of the changes to come.

He would listen to the peasants when they expressed their opinions of the government:

"Why do we have to have a *durak* bend our necks?"

And Nestor would lean forward and speak softly into the darkness:

"Cities are evil. Settlements are wicked. Towns are a curse upon the land. They are supporting the system of the *duraki.*"

The *Volga,* a virulent underground paper, proclaimed in the spring of the year of the Russian Revolution:

"Why shed a single tear for those felled by the just sword of our little father Razin?"

And Lenin was said to have declared in his cynical nonchalant way:

"Who would object to an honest anarchist's feats?"

Razin's name became a magnet overnight. Stories linked to his black, tattered flag were whispered across the land:

" . . . Wherever it appears, even the horses stand on their hind legs and whinny in fright . . . "

" . . . Like a torrent, his army will sweep across the steppe, without fear and without mercy. Hideous demons, slaughtering man and woman and child . . . "

" . . . He will stretch and thin his ranks, weakening the enemy's striking power, confusing his plans and strategies . . . "

"...Like lightning, he then strikes from the enemy's rear..."

" . . . He travels in a buggy drawn by four black stallions decorated with white silk sashes that drag through the mud . . . "

It was said of him with admiration that he drew from inexhaustible reserves of strength. When he was wounded—which happened now and then—a carriage with springs would carry him, his roaring voice muffled for once by the thick feather pillows he had stolen on one of his raids. He was driven by a zealot's vision, and but for the lunacy of fate, he could have been great. As it was, so he would claim, he had made long,

41

distant, devious strides, for had he not, as a fourteen-year-old boy, tended the cattle of the German landlord Johann Klassen?

Only when very drunk would he speak of those times when, briefly one winter, he had earned his keep in a Mennonite home—a small, dark, lean young boy who slept, coiled up against the cold, in a shed behind the cattle barn, who ate ravenously of the food that Mother Susanna packed into his basket every morning. To her distress, he would not wash himself for weeks on end, and was often heard muttering into his newly sprouting black mustache. He spoke very little to anyone, and the settlers in turn avoided his path. Ohm Klassen, puzzled and challenged by the dark intensity of the youth, had tried to be kind on occasion. However, beyond detailed instructions as to the work to be done, he had troubled himself little with the boy, for German Mennonites knew better than to be drawn too close to the alien culture from which he had sprung.

Once Nestor asked Ohm Klassen to lend him a book he saw on the kitchen table. The elder had nodded, but something heavy pressed upon his soul. Shortly thereafter, he found his daughter Katya, then a mere toddler, sitting astride the youth's grimy knees. The father's heart almost stopped.

"What was he telling you?" he asked the child, deeply troubled.

"Emperor Nikolai," babbled Katya, who was just learning to speak and delighted in the formation of every new word.

"What else?"

"Moscow," said the child, dimpling. "Petersburg. Wicked Czarina."

"Don't talk to him any more," the father said, quickly carrying her away in his arms.

He had felt compelled, that winter, to send the youth to a Mennonite school—a ragged, shivering, taciturn boy, an all too easy target for the German children, who had diverted themselves by chanting at the sight of him: *"Russejung, Russe-jung . . ."* The humiliation had cut deeply, for was he not brighter than any of those slow, blond, stubborn boys and girls, who bent their heads like sheep each morning in the prayer he despised: "Dear Savior, help me to be godly, so I can go to heaven . . . "? One day the teasing had become intolerable and Nestor had run out of school and straight to the home of Johann Klassen, seething with incoherent fury.

As he burst into the summer room, Mother Susanna looked up from her knitting and said sternly:

"Go and wipe your feet, Nestor. I just finished scrubbing these floors, and you drag mud all over the room. As a matter of fact, you should have left your shoes at the door so as to show your consideration."

The boy in his agony turned to Johann Klassen, who, as the elder of the village, was the man to whom one turned in distress. Nestor stood facing the man, his face contorted with rancor.

"Do what Mother Susanna tells you," said Johann Klassen, unperturbed. "Go outside. Scrape your shoes. Knock on the door. Wait to be asked in. Then tell me what you want, my son."

The youth swallowed. He did as he was ordered, wincing. He scraped his shoes on the mat outside, his face flushed scarlet. He knocked. He was asked in. Johann Klassen closed his Bible neatly. "The boy needs breaking," he said to himself. "Vanity before the Lord will not do."

"What is it?" he finally asked, having taken his measure of time before speaking.

The whole misery of his young life welled up in Nestor, strangled him, choked him, cut off his breath so that white circles danced before his smarting eyes. When he got hold of his voice, he began to curse.

He cursed loudly and vehemently.

Such a stream of filthy language rolled off the boy's young lips that Mother Susanna shrank back in consternation. Ohm Klassen expertly gripped the offender by the neck, almost lifting him off the floor by the sheer force of his enraged righteous zeal.

He had seldom used the belt on his oldest son Hein, and only occasionally on the lively twins when his conscience told him clearly that it was time again to reinforce obedience. He never beat his horses or his dogs. In fact, so even-tempered was this man that he had seldom tasted pure and livid anger. But this was evil. This was evil erupting from the body of a child, and evil had to be extinguished in the bud. His belt came down across the boy's tensing back in such a whipping flash that the buckle flew past Mother Susanna's head and landed, somersaulting, in a corner. He swung the leather again. He would have likewise disciplined his sons without the slightest hesitation. But his own boys, he knew, would not use unclean language—not in his presence, not ever! No Mennonite child would use the name of the Lord in vain as this vile Russian youth had done, besmirching everything that was sacred in heaven and on earth.

In all of his experience, the elder Klassen had never known such vileness possible—and that from the lips of a child! As he released the whitefaced boy, his hands shook from the force he had used, and he had to sit down for a moment to wait for his breath to return.

Nestor Razin shot out of the house like lightning, slamming the front gate shut, crying at last—in heaving, cursing, sobbing pain, blinded by rage and hate. He stopped only once, briefly, by the gate where little Katya Klassen played quietly in the shade of a tree.

He stood back a little, steadying himself. Then he kicked the child full force in the face. Deliberately. As hard as he could.

It was as if Hell's gates had opened indeed and spewn out the scum of human abomination, sentencing the whole of the Ukraine to die by the sword of Nestor Razin.

How easy had it been, in golden days, to pray: "Thy will be done." How agonizing it was now to speak such humble words as brother strife swayed back and forth across the land. Hordes of brutalized, brutalizing soldiers—Reds today, Whites tomorrow, Greens the following day—would burst into the

Mennonite settlements, flinging the gates out of their hinges, demanding that chickens be slaughtered and *borschtsch* be cooked in a hurry and well-fed, rested horses be lined up along the street. The unwashed, unkempt intruders would gulp down their food in a gluttonous greed, ready to scramble hell-bent through the back door at a moment's notice, for they suspected the enemy of lying in wait behind the large brick fences which framed the streets left and right.

Was it a pacifist people's fate to lie within the path of several contending armies, helpless strategically, and weaponless by edict of belief? Yes and double yes and yes again! It was a testimonial to the strength of the settlers' convictions that they held still as their villages were passed from hand to hand or were swept off the face of the earth with Bolshevik volleys, as their sustenance was torn away from under their very feet and given to bandits and murderers. Meanwhile Razin kept switching loyalties dictated by folly and fancy. Intoxicated by power and fame, he smeared their fences with a new arrogant threat: "I will torture the Whites until they turn red, and the Reds until they turn white." For Nestor Razin, whose thugs were daily roaming the streets, still took great pains with rhetoric.

No one had ever seen the Antichrist's face except Jasch Kovalsky whose word could not always be trusted. He had happened to come upon Nestor Razin one day, Jasch claimed, strolling along the streets of Melitopol on a Saturday night, without a care in the world.

"Do you know me?" Razin had asked, embracing Jasch with genuine affection, kissing him on both cheeks and heartily slapping his shoulders, "I am Nestor, the *Russejung.*" He had grinned. "Remember? *Russejung . . . Russejung?*"

Jasch had remembered only too well, not knowing where to keep his eyes to hide his embarrassment and fright. But Nestor had been jovial, had urged him into his hotel room, had ordered tea, vodka, cheese, and ham, and had demanded:

"Now tell me of my Mennonite friends. Tell me of Ohm Klassen Isaiah . . . what was it now? Five verse eight? Or ten verse five? Tell me of my bosom friends Peter and Paul. And how is little Katyushka?" He had roared suddenly, tears of mirth rolling down his bearded face: "I'll make them dance. Mark my word, comrade Jasch, I'll make them dance to the tune of their own parasitic life." Thus went Jasch's spine-tingling tale.

"Shut up! Shut up!" Katya had cried, putting both hands to her ears. Just this morning, looking out of her bedroom window, she had seen a small troop of the anarchist outlaws speed through the streets, a dozen of Red troopers close on their heels. One of their armored cars had roared past the square, splattering the Cornies statue with a thick shower of grey mud, but not before they let fly a bullet that struck a child in the cheek.

It was during those days of frayed tension that Katya had had her dream. It set her screaming in the middle of the night, and sobbing into the early hours of the morning. At first, she had no words at all to describe what she had seen. Against Gerhard's shoulder, she had finally stammered:

"I saw Father at the graveyard, and he placed his shovel here and there and everywhere, and finally he turned to me and said: 'There are too many of my people here. There is no room for me.'"

Much was made of this dream around the villages, even though Johann Klassen said calmly, trying to give comfort to his frightened child: "I have done quite a bit for my Lord. I should surely hope that there would be room for me in God's Acre once my time has come." But Katya had only stared at him and shook like a leaf. Thus it came to be known that there was more to Katya's dream than anyone could tell.

Rumor after rumor seeped into the lives of the terrorized settlers. Waldheim, was it not true, was richer than the surrounding Russian towns? There were more horses in their stables, more pigs and calves in their barns, more bacon and lard in their pantries, more flower and sunflower seeds in their attics, more sheepskins and carpets in their rich and sprawling homes.

"Do we have a choice?" the twins asked apprehensively. "A self-defense, well organized . . . "

46

"No. We have pledged non-resistance to our heavenly Father."

"Father, listen! Help yourself, and God will strengthen ... "

"Those who take the sword shall be felled by the sword. Thus it is clearly written."

Johann Klassen used all his influence to guard the doctrine of his ancestry against such powerful temptation. When it was clear that words alone would not suffice to contain the fervor of his sons, the elder arrived at a weighty resolution. The other village leaders had agreed: "All our money and gold. Every watch and clock we possess. All the flour and bacon and lard that we can spare. All the horses except the ones we absolutely need to work our land next spring. Everything. Just leave Waldheim alone. And leave our women and children alone. And do not make our boys reach for the sword and lose their soul's salvation."

It was a searching, two-pronged decision. Was he not, somehow, doubting his Lord by trying to buy security from a drunk and insane man whom Waldheim owed less than a kopeck? Only after his struggle was fought to the end did he tell his sons Peter and Paul.

"No," both said, and their jaws squared.

"Yes," said Johann Klassen, for he was not a man of many words in times when a few words more than sufficed.

"He sits in the eastern part of Melitopol," Jasch had explained, and had drawn him a map with seven arrows.

He went alone, as he knew he must do, choosing the early morning hours when silence was still upon the land so as to brace himself with proper fortitude for the offensive encounter to come.

Mean tongues had often insisted that the only worthwhile invention that had ever come out of Russia was the *samovar*. At this moment, feeling himself led into the very Cave of Evil, Johann Klassen was heartily inclined to agree. The samovar that caught his eye as he entered was a magnificent piece of beauty indeed—humming with comfort, shiny in silvery gloss,

47

spreading calm and security by its mere presence, sitting there haughtily on a small table amid the remnants of a breakfast and half a dozen dirty glasses, merrily reflecting the features of an amiably grinning Nestor Razin.

"A very good morning to you," said Johann Klassen with much poise.

"Well . . . well," the bandit said maliciously, and stared at the Mennonite.

He was armed to the teeth. He sat behind a heavy desk on which lay a pistol and two bandoleers of ammunition. His revolver hung at his side. The handles of two hand grenades protruded from out of his boots. A machine gun was strapped to his back.

"My friend and former master," said Razin, in biting irony. "What an honor, Johann Petrovich. What an honor, indeed!"

"He does not look like a bloodthirsty anarchist at all," thought Johann Klassen. "He is too skinny and too weak. And one can see the prison pallor." His Mennonite austerity revolted at the rest of what he saw. Nestor wore his hair in a low-hanging mane—raven-black, straight, greasy with pomade. His boots were polished to a high gloss, but his fingernails were dirty, and as he leaned forward to fix his eyes on the elder's face, he reeked of garlic sausage and cheap cologne.

The Mennonite chose his words with care, keenly aware of the weightiness of the concession. But he felt his heart at peace at last, and that feeling gave him confidence.

"Everything we own, Nestor," he said. "You can have it all. Except for the bare necessities. We need to keep some horses. And enough food to see us through the winter. But everything else is yours. Come and take it Sunday after next. It will be ready for you. I give you my solemn promise."

"But you see," replied Nestor Razin, fondling the pistols on his desk, "I can take it anyway. I don't need your damn promise. I can take it if I want. Your horses. Your gold. Your watches. Even your women."

Johann Klassen spoke carefully but with steadfast certainty:

"Nestor! You cannot take anything at all by yourself, for it is clearly written in Matthew ten, verse twenty-one: 'Are not two sparrows sold for a penny? And not one of them will fall to the ground without our Father's will!'"

"That," said Nestor Razin cruelly, "remains to be seen. That surely remains to be seen."

Was it thus written indeed? Johann Klassen was never to see with his eyes God's written promise again, though he did with his heart, to the end. He was found the next morning at the stairs of his chapel, his eyes dug out of their sockets by the anarchist's sword. When he regained his senses, he whispered through blood-crusted lips:

"God have mercy on us all."

Pacifist sons, guns in their fists, stood silent vigil between their homes and the neighboring Russian villages. Waldheim's young men, united at last in their outrage, took turns patrolling the streets, past the now dark and deserted chapel. Prayer meetings were held at first, to bless those sent out to kill. This practice was abandoned. It did not seem right. Nothing seemed right anymore in times of darkest anarchy.

Johann Klassen, inside the house, fought death, bitterly and doggedly. His body strained against the violence he had endured, for he came of a stock of people hardened to the rigors of life. His body still wanted to live, and so he fought.

"Nothing matters," the elder would whisper with difficulty, "except to forgive . . ."

The twins would listen with bowed heads, watching him struggle against the fire in his broken bones, weeping unashamedly. Later, in the kitchen, they would say:

"Pack us some food, Katya. We have to man the outposts for the next twenty-four hours."

She did as she was told, with averted face. She asked: "Where's my Gerhard?"

"We are relieving him; he should come back tonight. See to

49

it that he gets some rest. Let him sleep here, with Benny. His parents at home torment his soul. He cannot take much more."

After a pause, she whispered:

"Jasch told me Gerhard shot a bandit to death on Friesen's meadow. A young boy, barely seventeen, and said to be related to Razin."

"Don't listen to Jasch's exaggerations."

"Did he . . . " she started to tremble.

"Don't listen to him," they repeated. They stood with their arms around their sister.

"Think of Father," they said. With awkward hands they brushed the tears from her face.

"Be careful," she said, choked, closing and bolting the door behind them, taking her place at her father's bedside for the night.

Where would it all end? The land was exhausted. Every night the sky was lit by the fires of outlying villages too weak and isolated to protect themselves against the onslaught of diabolical greed.

The elder's blinded face turned toward his child:

"Get a pencil and paper, Katyushka. Write down this story for my children . . . " She could see him strain for command of his message. He struggled to focus on what he must say: "Much of my people's history has never been recorded. Therefore, we have no knowledge of past testings of our faith. However, it must surely have happened before. There are some traces still lingering in our hymns—pleas to heaven to guard against floods, against the dangers of the West-Prussian swamps, against drought and disaster . . . " His voice rasped on: " . . . only the very strongest could survive. Only somber young married people were permitted to enter this land—people with a solid reputation and some skills and money to make it in the East. And our great Czarina made very sure that no tramps or fortune hunters were permitted to come with the covered wagons. This way, along with our ancestors' baggage, came our craving for

50

order, our deepest inner longing for frugality and piety for the sake of healthy future generations . . . "

"Father, please . . . "

He said with an effort:

"We were compelled to acquire the wealth of the Ukraine since our reputation was so clearly tied to diligence which could not help filling our coffers before long. When one's reputation is so solidly founded on a rigid, immaculate life . . . Could we help falling in love a little with what we had accomplished by the sheer strength of our hands? We did not, however, accumulate wealth at the expense of losing our heavenly treasures . . . " His breathing was laborious. "The judgment visited upon Russia was not brought on by my people! Let that be clearly known!"

Katya took down this struggle word by word. It would be for posterity to judge!

" . . . Mennonite sons now stand at the gates of our villages, weapons in their hands and murder in their hearts—our boys who resisted the sword since the times of the German Reformation . . . Centuries of pacifist tradition . . . " His voice broke. He struggled for breath. He groped for High German words like a man drowning in his own blood:

" . . . I have fought a good fight, I have finished my course, I have kept the faith. Henceforth there is laid up for me a crown of righteousness, which the Lord, the righteous judge, shall give me at that day: and not to me only, but unto all them also that love His appearing, Second Timothy four, seven and eight . . . "

She, too, had something to ask of her Lord. She carefully closed the door to her father's room so that he would not hear and be still more distressed. She went to the window in her kitchen and looked up toward the sky, and she demanded of her God:

"As long as I can remember, he prayed with us, twice a day. Before I could barely speak a word, I had heard him pray a thousand times. Does that not carry some weight? Does that not count at all?"

51

She heard her father mumble indistinctly, as she stood there, enveloped in her own grief.

"... First John two, verse eighteen: 'Little children, it is the last time: and as ye have heard that antichrist shall come, even now are there many antichrists; whereby we know that it is the last time ...'"

The watch dog beneath the window yelped sharply in a short, painful, howling sound. "Hush! Oh, hush!" she whispered.

She felt her heart throb in her throat. For the third time, she went to check the lock on the door. Her fingers felt numb as she tightened the chain. She now knew that she was waiting. Whatever it was, she felt it coming. She felt its presence on the nape of her neck. She felt upon herself that which had been decided already; its unavoidability all but paralyzed her mind.

A single shot in the back of the house sent the heat into her face. A window pane splintered. She listened to the dull thuds of axe blows against the wall.

Mother Susanna said, quietly composed:

"I will go and see what it is. Stay with your father, child."

The door behind her back flew open. Katya recognized Nestor Razin at once, as he stood there, swaying against the light. Behind him, there were a dozen faces, staring at the girl. Her hand went to her throat.

"Where," said Nestor, "is that son of a whore, your father?"

Katya ran forward and seized the bandit by the sleeve. "You leave him alone," she stammered. "You drunkard! You vicious animal!" She clutched him, white-faced.

"Get out of my way." Violently, he shook her off. He stepped over the threshold. His men filled the room, pushing past her.

"My brothers will kill you!" Katya cried, hoarsely.

He did not answer. He shook her off again. Then he kicked open the door to the summer room.

"You are a pacifist?" he jeered. He spoke wildly. "Your men killed my brother. A young boy." Burning with fury, he raised his sword. With full force he let the blade come down on the old

Mennonite's face. "Your men caught him," he sobbed. "They meant to teach me a lesson." He stared at the blood that slowly stained the pillows. "They shot him," he screamed. His voice somersaulted. "They shot Sascha." He let the blade fall again, and again, and again, even though it was not really necessary, for the first blow had already killed the elder Johann Klassen, had neatly split his face in half on his pillow.

Katya moaned. Nestor Razin turned and blindly reached for the girl.

She fought him hard. But he was stronger; and he was insane with grief and desire. He raped her savagely as a dozen men looked on, leering, elbowing each other, shouting obscenities. Then he rose, cursing. As he walked out and stepped down the two stairs that led to the barn, the tip of his boot hit something soft and round. He gave it an impatient kick, and it rolled like a ball across the hall, coming to rest, grey-haired and bloody, at the doorstep of the room that had housed him as a child.

"And what do you have to say to that, Mamushka Susanna?" he asked softly under his breath. "Matthew ten, verse twenty-one?"

Gerhard Wall had to be told, and so he was told in the beginning. Afterwards, neither he nor Katya, nor anyone else in the village, spoke of this matter again. She put this burden onto his heart and out of her mind forever.

She saw him come along the neighbor path, carrying her little brother on his shoulders. She ran to meet him, stammering incoherently. He placed the child into her trembling arms and put his face to her cheek.

"I saved him," he said inaudibly. "We hid in a Russian village nearby until we saw them ride off with the loot."

"They are all dead," said the girl. "My father. My mother. The twins. Your family. All but one of Hein's children." She swallowed. "I was sure you and Benny were killed, too . . ."

"I fled out of cowardice," he said, showing on himself no mercy.

She said, after a while:

"Nothing hurts as much as seeing you cry."

"Katya . . ."

She shook her head: "God in heaven . . . " She swallowed. It took all her effort to say:

"Gerhard. Gerhard, my love. I am going to have Nestor's child. I know it."

There was a legacy to be preserved from the fires of the anarchistic days. Their children and children's children should know, and their children's children as well! Never should anyone forget what had happened in the wake of Razin's sword. After Katya had grown to be a very old women, she would still tell this story that stood sharply apart in her memories, and she would add nothing and leave out less:

" . . . Hundreds were called to die that night. Some were tied up and hacked to pieces. Others were shot and left in their blood. Three were hanged at the entrance of the village. We had a mass burial that week—I will never forget it as long as I live—that bloody, undignified pile of human flesh and hair. Those who could never be found were assumed to have perished in the flames of that night . . . "

" . . . the Lord had blessed my brother Hein, who lived at some distance from our home, with four healthy, beautiful sons. In the morning, he had sent the three youngest to the waterhole at the end of our village, and as boys will, they had lingered and loafed until it was too late to come home. So they asked to sleep in our hay shed. When the fires died down, my sister-in-law Lena carried home in her apron the remnants of her charred children . . . "

" . . . My great-aunt Maria, aged ninety-three, who lived on the outskirts of our town, owned a wall clock that had come to her family from the Vistula Plains. She could not bear to part with it and refused to hand it over. 'No . . . a thousand times no,' she told the bandits, for she was very stubborn and set in her own ways. She was kicked to death by their boots . . . "

" . . . Eleven farmers were hacked to death in a cow shed.

54

They were dismembered while their women and children were forced to look on. And after the horrid deed was done, the families were ordered: 'Each one of you now find your own . . . '"

" . . . the village Eichenfeld-Dubrovka saw every single male of age sixteen or older slaughtered that week . . . "

There were hundreds of gruesome, incredible tales, to be retold, relived, recounted—one by one by one! But if Katya believed that grief in one's heart is a license, she found in the weeks to come that she was very wrong. For she came to realize that her heavenly Father would go to great lengths to bring her to humble acceptance.

"Acceptance of what?" she would ask time and again.

The victims of the fiery night were laid to rest and resurrection, and it was afterwards that Katya set herself in stony silence before her Lord, to be married. The bridegroom stook trembling, haggard and old. The congregation could not see the Bible print for tears. Some tried to give her comfort, coming forward, stroking her heaving shoulders. The elder summoned from a nearby village, now that her father was no more, covered his eyes and left in mid-sentence.

"For what purpose, dear Lord?" Katya kept asking into the night.

She learned soon thereafter that the Lord had an answer of sorts, for a plague broke out among the ranks of the bandits late in the year. They came to her gates in a cluster, death already etched around their eyes, now seeking help from those they had tormented. And once again, they brought destruction. Seeing them there, Gerhard Wall told his wife in a barren, calm voice:

"They are our enemies, but they are very ill."

Katya replied with vehemence: "Let them die!"

The agony in Gerhard's face made Katya stiffen. But she cried out, facing him fully: "I can't do it! I tell you I can't do it!"

He looked at her without a word. She buried her face in her hands. But then she went and took an apron off the wall and said:

"May God help me. Tell me what to do."

Why should it be asked of her to wash the murderers' feverish faces, to bathe their filthy bodies, to comb the lice out of their hair? The illness now squatted upon the lives of the Mennonite settlers.

Over the graves of the young it was asked:

"How can God be silent to such wrong?"

"This is the opportunity to give testimony to our faith," Gerhard Wall spoke from the pulpit. "For is it not written, 'Bless them that curse you . . .'?" How could he find the inner fortitude to strengthen his grieving *Gemeend* when outside there were thirty coffins lined up beneath the acorn trees?

" . . . bless them that curse you, do good to them that hate you, and pray for them which despitefully use you, and persecute you, that ye may be the children of your Father which is in heaven . . . " he would say.

In his chamber, he would ask the question that was nearer to his heart: "My God, my God, why hast Thou forsaken me?"

He would hear Katya go into the shed on the pretense of having to scatter the hay in the manger so that she could clutch to a wooden beam and give way to the trembling of her body.

Jasch stumbled into Katya's kitchen, stared at her out of glazed eyes and moaned:

"It has gotten me now, Katya."

She wanted to scream: "Don't come to me. I am not strong. I can't take much more." But she said: "I will make you a cup of coffee. Then you have to leave. We have Benjamin."

He nodded. Slowly, he slumped to the floor.

She dragged his unconscious body to the side. He was a heavy man; she perspired with the effort. She rolled a towel around the *Voice of Peace* and put it under his head.

"There he is," she said to Gerhard Wall.

"Outside, there are two more," he replied. "Below the steps. They look very ill. They will not last till morning. Our hospital is overflowing. We will have to take them in."

"No," she replied, again.

But then she went with him and took one of the monsters by

the legs while her husband firmly grabbed his bony shoulders, and together they carried the dying bandit inside and bedded him next to Jasch, in the warm niche behind the oven that had always been her mother's favored place, and Katya gritted her teeth and fought a wave of nausea and turned to her husband once more:

"Now the other one, too."

"She is much too pale," worried the village women. "Don't let her work so hard, Gerhard Wall."

"She wants to work. It gives her peace of mind."

"Tell us when her time is near."

"I will."

"Katyushka, all things turn out for the best. You still have your man. You will have a family of your own. Many, many children."

To have a large family was the goal of a solid, orderly, heaven-blessed life. But of all the children she bore, only Sara was given to her to keep, and then Liestje, the gentlest, blondest of her children. Many years later, after her scorn had succumbed, she was given a son.

But for now, it was Sara.

"Why the name Sara?" she was asked. She had no reply. It seemed a name fitting for an infant of tender, finely chiseled limbs, a baby warm and quiet and soft, and really very pretty, a child who lived to grow up quite simply and naturally, an everyday Mennonite girl, a girl much petted and spoiled.

No one could have explained how this strange fact had come about.

Gerhard Wall was the first to take the baby's appeal with fervor. The very hour she was born, he said to his wife, tightly holding her hand in both of his own:

"She is a picture of a girl. She is very tiny, but she has long, black, beautiful hair. She has the sweetest mouth I have ever seen."

Katya did not reply.

"I love her already," he said helplessly.

She said nothing.

"Don't you want to see her?"

"No. Leave me alone, Gerhard. Please."

Stricken, he left. After a while, the young mother said with a sigh:

"Well. Bring her to me."

She rose on one elbow and intently searched the infant's face. She pushed the sheets down from her body and guided its lips to her breast. It started to suck, greedily.

Katya said simply: "That's that."

She did not smile upon her child. But neither did she weep. Nor did she ever weep a single tear over this matter in all the years that followed. It had happened and was over and done with, and she put it away from herself with steadfast determination. And life would go on.

Life did go on. Spring had arrived, but the skies were grey and low. Easter bells were persistently ringing in the faraway Russian villages. The wind danced with last year's fallen leaves. Jasch took his first steps into the garden and sat on the door steps, leaning weakly against the wall.

"Christ has risen," said Jasch with an effort to old Ivan.

"He has risen indeed," replied Ivan, walking hunched along the garden path, his face shiny with tears.

"Christ has risen," said Ivan to Katya.

She stood silently by her kitchen table, wrapping her brother's fragile body in a large bedsheet so she could gently and lovingly put him to rest.

"He has risen indeed," she, too, replied, and turned to Ivan and wept on his shoulder. After a while she let go of her servant so he could take the dead child out of the room.

Again she asked in wonder why it was that she alone was spared—she who knew herself to be of little spiritual substance worth preserving. She asked the question with a grim determination and persistence, for an answer she must have if ever her soul were to find peace again. What was the purpose in all of this and that?

58

"Wouldst Thou let me have a glimpse of Thy divine plan?" she kept asking. But she did not get an answer in those days.

It took the years of meagerness to silence Katya Klassen Wall. And silence it would be! She felt the very hush of a tomb spread steadily from coast to coast, from north to south, from one edge of the land to the other—a huge, impervious fog of destitution—while she stood trembling beneath God's left hand and listened to the message of this silence.

Hunger came slowly to her and her kind. It came much more quickly to those who did not have orchards, or some chickens, or a cow that had been recovered from the swamps once Nestor Razin and his thugs had perished from the plague and the bloody attempts at annihilation that preceded the arrival of Joseph Stalin and his silent, sullen men.

It had been a soggy, rain-shrouded winter, thick with a clammy humidity, too full of winds and restlessness. Only one-third of the winter wheat could be harvested; the rest was left to mildew in the fields. In early spring, the soil's sodden moisture was absorbed by a heat wave that was to last through the following year. It dried out their old, well-rooted apple trees and scorched the fields with a vengeance. Shortly thereafter, the skies started weeping again and could not plug up their tear ducts until late in the year.

"I am tempted these days to start the Lord's Prayer in the middle," Katya confessed one morning. "Give us today our daily bread, and tomorrow, and the day after that, and this winter . . ."

"That's all right," said Gerhard Wall. "Just as long as you pray, Katyushka. Even the skies above have lost their balance from the horror they have had to witness these past few years."

What was there to do but to wait for the following spring? Gerhard Wall took to the plow as soon as the land was thawed free of the ice. The war had sucked the laborers off his fields; the hands so long accustomed to the guns were now unwilling to hold the plain hoe. The workers of Poltava lay behind their

59

ovens in the straw, too weakened by hunger and indifference to come out into the sunshine and help rebuild what malcontent and infamy had willfully destroyed. And thus it would happen, predicted Gerhard Wall, that the Mennonite farmer who had once taken pride in helping to feed his land would now find himself starving to death on his own barren acre. His own people started acting foolishly those days—many of them, against his specific advice, had sold their horses and cattle for less than a week's supply of food, insisting peevishly that it made sense to liquidate the livestock so as not to use up the seeds for the following spring.

Before long, it was discovered by someone in the governmental ranks that the Germans were to blame for the famine, having wickedly mixed weed seeds with their grains so as to sabotage the reconstruction of the land. The Russian papers were seething with hysterical, spiteful accusations. At the sight of a German farmer, Russian children in the streets of Melitopol would break into a taunting chant:

"*Kulak* . . . Landowner . . . *Kulak* . . . There goes a *Nyemets kulak*, see?"

As long as Sara and Liestje were still small, Katya and her family managed somehow by living a week at a time, by stretching a slice of bread over six people and three days, by eating gruel and roots and mushrooms from the fields, dandelions that could be boiled and mashed, or poison ivy that could be used in casseroles and soups.

There were still the fruit trees behind the house, and the beggars now beginning to stream into Waldheim from the famished surroundings had to be kept at a distance. Those starving people, weakened into drugged, sluggish movements, looking as if caught in a perpetual daze, would simply sit there by the wayside, patiently waiting for Ivan to become indifferent in his own weakened doze, and fall asleep beneath the apple tree and start to snore into his beard. Then, stumbling and staggering, they would try to tear off the half-ripened fruit with a rake or the sling of a rope thrown over a branch.

Ivan, discovering the desperate thievery, would rise with shaky knees, take a deep breath, and with the help of a stick and a plentiful gush of his famous Russian curses, drive them back to the side of the ditch. There they would remain, watching him with glassy apathetic eyes, soaking into their yellowing bodies the anemic rays of the sun. And when a death occurred at Katya's door, Ivan would take a chain from the wall in the shed and drag the silenced sufferer away through the dust of the street.

Katya would later account for these years which gradually turned the entire Russian land into a silent cemetery by the infants she herself was forced to lay to rest as death reached out persistently for the weakest and the youngest:

"That was the year Susanna was born ... " she would recall with a sigh.

" . . . in the fall we handed back our Peterle . . . "

" . . . Maria was still with us that time . . . "

" . . . when our twins arrived, it rained. The Lord gave them to us one Friday afternoon, but he asked for them shortly thereafter, knowing that I had not one cup of milk in my pantry, or one single egg, or one spoonful of flour or lard, and therefore was too weak and feeble to nurse my little children . . . " The young mother would struggle with fierce determination to keep her youngest at her breast until a new one would arrive and force the older one away from her nipple, but as soon as she would reach for the bottle, the little faces would get their indrawn, pinched, serious look, and soon, she knew, there would be yet another little grave.

The last one died without a struggle a mere two days after he was born. She watched him die in mute concentration, with Sara leaning somberly against her knees. She felt no regret as life passed from the little face. She insisted on being lowered into the grave to ready the child for the resurrection, and proceeded to put some fir twigs over the tiny body so that the heavy earthen clods would not directly strike its face. The soil around her was cool and musky. There was a certain comfort in that smell. She

61

went back into the house, slowly and carefully so as not to waste her strength unnecessarily. She rested six times before she reached the stairs to her kitchen. As she opened the door, Sara and Liestje tumbled against her legs, grasping her around her knees, holding onto her, breathing heavily.

"Drink hot water," she said. "It helps for a while."

She leaned against the chalky wall, waiting for the dizziness to pass. This morning, Ivan had brought her half a barrel full of weed chaff he had been permitted to sweep up in a nearby government collective threshing shed. She would grind it down to flour and bake some cookies which the children could have before nightfall. She would have to be careful, though, to soften them with some meadow tea, for the children's teeth were loose in their gums.

"Stick out your tongue," she said to Sara.

The inside of the child's mouth was yellowish and swollen, despite the liquid of boiled fir twigs she made her drink each night. She sighed. The weakened skin on her calf, she saw, was already beginning to crack from the pressure of the unhealthy fluid stored in her legs.

"You can help me in the kitchen. I will let you lick the bowl and the spoon."

After some hesitation, she herself took a mouthful of the sticky dough, tasting it languidly on her lips. These cookies would certainly be edible. Between her teeth she could feel the grains of sand.

Ivan was a practical godsend in times such as these. Daily he would slouch into her kitchen to pull from his pockets some edible treasures—field mice, roots, bark off the trees. She had gritted her teeth when he came to her once, holding in his hands a set of live naked sparrows that had tumbled from a tree. She had been desperate enough, however, to close her eyes and throw them into a pot of boiling water. She had watched the children gulp them down, crunching the tender bones carefully between their loosened teeth. Once, she suspected, he had made her cook a piece of the cadaver of a dog, though he swore to her

62

by a number of Greek Orthodox saints that such insinuation was just the product of her weakened imagination.

"Sara, call your father in from the fields," she now said.

She readied the kitchen for supper. She still had a slice of dried bread, almost the width of her hand. She cut it carefully into six equal pieces, catching the crumbs in her apron. She set onto the fire a pot of leftover gruel. The family gathered around the table, eating slowly and with deepest reverence. Gerhard made her go to bed before it was dark because the knives of childbirth in her back were still fierce. But she woke early next morning, swept the stove, and heated the water for the pale chicory coffee. She held onto the chair and table with each step. Whenever she turned her head, the entire room would gyrate wildly for a few seconds before it would gradually go black. Slowly she moved along the wall, resting her cheek against the chalky surface here and there, waiting for the nausea to pass.

She forced herself to go to church before noon the next day. She was glad that she had taken the time to put her aching heart into the soothing hands of the Lord, for she returned home deeply comforted, aware of a peace within her reach, now that starvation and despair had silenced the mutiny of willful years and had opened the door to true solace.

She was sure there would be no more children. How could there be? Her body processes had stopped functioning. Her hips were as flat as a board. Her breasts were gone. Her hair had turned lifeless and ashen. She had not yet passed her thirtieth birthday, but she felt like a very old woman.

As bodily desires were silenced, a strong inner craving took hold of those still living. Many souls in the *Gemeend* experienced piercing, racking revelations that helped pinpoint just where they had erred in earlier, frivolous days. Many admitted to have strayed from the narrow but promising path. Many remembered that in their youthful years they had played dominoes behind their parents' back or had tried their exuberance at a Russian dance. Many confessed they had been impatient, too lax in their faith, too careless with their ancestral goods. They had yielded to gossip and slander, had neglected their prayers at night. Now they knocked on the elder Wall's door, one by one, with tears of regret in their eyes, more than willing to return to Mennonite austerity, begging humbly for his spiritual guidance in times of such barren, destitute grief.

Even Jasch, who in times long past was known to have jeered in disrespect, now became pensive and melancholy. Once, at dusk, he cornered Katya in the shed, telling her with fierce urgency in his voice:

"I wish I had what you have, Katya."

Against her will, she felt the color flush her cheeks.

"What do you mean?" she asked, unpleasantly moved, as she often was in his presence. She looked at him sharply. There was something about this man, of late, that made her ill at ease. Yet her occasional distrust of him disturbed and troubled her greatly, for she knew, did she not, his searching, troubled, two-sided heart?

"I mean your inner peace," he said softly, giving her a melting glance.

She stepped back, hastily. "Why don't you talk to Gerhard?" she suggested.

"The Holy Spirit moves me deeply," he told her, moving closer.

"It's about time, Jasch," said Katya somberly.

"I have a feeling I am drowning," he insisted. "I need to be baptized. I am in need of being saved."

"Why is it that I have this feeling that your conversion has something to do with the promised relief from America?" asked Katya. "There is talk that soon Canadian kitchens will be set up along the street to feed the hungry Mennonites. Is that why you are turning to the Lord?"

"I am a changed man," Jasch said emphatically. "You do me wrong, Katyushka."

"Changed—in what way?"

"I don't drink any more," Jasch answered, feeling pressured. "I have given up smoking. I haven't cursed in many a week."

"You have nothing to drink or smoke," replied Katya, not too impressed. "And as to cursing, what is that rumor that has come to my ears about your new Lutheran wife?"

Yes, Jasch was now a married man, having been wed in some haste to a girl named Marusya.

Marusya did not understand a flicker of Low German, having come from the area of the Black Sea where people tended to cattle and sheep. Katya had learned from her neighbors to the left that farmers living there had no regret for overdue debts and were disdainful of the plow. Marusya had brothers and sisters with strange, unfamiliar names: Rosemarie, Natalia, Regine, Hermine, Alexander, Eugen, Konstantin. But her arms were strong and her voice carried far. She was in charge of one of the children's homes which sprang up everywhere to take young infants off the hands of parents now driven into the collectives by hunger and despair. It was said, behind her back, that she had lured Jasch into the marriage bed with a pocketful of beans in those days of starvation.

Katya had smiled when this rumor came to her ears. The first time she caught herself smiling, she stood shaken, feeling her palms turn clammy from shock. Did this mean that she was now to live again? Yet who but her resourceful childhood friend would find a ray of sunshine amid the darkest of all clouds? And who was she to dictate to the Lord?

The following week, Jasch Kovalsky had firmly taken hold of the sleeve of a visiting elder from an outlying Mennonite village, and had found himself baptized and saved, even though the first frost had already set in and the river was already slightly iced over. Indeed, so zealous was Jasch in his new-found conviction that he insisted on being lowered into the chill waters not once but thrice, in honor of the Holy Trinity.

"Whatever it was," he was later to say, "it was a mistake. On hindsight, I am sure that what seemed a revelation to me then was nothing but a case of indigestion."

65

"Indigestion? During the famine?" asked Gerhard Wall in firm reprimand.

"Conversions on the deathbed never count," retorted Jasch, thus putting a stop to the elder's annoying concern.

As long as it was still safe to speak one's conviction, Gerhard Wall patiently tried to reclaim the lost sinner, but Jasch shrewdly resisted and defended himself:

"You preached too strongly of floods and damnation. You had the whole church in a hyponotic trance. I was just swept along, thinking for a moment that I had come to a decision. But in a few days, not a trace of that feeling was left."

And now he sat in Katya's kitchen, warmed his hands on her stove, drank her coffee, stretched his feet along her fire, and had the audacity to suggest:

"Let go of your foolish beliefs. The Lord won't help you now. Join our cause. United, we can do more than your God has ever done for Russia."

She looked at him with contempt. She was not so weak and so doddering as to foolishly join the Bolsheviks, who were known to be morally hollow and utter braggarts to their teeth. What an outrage to be asked to join the cause of the Soviets, to renounce one's beliefs, to become a slave to a fiendish, debased, putrified state! Was this not just like Jasch, who never knew right from wrong, to sit there in his favorite chair, repeating himself as he always did when he thought persistence was needed:

"Let go of your beliefs. Your God won't help you now."

"Oh, Jasch!" protested Katya. "Please. Just shut up, will you? At least in my very own kitchen."

He shook his head sadly at such stubbornness. After a pause, he tried another angle:

"Tomorrow, we will celebrate the October Holiday. An important national event for you and me, Katyushka."

"Not for me, to be sure," said Katya, unimpressed. She dropped the towel with which she was drying the dishes, and went to his chair and stood close to him, so that no passer-by outside the door might hear and turn a casual conversation into a false denunciation that might take months to clear away from her name.

"You stole my Sunday from me!" she said sternly.

"I pride myself on a ten-day work week," replied Jasch with stiff formality.

"You can't get rid of our Lord by stealing away His day. How dare you, Jasch Kovalsky!"

"What nonsense you speak, Katyushka."

"Aren't you ashamed of yourself, to be a thief of time?"

"There are quotas," replied Jasch, defensively. "There are norms we have to keep. I look at the calendar and the blood stops in my veins. From where am I going to get two hundred percent of last year's harvest to fill the orders I have been given?"

"Let your people work six days. And rest on the seventh. That's how."

"We strive to be efficient," he said.

"Efficient," exclaimed Katya, scornfully. "Just what is it that you call efficiency? I have listened to the nonsense that goes on in the collectives. This system you are pushing is senseless and wasteful and you know it, Comrade Jasch. What used to be work gladly undertaken and willingly done will now become duties dragged along by the hair. What do you know about running a collective of several hundred men? Walls will cave in, roofs will break down, and further disorder will decay our weakened land. The lazy ones will have to be carried along by the diligent ones, for wages now have a bad name, and good pay will no longer be an incentive for hard, decent work.

"The peasants are complaining: 'We were promised land, and this is why we joined. Nobody told us the land we were to own would belong to the state.' And they are asking, and rightfully so: 'What's the use? We won't get to reap the harvest anyway. So why tighten screws and sharpen plows and waste one's precious energy?' Jasch, listen! The proletarians now sit in kitchens that are not theirs, they eat bread the grain of which they haven't planted, they sleep in beds when all their lives they slept on earthen floors. Is it any wonder that insecurity and guilt will cause their souls to twist?"

She had watched them in the yards of the collectives, dawdling away precious minutes, glancing at the clock, and complaining loudly about a long array of maladies, mysterious aches, strained calf muscles, toothaches, and nausea. They compared their grievances in loud, accusing voices, worrying about each other's quotas, bragging about connections with powerful Soviet officials. In the fields, meanwhile, there remained large stretches of uncut wheat, more than ready to be reaped, already blighting from the dew of early fall. Even formerly diligent, hard-working peasants like her own old Ivan would tell her slyly:

"Why should I break my back, Katyushka? Why should I bother cleaning my house, or weeding my garden, or sweeping my cellar? Why should I risk having them think I want to be a *kulak*? Am I itching, perhaps, to go to Siberia?" The very word would bring the pallor into Ivan's shrivelled face.

"Were it not for the *kulaks* like your family," said Jasch, "we would have won our class struggle years ago. As a matter of fact, that's why I am here, Katya Wall. I have the district police officer and the investigating official of the Soviet outside in my buggy waiting for my orders."

"Investigating what?" cried Katya resentfully. "I am sure that there's no needle in this house that you don't know about and haven't registered. What is there to investigate again? These past three months you have counted at least fifteen times every plate and spoon that we own."

Jasch considered it beneath his dignity to reply. He was now a pillar of the Soviet State. He motioned through the window. The men who had patiently waited outside climbed down from their seats and stalked into the barn. Jasch followed them with an ominous frown on his face to cover up the fact that inwardly he was blushing. Did he enjoy what the Soviets had ordered him to do when it came to his very own friends? Rummaging through Katya's shed, peering into her

68

closets, opening her pantry, looking into her barn, dictating to his subordinates what was his duty to dictate? It had to be done by someone, was that not true? Why did she try to complicate his life by her resistance?

"Four grown pigs."

"Sixteen piglets."

"Two self-binders and four cultivators."

"Three pantries full of food."

"Enough linens to clothe five proletarian families."

His horse was tied to the gate, exhaling foggy clouds and moving its body in discomfort beneath the icy blanket on its back. Katya, to show just what she thought of Jasch's attempts at self-aggrandizement, turned her back to him and went outside to rub the mare's back with a brush. Jasch might be in charge of the betterment of all humanity, but he still did not know how to tend to the needs of a beast.

Thus, by ill-conceived, devious, treacherous means, a dazed Russian land began to stir for reclamation. And weakened by destitution, it now possessed no means with which to rebuild what anarchy and discontent had so capriciously and willfully destroyed—nothing save words: cheap words, plentiful words, evil words, atrocious words flanked by the hammer and sickle, words aimed straight at the minds of malleable children, words that rolled off the presses day and night proclaiming with a vast amount of ink and paper that Christ was now no longer Christ but an ordinary human being whose teachings were the opiate of the masses.

Were Mennonites to stand defenseless and see divine truth defiled and disgraced as Bolshevik barbarism readied itself to squash living, quivering souls and their sacred institutions? Were they to stand by idly and see their own dear children—too young and innocent to understand the blasphemy—help spread this poison with their eager little hands? For fences and gates, it seemed to them, no longer existed for purposes of order and expediency. They were there to be smeared over with obscene proclamations jeering at eternal truths:

"We'd rather be allied with the Devil than with God, because the Devil is against Religion, and so are we."

"We leave Heaven to the Angels and the Sparrows, for Ours is the Future here on Earth."

"Neither Czar nor God nor Tribune can save us. Why not save ourselves by our own collective strength?"

The wind, at times, would try to shred this sacrilege to pieces, but the next morning would see a new cluster of school children dispatched to tack another batch of printed profanity to the old whitewashed wood, to propagate the offensive message. Soviet arrogance continued to snare the trust and confidence of the unsuspecting people of the land.

Such shameless desecration rose from the depths of atheistic insolence! Was she, Katya Klassen Wall, though only a simple Mennonite woman, to stand defenseless as the despised crossed symbol of the rebellious working masses appeared in every storefront window, on every wagon that rolled through her streets, on every tree trunk left unattended, in the very sand beneath her feet, where idle hands, not knowing better, would etch it in the soil on languid afternoons? Katya, whenever she saw it, would shudder and move as far away from it as she could. At night she would take a pail of paint and brush and walk out to undo as best she could what Soviet malice was forcing upon her and her kind.

She wholeheartedly agreed with her wary brother Hein, who just the week before had likened this symbol to the measles:

"It appears in every family, no matter how cleanly one tries to live, and how separate from worldly temptation. It invariably seeks out our youngest, who are not yet immune through solid knowledge of Biblical truths. We are mistaken, however, to think it as harmless as measles, that come and go and leave little lasting pain. It will not burn itself out as measles always do. Many a night I am haunted by dreams that show me how it multiplies before my very eyes from viciousness and spite, moving in on me, hacking away at my feet . . . "

The elder Gerhard Wall smiled wanly at such unexpected vehemence. Hein was not a man of easy tongue. He was a farmer set doggedly but squarely in old-fashioned ways, distrustful of even a likelihood of better times.

"Don't you read the papers, Hein?" Gerhard would at times admonish him gently. "The newspapers and radio announce that starting with the First of July . . . "

"What papers?" Hein would cry, contemptuously. "The *Voice of Peace* died years ago."

"The *Voice of the German Worker* . . . "

"Empty promises," scoffed Hein, "good for nothing but to throw sand in people's eyes and to distract them from the sinister intentions of the Soviets. You sound like Jasch, Gerhard Wall. Shame on you for being so yielding."

"You do me wrong," replied the elder Wall calmly. "Why, I would be the very last to yield to godless slogans. As you well know, Brother Hein. And, please, don't liken me to Jasch."

Jasch Kovalsky, to many in the village, had turned into the very incarnation of the elusive, invisible erosion that kept on wearing down the settlers' confidence and hope. It was difficult to say just what he did that seemed so disturbing, except for certain irritating habits he had of late borrowed from the hoodlums who were steadily attracted to his hut. Stopping busy people in the streets with heartfelt shouts of "Comrade!" Slapping them on their backs left and right, forcing into their hands torn leaflets from his bulging pockets. "Join our Glorious Communist Cause!"

Well, that was Jasch, who made a perfect fool of himself aping the dissidents' voices, their turns of speech, the way they clustered at corners. When he smiled—and it seemed he always smiled of late—he flashed two golden teeth. Last winter, while many had doubled over from cold, he had stalked about the streets of Waldheim, wearing a new sheepskin and brand new felt boots on his feet. On his belt now glittered the hated, five-spiked star. He would make his unwelcome appearance in this homestead and that, peer around suspiciously, shake his head in disapproving disdain, kick a tractor wheel in passing, and exclaim in pointed contempt:

"A German trademark, eh?"

Many things about Jasch troubled the hard-working settlers. Hein had seen him once making a speech, the mere sight of which had been enough to make him lose his appetite for days. Hoping to hire him for an urgent task to be done on his farm, he had knocked on Jasch's door one evening. No one had answered, though many voices could be heard inside. Hein had pushed open the door and walked in. Applause had blown into his face, for Jasch, at this moment, was entering the room from the opposite side. So many people were crammed into the low-roofed hut that Jasch had not noticed Hein through the thick tobacco smoke. Hein had stood by the door for a while listening.

Someone had pushed together two tables and boards to make a provisional podium on which Jasch, thus raised above the upturned faces, delivered a somewhat hysterical speech, the content of which he, Hein, could now no longer recall except for words like "traitors," "liquidation," "kulaks," and "Siberia." Jasch, fool that he was for an audience, had ended his folly with a poem—composed by his very own pen—that promised miraculous equalization. The no-good loafers in the room, who had nothing better to do than to be entertained in this fashion, had applauded every word he said. Jasch had finished, Hein told Katya, chagrined, by calling himself "a friend of the truth."

Katya nodded. "Yes, Hein," she said. "I know. I know about Jasch."

She, too, felt frightened of late.

Just last week, wanting to borrow a cup of flour from Ivan, she had walked to his home after dusk. She had thought nothing of the tightly drawn drapes at first, for she knew about Ivan's violent fear of sorcerers that might come and snatch him in the dark. She had not been able to resist leaning forward and peering through a tiny slit in the window, for she was—like all good

72

Mennonite women all over the world—suspicious about anything that was purposely hidden from the eye. She had seen Jasch stand by the table, a cup of steaming tea in his hand, his face flushed purple with eagerness. She had leaned closer to see what so held his attention—in fact, she had pulled up a little milk bench to stand on so she could scrutinize him better. Spread over a table was a heavy scroll of paper, which from her viewpoint looked like a map of her village. Jasch was studying it intently, every once in a while taking a sip of his tea as if his throat were dry. And the night breeze at this moment had moved the curtains just long enough for her to see that he was not alone. With him was a well-known henchman of the nearby Soviet secret police.

It was then she realized that Jasch's duty was not to tabulate the columns recording the success of the collectives, as he had boasted to her time and again. His task was to collect and to categorize accusations. For accusations were now a deadly fact of life, aimed at the old and the young, the rich and the poor, the wise and simple of mind. These accusations, routinely delivered with a goodly measure of Russian profanities—for shouting and cursing had proven an efficient means of quick intimidation—could set a German settler to trembling and stuttering, cause him to contradict himself, and land him most expediently in prison for being an Enemy of the People of the Glorious Russian Land.

"Brother mistrusts brother," complained Hein. "Children turn against their parents. Treason is suspected everywhere. It is dangerous to ask a simple question. It is dangerous to wonder. It is dangerous to think."

Hein was an awkward, sullen man, aged far beyond his years. He had lost three children to the revolution; another one had died from typhoid, and even though new ones had since been born and had taken the place of their brothers, in his home and in his heart his grief stood stark and fresh. With distrust and bitterness he watched and nodded as government agents began to move in on the outskirts of the settlements so they could eye the German farms in order to make collectives out of them. And he had become one of the first of the many frightened colonists

73

whose ears were keenly attuned to what was now echoed across the great waters, and what struck a responsive chord in many a Mennonite's home.

Hein took care not to miss a single meeting in Nikolaifeld, where it was argued with stark persuasion:

"If in front of us a door opens, and behind us one falls shut, then that is most surely a sign of the Lord."

What good did this land do them now? No longer was ugly, jealous talk confined to the cover of night. In broad daylight it was now said that one could take away one's neighbor's possessions according to the Communist dictates of the land.

"Let's flee while there is still time. Let's go where our brethren are who were wise enough to foresee the afflictions that have befallen our people. Let's go as a group to Canada."

There had been previous years, to be sure, when Mennonite confidence in Russia's promise had been shaky. Two decades ago, there had been a dispute over a single word in the contract which had originally drawn them to the plains of the Ukraine. Deceitful men in the emperor's palace had broken a sacred promise and demanded that they shed blood for princes and kings. Many declared that after such treachery, Russia could never again be trusted. The word "emigration," during those years, had acquired a magical pull—a pull of such persistence that within the span of a decade, according to the archives, one-third of the Mennonite populace was thus extracted from their midst.

This was recalled anew.

"What about our responsibility to the Ukraine?" their elder asked in sorrow. "Can we, as exemplary farmers, forsake our obligation to our violated land?"

"You can't be serious, Gerhard Wall."

Oh, but he was! The Cornies Statue still stood in the middle of their village and symbolized, for all to see, what German diligence, German determination and German perseverance could do. He drew strength from the sight of it every day he looked out of his window. He tried to appeal to his fearful,

74

restless brethren in the *Gemeend* by reaching deep into their past, by reminding them of their pride in their stately farms, their churches, and their schools, in which their children were taught the way of the righteous. This was the place where they had been born, where they had lived in peace and security save for the last few insane years, where they could count on finding dignified rest for their mortal remains when the measure of their lives had run its course. His pleas, however, were in vain, for he was told:

"Even the tombstones are dragged away and the graves are flattened so that the goats of the collectives can graze on their surface."

"It is true we have been ravaged. But we can rebuild. We have our land. We have our tradition. We have our German language that welds us together into one community. And I have a feeling—I feel it in my heart—that sooner or later our *Vaterland* will come to our aid. Germany will pull itself up by its bootstraps."

"Germany lies with its face in the dust!"

"As the guardian of your inherited spiritual goods," cried Gerhard Wall heatedly, "I am telling you this: They are not defeated yet! Not Germany! Imagine how we will rejoice when German help arrives! We can count on Germany. We can depend on our *Vaterland*. We always have! Sooner or later . . . "

The *Vaterland*, of course, was still theirs for the taking. Germany, in fact, was ever-present on the horizon of their hope. It was true, to be sure, that for many years now not one single whisper of a message had come to them from Germany. Only once, briefly, at the end of the war, as the front had rolled over the Ukraine, had German troops appeared in the settlements: men of hard determination, grey-eyed, tall, and quiet. The Mennonites were shy around these men even though they spoke the language—a clear, concise High German that felt like a breath of fresh air. The settlers had treated the young warriors as highly revered guests and had opened their homes and their hearts to these boys who had come to their aid, and for the brief period when German troops had patrolled their streets, there had been relief from the harassment of Razin.

"Dear brethren! Let's wait a little longer. Let's give Russia the benefit of the doubt! Last week, at Ensen's wedding, didn't we sing again our favorite German songs? I counted eleven, as against seven that were still sung in Russian. That is progress, to be sure!"

"Yes, and it was rumored afterwards that many traitors had mingled with the guests."

"Surely you exaggerate. There are no traitors in our midst."

One of them stood up heavily.

"Listen," he said. "I know for a fact that I am being blacklisted. For praying in High German with my children. For having owned a German map. For having bought a tractor built in Germany. I can't stand this pressure. I am forced to lie, to deny my German ties, to forsake my God and my beliefs . . . "

"Times will get better. Why, things are vastly better already, from the way they were a year ago. We are now sowing and reaping again. Everything may fall to ashes. But land cannot be robbed or burned or destroyed. Our land is still ours to work."

"Even if we are forced into the collectives?"

At this an old, well-respected settler stood up with shaky knees and shook his fist and cried with stark emotion: "Better dead than Red!" and it became a shout of anguish and determination that drowned out the voice of Gerhard Wall.

But Gerhard, of late, had become a very steadfast man. The worst, in his eyes, was over indeed. There was now a song in his heart. Once again there was happiness in his voice. Once again it was high summer. The wheat on his land stood taller than his shoulders. The twining plants in between were already yellowing from the heat. Behind him lay many long, rigorous, frustrating winters. But when his need had been greatest, God's help was nearest, as he had known it would be. He had known this with a certainty when early this past year a silken wind had sprung up from the south to lift his farmer's heart and signal the start of yet another wondrous spring.

How beautiful this inner awakening had been! He had walked across his land slowly, the scent of the freshly plowed, still fuming fields in his nostrils and in his veins. It had made him a little drugged, for he was still weak of body and emotions from the devastation of past years. Now he relished the odor of the earth, imagining the marvel of light green tips that would once again sprout undisturbed, imagining the gold haze when the pollen would lie in waves over the ripening fields, thinking of the rich rewards of harvest time. He could close his eyes and imagine Katya at the edge of the field, taking a handful of grain to test its ripeness between her fingertips. She always knew when it was time to harvest. She needed no calendar except her senses of sight and touch and smell.

This morning, she had packed him a basketful of food: meat cooked as well as thoroughly cured, a large pot of borscht, a bag full of zwieback, three hard-boiled eggs, and a small jar filled with tasty, slightly salted sour cream. Very early he had left for the acres. She would follow him a little later with the fodder and the water for the mares.

In the chambers along the village streets there sprouted a new crop of blue-eyed, fair-haired children.

"The women are always expecting," he mused. "Women are so much stronger than men." Last week, he had heard Katya whispering with the midwife behind a door. Would it, this time, be a boy?

His eyes took in the promise of the land:

"It is mine," he said. "It is my land. It grows the bread for me and my family. No one is going to scare me away."

Hein, soon thereafter, knocked on his door, sat down heavily at Katya's table, put his head in both of his hands, and said to his sister with a shudder she could see ripple along his back:

"Today I sold my homestead. My uncertainty is over now."

Gerhard went out of his home and into the night to hide the fact that his heart was aching.

77

Katya had to sit down with Hein to give him comfort with her presence, listening to him as he nailed down the coffin of his past:

"Now all that is left for me and my family to do is to sew our bedding into big bundles . . . "

Many years later, Katya would tell of those days.

"Thousands fled. Like thieves in the night, they sneaked through the orchards, knocked on my window, and whispered: 'Is it safe to come in? We are departing tonight. We came to say farewell . . . ' Behind them, they left the table set and the lamp burning. We later found their horses by the railroad station where they had tied them to the gates . . . "

"Was it that dangerous to flee?"

"Yes. Yes, it was, toward the end. Only dimly did it dawn on Russia's leaders as to what was taking place in the Mennonite settlements. But when this was realized . . . when the government tried to step in and plug up this drain of German farming skills, it was far too late. For by then it was crystal clear to many of our people that they were indeed much like the Children of Israel trying to escape the dangers of the Red Sea. Thousands upon thousands stood before the gates of Moscow, pleading for passports. Never before, and never again in our entire history were Mennonites given so much attention and sympathy as during those days when the eyes of an outraged world were turned upon the refugees, who were, by sheer numbers, an embarrassment to Soviet Russia and a plea for help to every German heart. We heard that flyers were distributed all over Germany proclaiming: 'The fate of one German is the concern of every German.' For Germany, once more, stood squarely on our side . . . "

There was only one letter which gave a glimpse of the fate of the departed.

"...We were confused and nauseated by the endlessness of the sea," Hein wrote from Canada. "The ship heaved and snorted like a dragon, the chimney billowed smoke over our heads, and we were lonely and lost.

"In Montreal we would have been lost for sure, had it not been for the special buttons on our coats. Someone always grabbed us by those buttons and led us to the right train. And everything is different here. The crows make different noises, and the field mice have shorter tails, and the sun, it seems to me, rises in the north.

"Our home is a one-room hut of prairie grass that someone built on our land. It looked desolate at first, but soon we had a fire going, and we burned the dirty paper that was stuck between the logs. Inside it is now warm and cozy. I cut down a cord of poplars the very first week, and sold it as firewood in town. That gave us some money for food.

"We struggle hard. Most of us are deeply in debt. For two bushels of grain that we sow in the spring we have to repay three in the fall. Difficult times are ahead of us, but Katya! What a wonderful, secure feeling for a man to be on his own land, even though it is nothing yet but wilderness and sky. I hold my plow for fifteen hours at a stretch, and at night I cannot open my fingers to hold the cup of coffee that is waiting for me in the kitchen. We have flour, lard, salt, and sugar in our pantry, and along our porch, I have stored more firewood than we will need. Two cows supply milk and butter. In the city there's a German store where I will buy gloves for the winter. We reached the soil of Canada with barely two dollars in our pockets, but we were met by friends.

"We wish you could have come with us, for we worry greatly for your safety. Our train was one of the last to pass the Red Gate at the border of Lithuania. Before we rolled to freedom, all wagon doors were bolted shut. Guards stood outside on the running boards, pushing us back with their guns as we tried to look out of the window for a last silent farewell . . ."

"Two days later," Katya would recall with a sigh, "Russia bolted its doors and sealed us inside, as good as dead to the rest of the world."

3

Someone had nailed shut with big, rusty nails the entrance to Gerhard Wall's chapel. A notice was stuck to the wood informing him curtly that God's message, in whatever form or fashion, was no longer welcome in the land. Holding the piece of paper in his hands, the elder walked to the back of the building. The wooden fence had been torn down in order to cut a road to the rear of the village. He came across a Russian worker dismantling the steps, who informed him between thuds of his axe that the building had been singled out to be converted into a restaurant, with gaudy blue tiles from wall to wall and with shelves to hold bottles and glasses.

"Who ordered it?" asked Gerhard Wall. But he knew. For it was Jasch Kovalsky now with whom he was forced to plead when it came to matters pertaining to the welfare of the *Gemeend*.

"You can't take away my church, Jasch," he begged, frantic for once.

"And why not?" asked Jasch. "It is by far the most convenient building we could find. We need a meeting place for our assemblies."

Jasch's power had grown vast and persuasive. Some had heard that his new allegiance had briefly landed him in prison to be purified and washed clean of any lingering religious convictions. Truth or gossip, Jasch did nothing to counteract these tales. On his return after a mysterious absence of more than a year, Marusya had greeted him with wails of distress, for both his horses, she informed him loudly, had fallen ill to a sudden disease. He had gone and called on a comrade here and there to ask for assistance in his predicament. As a result, his name and picture were splashed across the pages of the paper as an example of proletarian need. It had helped him to secure work to his liking.

He was a man meticulous with lists. He loved paper with a

passion. He loved columns, rows, dates, names to be manipulated, shifted here and there, filed away, crossed out of existence. Before the week had passed, he was in possession of a big rubber stamp which would be pressed with great efficiency against anything that was written and handed to him by subordinates whose cowed behavior flattered his vanity. They made sure this rubber stamp was always at his fingertips, for his moods depended on its presence.

In bold, sprawling letters he would sign the name he had always despised, hot with the knowledge that five, ten, fifteen, twenty-five years—perhaps a lifetime—had at this moment passed through his stubby, thick-set fingers. He was an all too willing instrument. It was not even blunt vindictiveness that motivated him; it was simply that he who always bent readily to the slightest wind, was of no substance to withstand the storm of communistic zeal.

"I am here to collect your taxes, Comrade Wall."

"I have paid my taxes already. As you well know, Comrade Kovalsky."

The amount Gerhard Wall had paid the previous year had been staggering. As the shepherd of his people, he was now officially classified as a Parasitic Element, and the voting right was stricken from his name. The family had been forced to sell four of their best horses and two of their cows. The rest of Katya's silver had been traded in on the market. The *Gemeend* had helped with the rest.

"I am here to tell you that there has been a regrettable error in the bookkeeping, and that once again you will have to pay the amount, Gerhard Petrovich Wall."

To substantiate his claim, Jasch now pulled a letter out of his pocket. It had no date and no name. The rubber stamp was unreadable. More than half of the handwriting was blotted out, but there were numbers and scribblings in the margins resembling a secret code.

"That is a forged document," said Gerhard Wall.

Jasch found the remark disrespectful. He therefore felt

81

compelled to reply, more sharply and threateningly than he had meant to speak:

"Be very careful what you say, Comrade Gerhard Wall. The Soviet government is patient and just toward its citizens. But there's a limit to the harm it will tolerate from dissatisfied exploiters like yourself." And the inspector, a crude oafish Russian who in past years had been a herdsman in a Godforsaken little Russian town, now slapped the dignified elder of Waldheim on the back and on his shoulders, left and right, and yelled in hilarious glee:

"Are you going to pay, or are you going to try Siberia for a change?"

Siberia!

The chill menace was to loom for many years in the center of their troubled existence. There were devious minds now at work, hands seeking out all of the men in their prime, often the old, sometimes the senile, and—ever more frequently—boys not yet men. The invisible hand that ordered thousands of them into the frozen darkness of the arctic night was not satisfied with taking present lives. It aimed at stopping future generations.

Malevolent powers were at work in this matter, faceless men taking their secret orders from silent, faraway cities, invisible fingers that took down words, phrases, a casual remark here and there, words said in anger, in jest, or in frustration, words meant as teasing, or a greeting in passing, or an incidental commentary on the events of the day. But once on paper, these words would take on a life of their own, would turn into fiendish monstrosities, capable of pushing lives, old and young, into the pit of political exile, to perish without a sound or a trace from the face of this sorrowful earth. A generation of children grew up with the daily presence of fear—a dread and terror capable of stopping heartbeats and coagulating blood and magnifying sounds, so that an unexpected step on a stairway or a knock on the door would send tremors along the streets of a village.

The bleak finality that was Siberia came to them in dismal bits and pieces through messages that somehow found their way into the colonies in censored letters which outwardly told little, but which, on closer inspection, revealed an outcry of human agony—fragments of nonsense words which had to be pieced together by the bereaved relatives to be understood, words to be read backwards, interpreted, and decoded, slips of paper to be inspected for hidden needle pricks—every single message revealing a silent horror which by its very muteness was all the more a desperate call to heaven for deliverance from such brutal, arbitrary might.

" . . . When we arrived at our destination, there was nothing but dark, forbidding forest, nothing but ice and snow beneath our feet. . . . "

" . . . we spent hideous nights outside, without shelter of any kind. Our faces are burning with fever; our bodies are tormented by lice. . . . "

" . . . on our arrival, we had to barb-wire ourselves so no one can escape. . . . "

" . . . our toes are turning black. Our clothes, wet from the day before, are frozen stiff before we arrive at our working place . . . "

" . . . men are dumped in graves half alive if it is thought they are too weak to last out the quota of the day . . . "

" . . . those who try to flee are cut down by the machine guns of the guards . . . "

Gerhard Wall would sometimes walk along a village street where on one single hand he could count off the homes not yet orphaned. They always came at night! He dreaded the night! A van would roll along the street, halt here and there in arbitrary fashion, and many a heart would stop beating at the sound of the wheels. There would be the thud of rifle butts at a door, then shouts and curses and obscenities. And then a wailing would begin that could be heard from one end of the street to the other. The van would leave after a while, having drained the village of yet another ten, twenty, thirty men, leaving children orphaned, women widowed, young girls without a chance for motherhood. And after a while, the night's silence would deepen.

How easy it would have been, during more than a decade of steadily mounting terror, to let go of one's God, to side with the unbelievers, to join in blasphemy and try to hold on to the pulse beat of tormented life. But Gerhard Wall knew that his people did not—could not—renounce the very fiber of their being. God had bound them over, and God would rescue them and slay the fiend. Was it not written in Psalm seventy-two: " . . . he shall judge the poor of the people, he shall save the children of the needy, and shall break in pieces the oppressor . . . in his days shall the righteous flourish . . . he shall have dominion also from sea to sea, and from the river unto the ends of the earth . . . and his enemies shall lick the dust . . . "

From where such help would arrive he did not know, unless it should come from Germany. But did it matter? It sufficed that help of some kind was promised. He was thankful for this certainty, for often he himself felt weak in his faith. The grievous burdens of a broken, terrified *Gemeend* rested heavily upon his shoulders. He had been thrust into divine service before he was inwardly prepared to take on the full dimensions of this laborious task, and before he knew it, a year had passed, and another, and soon five years had gone by, and then ten—and the good ones, the strong ones, the older Mennonite leaders on whom he could have leaned for guidance and support, had all been sifted out from under his very hands and perished in the night. Those were the ones he needed! Those were the ones who by their wisdom and example could have given him sustenance and backing in this wretched time of spiritual and moral disintegration. It was the simpler people who remained, and that was one of the reasons he felt so overwhelmed now when everyone leaned on him who was so mortally weary himself.

Sometimes, in morbid castigation, he was driven to the place where his chapel once had been as he remembered it so clearly—built stoutly for posterity to come, paid for to the last of its sparkling windows, kept immaculate by the women of the *Gemeend*. Now it was but a violated shell of an edifice—dirty, defiled, and neglected. At the side entrance he saw three empty barrels—beer containers, he supposed with a sigh. The staircase in the back had sunk to one side. The rain had washed off the paint from the gutters and the window sills. He bent down to pick up a broken flower pot and set it to the side.

It was the same sad, heart-breaking sight in Muntau and Tiegenhagen and in the villages beyond. Club houses, stables, granaries, and theatres had been built of what were but the skeletons of former places of worship. He knew of one that had been torn down because the strong red bricks were needed to fence a pigsty in the collectives.

"I must bring my message to bear upon the young," he would tell himself time and again.

Those were the precious ones, the ones still malleable.

Every night, he would casually walk along the village street, hoping to find a brave soul willing to hear him out without fear. His own son David, he knew, was still too young to have been totally contaminated by the heretical dogma of the Soviet schools. It was still possible to talk to David. It was all but too late for his daughters. Sara and Liestje already had a picture of Joseph Stalin hanging above their beds. He still harbored hope that he, their father, could salvage his girls if only he kept trying persistently enough to find words to reach their yearning, impressionable souls. Yes, he would try as best he could. He could do little but keep on trying.

He knew that the crashing, flamboyant ideologies were visibly hardest on Sara—this child of his whose eyes were hungry for praise, who knew full well that her young beauty was underscored by the glittering *Komsomol* star on her shoulder, who by her very charm and grace could manage to wiggle by the profoundest truths without so much as a nod of acknowledgment that spiritual substance was lacking in her life.

Gerhard Wall knew without a trace of doubt that he loved his oldest child with a love that knew no reservations. Even when she was gone, he was not free of her presence. He would seek her out in order to feel the never-stilled pain, the way the tongue is

85

forced to seek out a tormenting tooth, just to make sure life was still there, the pain was still there. He had learned to draw strength from the knowledge of his love, for whenever he felt that he was weakening on behalf of his Lord, he need only look at Sara's strangely shaped, slightly surreptitious face to be reminded of the night when he had fled from God's scythe and thus by his cowardly action had bound Katya over. What had happened was not Sara's fault. He loved Sara. Of that he could be sure! There was soothing penance in this love.

He waited for her by the window each day. He loved to watch her appear around the corner and walk by the Cornies Statue depicting the legendary agrarian genius of the Mennonites. Previous generations had put up the sculpture in recognition of a God-sent mind who, in his time, had imparted to the settlers so many innovations that certain persons, even then, had speculated about a pact with the Devil which must have gained him his uncanny wisdom. How else was it possible that his windmills had run so smoothly that a child could set them in motion by the mere force of its breath?

He had believed in many things that must have seemed strange in his times. He had held that the land should rest every fourth year to replenish itself—that it would repay such consideration with seven-fold richness the following year. By example he had shown the Mennonite settlers that such land would store up the moisture beneath and starve out the weeds on the surface. Future generations had religiously followed his advice, leaving the acres in thick, loose clods so that the water, during the fall, could sink in, and the frost, in the winter, could crumble it, and the next year's sun could draw out a richness of grain that made the Russian neighbors exclaim in superstitious envy and awe:

"Do the Mennonites have a separate God?"

"Perhaps no separate God, though certainly God's blessings," thought Gerhard Wall, remembering the cherished legacy.

Now in the Soviet collectives whenever one saw cattle that

were red and strong of meat and generous of milk, one could be certain they were the *krasnaya nyemka*— "the lovely German creature" that Cornies had imported.

Yes, this outstanding man's powerful seal was still upon the land. He had planted scores of trees to control the underground water table. During revolutionary days, many of these trees had had to fall, and the officials now lamented bitterly that this had been a wasteful, hasty mistake, for the winds now had free play and carried away the finest layers of the soil, to everyone's distress and remorse. The acknowledged wisdom of this man thus was probably the reason why the statue was still left alone when so much else of German heritage had had to fall—most likely because it gradually dawned on the fumbling Soviets that there was careful purpose behind the smooth, efficient beauty of German inventions.

There was Sara now, coming along the street, as always the center of attraction of half a dozen boys. She was very popular among the youth of the village. Her emblem was flashing in the sun. She walked briskly, her eyes sparkling from animated talk. She was most certainly a beautiful sight to behold! He could hear her laugh with her friends.

Gerhard Wall leaned forward in anticipation, charmed by the glow in her face. Her eyes danced. Her entire lovely face now turned into a dimpled, mischievous smile. She stood back a little, swinging her foot. She puckered her lips. Gerhard Wall turned white as he saw her spit in the dust in front of the statue. The other youths applauded.

The elder waited for her by the window. He waited patiently until her friends could no longer be heard. He closed the door behind her as she walked in with her light, agile steps, and then he also closed the three windows that faced the street, as well as the one in the rear of the house. He did this precisely and methodically while she stood there waiting for his greeting. He turned to her slowly and struck her across the mouth with all the force at his command. The blow sent the girl reeling the length of the hall.

"Get out of my sight," he whispered, hoarsely. "Have I taught you so little all these years?"

He stood, stunned by his own violence, while she fled sobbing to her room. Only much later could he speak.

"Child, forgive me," he said, humbly. "I lost my patience—shamefully! I am heart-broken, Sara, to have struck you so hard."

"To have a *kulak* for a parent," sobbed the girl, "is worse than being dead."

He sat by her bed, stroking her shoulder. What could he say? He cringed at the denunciation. A *kulak* was one who traded off the sweat of the land, who gave his miserly wares with his left hand and raked in thrice the profit with his right. He was not such a man. He never had been, nor had any of his people. Cornies had not been such a man. Cornies had not worked for his gains alone; nor, for that matter, had he worked solely in behalf of his people. He had, in fact, openly sought out the Russian serfs, had looked into their vermin-infested lives, had scolded them harshly for loose living, had taught them cleanliness of body and made them feel the joy of cleanliness of mind.

" ... he was no *kulak*, Sara, though he owned land enough to feed three hundred workers. People felt glad and fortunate to work for such a man, for the abundance of his inner being spread over all who came in contact with his mind . . . " Was she listening? Her sobbing had subsided. "Even then, Sara, people did not always approve of a self-restrained, self-disciplined way of life. Not all were fond of this hard-headed man and his peculiar theory of how good land should be honored. And Cornies was very obstinate in his own well-meaning way, I have to admit! He was not at all above enforcing his views and beliefs by means of a swift and sharp-cutting whip which he carried around for good measure. One settler, to spite him, had planted his trees head first. Imagine! Cornies thought it expedient one day to seek him out to teach him a lesson he would remember. And just at the moment when this sinner bent down between the weeds to search out his miserly trees . . . "

88

Sara smiled faintly at this tale and was now willing to turn around to face her father fully.

" . . . Imagine what happened! His rear end must have stung for days! But such punishment was for his own future good, and the negligent farmer realized this fully. Cornies' favorite saying was borrowed from Frederick the Great's many maxims: 'You have to force people to their happiness.' He was a full-blooded German, you know, quick to strike out when blocked since he knew himself to be right . . . "

The elder's voice was very eager now:

" . . . He came from a soldier's town, you know, somewhere in the North of Germany? Sara? Are you listening? As a matter of fact, he was not even truly one of our own, for most of his ideas seemed far too worldly to our forefathers. Our own church elders turned against him in the end, and he was forced to leave the *Gemeend,* a bitter and taciturn . . . "

"Father, my face is hurting!"

" . . . I said I am sorry! Child, what we had in this man was a heaven-sent genius, whom even our own people, never too kind to those with exceptional gifts, would distrust and denounce in their stubborness. As a matter of fact, Sara, he was an unbeliever of sorts! It took him longer than most of us to struggle through doubt and temptation to the certainty of Mennonite belief, for he was a bookish person and of a heady temper as well! He died more feared than loved, but he left his mark upon the land. And once he rested beneath his hill, everyone was forced to testify that in this place there slept a real man of God . . . "

"There is no God," said his beautiful daughter, matter-of-factly, her eyes now calm and serene.

" . . . it was his misfortune that he lived in a time so critical of his capacities, so jealous and suspicious of his gifts. Once, he even went to Petersburg . . . "

"It's Petrograd now," said Sara, pointing to the map which held nothing beyond the borders of Russia.

He took her lovely face in both of his hands. He said, feeling his voice tremble:

89

"Child, watch your tongue. Don't ever—ever, Sara!—speak to anyone about our disagreement in this matter. Please listen. Listen carefully. I am an old man by now. I have to speak my mind to my own children whom I love. I cannot help myself. Listen to me. I have to speak because my Maker has ordered me to speak in His behalf. I have no choice. But close your ears if that is what you have to do in order to survive. Close your eyes and your ears and your mind if that is the only way you can live. But please, for God's sake, do hold your tongue."

"Don't worry," said Sara. "I won't turn you in. Just don't hit me again, Father. Don't ever strike me in my face."

He said to Katya, the way Ohm Klassen had said to his twins: "My house is shaking."

It broke Katya's heart to see him like this, sunk into himself with bitter grief from being wounded by one of his children. He would not even look at her then; he would sigh and go into his room and pull the door shut behind him. She would hear him move the heavy chest of drawers to the side to take the Bible from its hiding place. She thought she heard him weep in the darkness. If she strained, she could hear his voice through the walls:

"How can I put up with this destruction of inner convictions? I know I will lose my children unless I find a way . . . a way to put their feet upon some solid ground that will withstand . . . My eyes are on the window, for fear a traitor will pass by . . . "

What could she do but join him silently in his distress? He reached out for her in the dark and held her close to himself like a man drowning:

"Katyushka. We are no people without our German bonds. If we deny . . . if we forget from where we came, the wellspring of our essence will dry up. What can I do to stop the plunder of our past? I am not up to such an overwhelming undertaking. My church has been closed, given over to profanity and dirt. The men who had a hand in crafting our lives are silent in their graves. I am too weak and too unlearned. I lack the means to combat fear. Torture can break me in less than two days . . . "

"You can baptize in the barn," said Katya. "You can read the word of resurrection at a coffin, for in the sight of death no one will dare to give you away. Burn your Bible. You don't need it; you know more than half of it by heart."

"I am so full of fear," he repeated.

"The Lord is my shepherd. I shall not want . . . "

"It is but a matter of time," he replied.

She knew, as he did, that sooner or later exile to Siberia would be his fate as well. It was but a matter of time. And time was running out. It was no longer sufficient to talk of spiritual tidings; that was as good as throwing God's precious words to the wind. More concrete, immediate help was needed. There was destruction, decay, destitution wherever one turned one's eyes. When she now sent her own son David to the store to stand in line for a glass of sugar or a loaf of week-old bread, the little boy would elbow left and right, reprimanded by not a single one of the adults, for youthful insolence was now declared a virtue by the state. Parents no longer dared to discipline a child that needed discipline the way a tree had to be trimmed of its wayward branches. There was loud, lewd singing in the streets lasting far into the night. The Devil only knew what went on in the bushes. With the Russian language had come the Russian vulgarity—the loose cursing and swearing so offensive to a people accustomed to account for every careless word. Youths of decent German descent, now Russian students in the cities, would come home on vacation and walk by her house, arms around each other, breaking into singing at the elder's sight:

"We leave heaven to the sparrows and the angels, for our future is here on earth . . . "

"Katyushka, what am I to do?"

She said mechanically: "Yea, though I walk through the valley of the shadow of death, I will fear no evil, for Thou art with me; Thy rod and Thy staff they comfort me . . . "

"I am comforted that I can talk to you, dear wife, for you are of stout, certain mind. You listen. And you don't condemn.

91

Katyushka! I am no longer certain of my God. I am no longer
certain that the Almighty is holding the steering wheel of my
ship-wrecked life. I can no longer retain my thoughts. I forget
what was clear a minute before. My words no longer suffice. My
thoughts become lost, for my eyes are glued to the window. I am
utterly drained of my spiritual strength."

Katya said calmly:

"There is no longer a *Gemeend*. But there are still its hungry
members, and you know it, Gerhard Wall. We can no longer
count on God's voice. However, we can count on His promise."

But he could not stop; a torrent of doubt demanded to be
released:

"I worry whether our foundation with withstand . . . "

"Others have felt the same. Didn't Jonah try to escape God's
hand? And didn't Elijah groan and moan? And didn't Jeremiah
curse the very hour of his birth? And what about Job and his
struggle? We all doubt. But why talk about it and thus give
substance to doubt and open a door through which Satan can
enter?"

"I am so tired of being the Lord's dispatcher." His hands
were like lead on her shoulders.

"Gerhard," said Katya. "You have to promote a visible
cause, something the young can feel and grasp with their own
hungry hands."

He said, after a pause:

"There are rumors, Katyushka."

Immediately, she went to pull the drapes shut at the tone of
his voice.

"In Germany," he whispered, "new uniforms are mixing
with the old . . . "

She stood in a quaking shiver. She knew. The *Vaterland* was
beginning to stir. The *Vaterland* was beginning to feel youthful
strength surge through its veins. Lord! Could it be true?

"Oh, Katyushka. What's happening in Germany?"

"Speak of Germany," she said with a helpless little sob she
could not manage to swallow in time. "That is a message the

92

young will understand. There is your answer, Gerhard Wall. Right there. You have known that all along, haven't you, dear? Sooner or later, Germany will come to our aid . . . "

There was a way. There was still hope. Nothing but the tiniest flicker of a promise, barely enough to keep strength faintly pulsating, barely sufficient to shelter this tiny flame of hope for survival in the midst of a hideous hurricane of vicious destruction. There was a way to keep it alive by seeking shelter and strength in Germany's poetry, in Germany's songs, in those rare guttural sounds of German awakening that filtered through the horrendous noise of atheistic blatancy—talk of a powerful, volatile man risen from the very depths of German stock, a man of whom they knew little beyond fragments of passionate rhetoric, a man whose very name they did not know, but who was, they understood instinctively, right at this very moment rallying young German forces in their behalf. Yes, by God in high heaven, there was a way!

He, Gerhard Wall, might have been drained and wasted, but he still had a son. He still had a boy young and willing. He and the boy would sit on the door steps, and he would pass on to the child his hopes and his longings. and the child would whisper back to him those precious sounds of magic, and he and the boy would be one. His son could still be taken by the hand, be led into the woods and stand in awed reverence while he, his father, would break off a twig from a fir tree and put a match to it and have him smell the sharp, pungent scent of the spark-throwing needles, and tell him in a voice raw with emotion:

"This, David, is the smell of Christmas in the *Vaterland* . . . "

4

Sara, in many ways, was of a fortunate disposition. She managed to bob through much of her life like a glittering, dancing bottle cap on the surface of a ferociously racing river—accidental in her place, without much substance and solidity, but indestructible in her own way, too weightless and unimportant to be hurt, overlooked in the concerns of the day. She understood instinctively that she could always count on having her transgressions forgiven in exchange for her lightheartedness in times when ease of mind and a light-hearted laugh were rare commodities indeed—so scarce as to be absent in the troubled lives of the people that she knew.

She was very pretty, to be sure. In fact, she was easily the most beautiful girl of Waldheim, and probably of the neighboring villages as well. She was so very different from any other child that they had ever known that allowances were made for Sara by mere virtue of her lovely, clear-cut face. Even as a very young child, when Katya had held her in her lap during services, those around her found it difficult to concentrate on the solemn word of God, for she distracted them with her huge unblinking eyes and her teasing, flirting smile. Mennonite children were forced to sit and to listen in reverence to that which flowed from the pulpit on the day of the Lord. But if a sermon was stretched a little too long or was too repetitious, it was Sara and no one else who could just slide off her mother's lap and gently tiptoe along the aisle and wait in the sunshine outside.

Now she stood amid a darkness not dark to her eyes, a ready expectancy in her face and a deep-seated certainty in her heart that no matter what might come her way that could not be helped, the currents of her young world would carry her safely.

"Guess what, Mother! Yesterday I had myself married to someone from the settlement of Sagradovka."

"You did what, Sara?"

"I was married, Mother."

Katya was silent to such news. What was there to say that would make a difference? A young man whose name she had never once heard before—a meek, blushing, quite pleasant young fellow, she learned to her relief—had taken her child up ten steps to a place called the Marriage Palace where a woman judge had curtly pronounced them tied to each other for life.

There had been a very solemn ceremony, explained Sara apologetically, with an eight-and-a-half minute lecture on how to live up to the stringent dictates of Joseph Stalin and his creed. There had been music in the adjoining room. And a photographer had taken half a dozen pictures. They had had to sign five long, fine-printed papers before they were permitted to shake hands with each other and with the other people in the room. They had spent the rest of the afternoon searching for a place to live, since Franz was promised work in a factory supplying felt boots to the Red soldiers. Would Katya mind if for the time being they occupied the summer room?

"Even though he isn't Mennonite, he's German, to be sure. That's almost more than one can ask,"said Gerhard Wall, glad to find out that his new son-in-law's ancestors had come from Bavaria more than twelve decades ago.

"His parents never owned a thing," announced Sara with proud satisfaction. "Not a thimble! Aren't you happy, Mother? Be happy for our sake. We are legally married, you know. We could have just chosen to live in free love."

"I suppose so," agreed Katya, with a sigh.

Free love could mean this or that and make you cringe in shame. The courts were overrun by women demanding alimony after one of the partners had shamelessly broken the Soviet vows, whatever there was to be broken. Their children, having become homeless through their folly, were roaming the streets of the Russian cities, forced into a life of thievery. Was this young fellow here, perhaps, one of those who took wedded duty to be a temporary diversion? He was no Mennonite—who was he, anyway? He startled her every time she walked into her kitchen and saw him sitting there. This marriage remained unreal to Katya although she came to like the shy stranger quite well and spent many an afternoon ironing his shirts and mending his socks while he sat by the window waiting for the letter that was to arrive from Melitopol, willingly supplying answers to her anxious inquiries about the customs and mores of the place from which he had come.

95

She glanced in his direction every once in a while, and felt reassured the more that she looked. Yes, as a mother she would have to admit that Sara had done what any sensible girl her age should do—she had found herself a quiet and decent young man who obviously loved her well enough, and who might even be so indiscernible as to escape exile in these trying, sorrowful times when young manhood had become synonymous with willful, arbitrary deportation.

Yet her heart revolted. How could it be right to take one's life's decisions past the *Gemeend* and never bother to register with the Lord one's love ties with another human being? In the life that she herself had known, the church had dictated, had controlled the very flow and rhythm of life and had wielded consistent power over each family. Every birth, baptism, wedding, every death was carefully recorded in the book of the *Gemeend*,—even the names, first and last, of those people who had fled to America more than a decade ago.

To her distress, she kept forgetting the name of the young man who claimed to have married her child. The only reality that Katya could grasp having come out of this hasty, superficial, spur-of-the-moment union was a child—a precocious girl with soft brown curls, a serious mouth, and wide-set, questioning eyes—a child of keen perception whom Katya loved with utter abandon for the rest of her burdensome life.

"Let me have her," she pleaded with Sara. "Life in the city is unhealthy for a child."

"Sure," replied Sara, nonchalantly. "We named her Karin. Isn't that a pretty name? As she isn't really all that pretty a baby, she needs an ornamental name, don't you think? Why, when she was born, she did not even have a single strand of hair. She looked like a scalded monkey, to be sure."

Karin! What an unordinary twist of one's tongue! Had the name come from a book—or worse!—from one of those moving pictures the Devil had recently invented? It took Katya a month to even remember its sound and its spelling, though it took her only two minutes to understand most fully and comprehensively

96

the total blessing that had once again been bestowed upon her by a benevolent though shrouded divinity. And it was just as well, she now admitted gladly, rocking the baby in her lap, for Sara to have been married so hastily, for she might never have had another opportunity to get herself a man. Indeed, many a young woman was not so lucky. Certainly Liestje was already beginning to resign herself meekly to lifelong solitary spinsterhood, since she was shy and unassuming, and of a pale, plain face as well.

For when Karin was five years old, a wave of deportations swept the country such as the worst years of exiling had not yet seen—in the wake of the sudden announcement that Germany, once again, was at war with the Russian land.

Only a very few men managed to escape the indiscriminate mass manhandling that was now to take place, that took the timid stranger, before long, from Sara's side along with hundreds of thousands of others who soundlessly perished as if they had never lived at all. Only a handful of men saved themselves— those who could fade into the cities as sought-after craftsmen, or those who had wisely married a Russian woman with high-ranking government connections, or those who chose to arrest so as not to be arrested, or those very few whom a quirk of fate had temporarily bypassed—men like the elder Gerhard Wall, who still stood under Jasch's dubious, ambivalent protection.

There was the unassuming Mennonite Ohmtje Wiens. In his seventy years of life he had never uttered a sentence other than simple Low German save for his awkward talks with the Lord. Now he signed his unsteady name to a 15-page document of treason that found him guilty of treason for having participated in a plot designed to sever Armenia from Soviet Russia. He did so after one of his sons was sentenced to death for having planned to bomb a Communist meeting in Tokmak, and another one for having hidden a German sword beneath his attic stairs in order to do away with Soviet might, after his two grown daughters, girls of immaculate reputation who seldom left the house, were found to have been involved in an unchaste relationship with a well-known counterrevolutionary who, to the best of anyone's knowledge, had never set foot in Waldheim, and after his youngest son, a boy of fifteen, was executed behind the house for good measure.

And there was the highly respected Mennonite Fritz Friesen. At one time or another he had employed a shiftless Ukrainian servant girl who now came forward, remembering that he had told her of having harbored a White terrorist for the duration of three nights. It made no difference that after the old man was taken away to be silenced it was discovered accidentally that his ill-fated guest had not been a soldier of Wrangel's Army but a typhoid-ridden bandit whom he had taken into his home in Christian concern and who had died in his bed the following day.

Gerhard Wall's neighbor to the right, it was meticulously documented, had dug a deep well in order to poison 23 Ukrainian workers after having exploited them for capitalistic gains for eight years. The one to the left had slaughtered a pig seven years ago and had secretly sold it in order to buy seeds for his fields, instead of giving his profits to the collectives, thus undermining the reconstructive efforts of the land. This one had purchased a bag of corn at the market for twice the legal price, and that one had walked out in the middle of a Soviet meeting and thus stood accused of disrespecting the Soviet will. There were those who had collaborated with the enemy by serving as medical helpers during the previous war, and those too old or too stubborn to work on a Sunday, or those unfortunate ones like young Hans Letkemann who had a serious speech defect and could not make himself understood as he tried to explain in gurgling terror that the crime he was accused of having committed could not have been his because he was born the following year.

People no longer dared to nod a greeting across a neighbor's fence without catching the deadly danger in the air. It became a way of life to whisper at the supper table, to pull the curtains before any word was said. A slip of the tongue, a misunderstanding, a sudden silence, a suspiciously disrupted conversation was

98

more than sufficient to throw an entire family in jail. The settlers found themselves accused of having plotted to blow up bridges and buildings and having signalled a German war plane by lighting a match in the fireplace. To begrudge one's neighbor's efforts and to say, "Are you itching, perhaps, to gather riches of your own?" meant seeing him arrested the following night. To envy a friend his strength of conviction meant to accuse him of praying for divine intervention to do away with Stalin and his men. One could simply happen to overhear a neighbor sigh and charge him with a defeatist attitude. Denunciations multiplied like rabbits in the barn.

There was a time when Gerhard Wall had thought that he knew the absolute limit of human brutality—to see an innocent man put to the wall of his house and to watch his body be riddled with bullets. Quick death, to many, would now have been mercy indeed. He knew of men who spent weeks, months, even years in incarceration, often held sleepless for many nights by devilish malice—men who, if ever released, were broken, crippled for life in body and spirit and mind. Wasn't he one of them, many a time? Dozens of times, these past few weeks, he himself had been torn out of his sleep to be taken to yet another drawn-out, tormenting, utterly senseless interrogation.

"See this file?"

"Yes, Tovarich."

"It contains the documented proof that on April the twenty-second. . . . "

Accusations. Insinuations. Threats. Persuasion. Intermittently the agonies of solitary shackles. More frequently, incarceration in a room crammed to the brim with other wretched lives—where men stood silent for days, shoulder to cramping shoulder, leaning against each other, swaying from utter fatigue, retching from the smell of human excrement, where men lost their reason, their sanity, their faith in a God who had covered His face eons ago, where men died standing, held in place standing unnoticed for hours. Once in a while, the gates might open a slit and permit a glimpse outside where thousands of women sat patiently holding their bundles to their knees, hoping for a chance to ease the burdens of their fathers, their husbands, their sons, hoping for a decision—any decision—that would put an end to the agony of waiting and not knowing.

" . . . for having enticed your loyal servant Ivan to sow weeds, thus helping cause the Russian famine. . . . "

" . . . for having knocked Stalin's picture off the wall with your elbow . . . "

" . . . for having praised the vices of imperialism from the pulpit . . . "

It was a deadly serious game—night after night, week after week. Was there an end? He knew why he himself was spared—for whatever a stay of execution was worth to a man fully sentenced—because there was Jasch, sitting behind his desk, right hand to the official interrogator, pen poised between his fingers, looking about with a bored expression, trying as best he could without endangering himself to ward off the inevitable fate of Katya's husband Gerhard Wall.

"There are scores of witnesses who will testify to the effect that on November 15 of 1915 . . . "

"I didn't yet minister from the pulpit in the fall of that year. My father-in-law was then still alive."

"Didn't you tell your congregation at one time: 'Thy *will* be done'? With this certain insinuating inflection in your voice?"

"If I did, I was not speaking of the Emperor Friedrich Wilhelm. I could not have made reference to the abdicated German ruler because . . . "

"We know of your secret connections to Germany. We know of whole strongholds, entire nests of German spies along the Russian border. We know of plans for secret networks of tunnels. There isn't a German alive who doesn't in his heart hope for the downfall of our glorious State . . . "

Gerhard Wall tried to steady himself with an effort. Could there be any substance to those rumors? Was this man who at this very moment was believed to be rallying the youth of Germany beneath his flaming flag perhaps . . . ? He would have to pull himself together! He could not afford to be side-tracked by wild, soaring, irrational hope! Tiny droplets of perspiration stood on the elder's forehead and upper lip while he struggled as best he could against the sucking quicksand of false denunciations. He forced himself to stand erect, to focus on details. There were three tables in the room. Yes. One. Two. Three. They were covered with red cloth. Red was the color of Germany's flag. The secretary yawned. What would he give for an uninterrupted night of sleep! There was a fly buzzing against the window. A fly this late in the year? Where did it come from? Why was it still alive? All other flies had long since perished.

"What is your name again?"

"Gerhard Petrovich Wall."

"Why were you arrested?"

"I don't know."

"What are you saying?" The voice became more threatening.

"I don't know, Tovarich."

"Are you implying you believe we have arrested you illegally?"

"Yes, I do."

"Throw him into solitary confinement. He is accusing us of abusing Soviet power . . . "

"No, Tovarich. I just said that I haven't been told the reason for my arrest. I need to know what I have done."

"So you admit that you have done something wrong?"

"No, that's not what I said at all."

"I think you are indirectly slandering the Party."

"That was not my intention."

"Does the Party have to account to you?"

"No. I have no concern . . . "

"You have no concern?" This time, very gleefully. "You don't care? What are you implying, Gerhard Wall?"

"I am concerned. I worry about what . . . what you are trying to prove."

"I have to do nothing to prove your guilt to you. Nothing at

101

all. I can just sit here all day and twiddle my thumbs and wait for you to prove your innocence to me."

"I am innocent, Tovarich. I have known nothing of Germany for the past twelve years."

"You lie!" This time it was a shout.

Gerhard Wall fell silent.

"Speak up!" fumed his tormentor. "We are not through with you yet. You still stand accused of the following—Number one: Of having a brother-in-law abroad—what is his name now? Hein Klassen, living in Winnipeg, Canada—who used to write slanderous letters derogatory of the Russian Government! Number two: Of having had, above your bed, the picture of the German Emperor of whom you were so enamored that for a period of two years and seven months you wore a mustache exactly like this imperialist *Nyemets* pig! Number three: Of having . . . Oh yes! Here it is! . . . You stood there leaning against the fence on August the second this year talking to your neighbor Aaron Bergen, and a passerby heard you say . . . "

Incredibly, after five hours of torment, he was suddenly released to go home. Katya heard his footsteps in the hall. They halted by the door. He must be leaning against the wall. She went to him, helped him into the room, pushed him onto a chair. Without a word, he sat there, his eyes fixed on the bare spot where once had hung the cross-stitched words: "Lo, I am with you alway, even unto the end of the world." He sat, his head lowered onto his chest, his face pallid. The last rays of the evening sun betrayed the hole where the nail had held the frame. She would have to paint over the spot again so as to forestall suspicion. She sat there opposite her husband, dressed in her best black dress, waiting for him to speak.

He said: "In the prisons, one is always near the gates of eternity."

She answered, "They may tear us from our soil, but never from our God."

He rose. He put his suitcase in the hall. "They will come again," he said, inaudibly. "This time I won't be back. I know

102

it." They looked at each other. "Katyushka. There is talk that all villagers will be deported within a few weeks. Something must have happened along the German front." He clutched to her suddenly, his voice hoarse: "I think the Germans are coming!"

They waited.

Late in the night, there was a knock at the door. There was time, thanks to the beloved Lord, to say a silent farewell to the sleeping children. How often had he stood like this, wondering if he would ever see them again? He stood by their beds for a while, silently looking at their faces.

When he did not return the following day, Liestje offered to go to the interrogation building. But Katya shook her head. A chill wind had sprung up, for it was late in the year. Liestje was of tender lungs and sickly disposition. She, Katya, would ready herself to go. Dizzy with dread and foreboding, she packed yet another bundle of clothes, a small pillow, two pairs of socks. Perhaps she could smuggle these items into her husband's hands if Jasch would help her discover a guard willing to let himself be bribed with a small pack of tobacco she had traded from Jasch just last week for this purpose.

"Don't wait for me," she said to her children. "It might be days. Liestje, be sure to give Karin her meals. David, stay close to the house in case we have to leave. Sara, pack our bedding."

Many hundreds of women were already waiting outside the prison gates. She managed to push herself through the railing where she could see Jasch by the door. She tried to wave at him, to make him notice her, but he stood there, a guard at his side, a list of names in his hands, frowning disconcertedly.

She tugged at his sleeve. He shrugged her off, coughing in discomfort. But in an unguarded moment, he bent close to her face and whispered:

"Several of the accused were shot at dawn, but Gerhard was not among them. I am quite certain that he is still alive."

She sat on the floor like the other waiting women. She waited there all day, watching the letters of the alphabet

103

diminish in Jasch's hands. When she had almost given up hope, she heard her husband's name called from the door.

She struggled to her feet. Gerhard Wall came slowly down the steps, supported by two men. His head hung loosely on his chest. His nose was swollen out of shape. A band of blackish, crusted blood ran across the back of his neck. Could this be the man who had said a hundred times and more that others' sorrows were his own? A tremor went through the waiting women. They had all known him well. To suffer a loss meant to knock on his door any hour of the day or night in order to weep in his presence and be certain of two arms that gave comfort, of eyes that were softened by love and compassion, of a word from the wells of the Bible that promised relief, of time for spiritual searching. His beard had grown out, but even so, the weeping women realized that this was a face robbed brutally of human dignity—it was a vacant face, a face that was no longer Gerhard Wall, the staunch defender of his faith, the loyal shepherd to his frightened, hurting, diminishing flock. These were the features of a stranger who on the rack had left a lifetime of deepest faith.

Katya called out his name in a wail, struggling wildly, fiercely against the many hands that held her back. The elder lifted his head with an effort, and briefly, his own empty gaze met her own. He whispered, lifting all ten of his fingers:

"Ten years . . . "

"Gerhard," she called. "Gerhard. Gerhard. My love. My love. My love. Oh, my love." She was not a woman given to easy endearments. Never in their closest moments had she felt free to speak such words of love and affection as now poured forth from her lips unchecked, while she was choking from tears, from grief, from rage, from Jasch's heavy hand over her face, from his tight, fear-stricken voice in her ear:

"Hush, Katya. Hush! Be quiet, for heaven's sake! Do you want to get arrested, too, here on the spot?"

Someone handed her a bundle of dirty, blood-stained clothes. She stared at them, blinded by tears. In one of the sleeves she found a scribbled note pinned to an inside seam: "I will write to you if I can. I will use the name Kamarov."

She committed that name to her memory. Kamarov. She knew no one by such a name. Kamarov. She was not to forget! It was a strange monster sitting on her tongue. She hated it; it was alien, bitter, incomprehensible, not part of herself or the man who was now led away.

She stared at the paper in her hand. Kamarov. She must not forget! Gerhard had always teased her about her poor memory for Russian names. But this one she must not forget! She must always remember the name Kamarov. How else was she to find her husband in the endlessness that was Siberia?

And though she imprinted it onto her memory in an utter gesture of will, she was never to hear it again—not in the weeks to come, not in a year, not in ten, not in a lifetime, not ever.

Book Two
Sara
[1941—1945]

5

The old woman had lost her crutch in the darkness; her hands trembled as she tried to steady herself against the rusty wagon walls.

"Hurry up! *Davay! Davay!*" a guard shouted loudly, letting the rifle butt fall cruelly between her shoulder blades. The blow sent her staggering into the river of human wretchedness piling up along the railroad tracks. A long, rattling train pulled away, overflowing. Another one pushed in, backing up to the shrinking lines on the ramp, sucking up a steady stream of people.

Notice had come the previous night that the outlying villages had ceased to exist—that all had been drained into the waiting cattle trains. The deadly edict, by early morning, had been affixed to Waldheim's people. Now it was night—a night as dread, as dark as Satan's vile bowels.

Katya sat, numbed, on her bundles of bedding, both arms folded around Karin's shivering body. To her right crouched Sara, silent and pale. On her other side were Liestje and David, clutching hands for comfort, watching the henchmen of the Soviets push people roughly into the heavily guarded wagons.

"Ens."

"Fast."

"Jantzen."

"Unger."

Each name stabbed Katya's heart. She knew them all. Anna Ens, her neighbor and her childhood friend. Johann Fast whose wife had been her schoolmate. Old Auntie Jantzen, her dead mother's cousin, a woman bent with age and grief. Paul Unger's wife amid her many sickly children. Family after family, clinging to each other in terrified clusters so as not to be ripped from each other for life.

A sudden beam of light struck her face.

"Katyushka?"

109

She turned, blinded by the sudden glare. "Jasch? Is that you, Jasch?"

"Yes, Shhh."

"Where will we be sent, Jasch?" She could vaguely see him push against the stream of heaving, struggling, staggering people.

"I don't know. Siberia, most likely. Perhaps the Ural Mountains or Tashkent." Reaching for her scarf, he pulled her to himself, pretending to tie the knots about her back. "Come closer,' he hissed, urgently. Against her ear, he whispered: "The Germans have overrun the steppe...if we last till the morning..."

Katya felt her mouth go as dry as parched cotton. She could see that Jasch was stalling as he moved about, loudly calling names off the scroll of paper he held in his hands.

"Thal."

"Tersen."

"Vogt."

She grasped Liestje by the arm:

"Listen, child!"

The night suddenly hushed. It hushed as a canary might fall dumb before the glimmering eyes of a cat. A heart-rending poignancy was linked to this stillness. Life hung suspended from a spider's fragile thread. People burrowed into the straw. Had there ever been hours, minutes, seconds as cruelly long as these? This night, most certainly, was part of God's eternity—a boundless, unmeasurable, unfathomable streak of everlasting time.

Out of this darkness, gently now, there came a distant humming.

All faces turned upward, toward the approaching light of the sky. A Russian plane, flying low, arched like a meteor along the rapidly discoloring horizon, its wings and fuselage torn to shreds, trailing a tail of blackish smoke. As it disappeared beyond the tree tops, an explosion, hard and final, ripped the silence and ended in the shattering of many windows. Now, with the racing

110

light in the sky, there appeared eleven, thirteen, sixteen Russian bombers. And in ferocious pursuit—like swishing, bristling little wasps—came darting from the clouds a handful of sparkling German hunters, flying so low across the barren fields that it seemed they intended to take off the tips of the old acorn trees with a clean sweep of their glittering wings. By now, it was light enough to try to comprehend the inconceivable—to realize in stunned disbelief that the railroad station stood deserted of the Soviet tormenters.

Katya held onto Karin with cramped fingers, unaware that the child was writhing under her grip.

"Sara, find out what is . . . is happening," she managed to whisper after a while.

Who else but Sara could be entrusted with such a suffocating mission? Only too glad to escape the night's clutching horror, Sara ran as fast as she could, her heart like a fluttering bird in her throat. It took little effort to squeeze her slender body through the bars of the locked iron gate. She took a speedy short-cut through an unharvested corn field, trying to reach the main road to her left, feeling the stiff canes battering her knees as she hastened along. Parting the last swish of dry, brittle stalks, she found herself facing an apparition—a young man in a strange, grey uniform who stared at her in startled surprise, stuttering in broken Russian:

" . . . I tried to cross the bridge over there . . . there was fire from the left . . . I must have lost my way . . . "

She chewed her lower lip in vexation. Was this a provocator, disguised to trick her into an imprudent remark? Was he a spy placed here by the Soviets? She tried hard not to show a reaction that could be twisted into a noose for herself. She squinted at him against the sun, trying to read his expression.

"Which way to the main road?" asked the young soldier politely.

He wore a strange, hooked emblem on his sleeve. His eyes were attentive on her flushed, bewildered face. He smiled reassuringly.

111

"Turn right," she said. "Go three blocks to Ohm Friesen's..." Carefully, she took two hesitating steps, swallowing. "*Nyemets?*" she asked in a tiny voice. "Are you... are you a German soldier?"

He gasped with surprise at the German sound. She stared at him, eyes wide open. Then she nodded, feeling her palms dampen from shock.

"I speak Ger . . . German," she whispered faintly.

"Suppose you show me the way?" he asked. He motioned to the back of his motorcycle. "Grab me tight around my waist."

Her arms went around his body. There was a prickling in her veins. The motorcycle spewed smoke and noise. Her long hair fluttered in the wind. Reassuringly, his armpits held her trembling fingers.

"My name is Karl-Heinz," he shouted against the suction of the air.

She remained silent, holding him fast, wet as a chick from the morning dew. After a while, she leaned forward to whisper in his ear:

"How could you come so swiftly?"

His laugh stood ringing in the air:

"You aren't used to crazy ones, are you?"

"There is the station now," she said. "Turn right. My family is waiting to be exiled."

"No one is going to be exiled," shouted Karl-Heinz, skillfully making the turn into the street.

Katya, at the sight of them, gave a strangled moan. She came staggering toward them, shaking Karin off her lap, swallowing her sobs, treading on air as if running through hollow, empty space. A sound came from her lips that might have been laughter or tears—she did not know which, nor did she care, Oh God! why should she care! On the last few steps she stumbled, and the tall soldier sprang forward from his motorcycle and caught her in his arms. Against his epaulets she pressed her broken, crumbling face.

She heard Sara say in a tiny voice:

112

"Mother, let go of his arm . . . "

The young German warrior patted her white hair, a little embarrassed, murmuring reassuringly:

"Now. Now, mother. Mother, what is there to cry about now? Now we are here, mother. Now we are here."

A resurrected, jubilantly patriotic *Voice of Peace* proclaimed that with the appearance of the swastika, a new millenium had begun.

Need anyone be told?

Only in passing had Katya noticed the strange, barbed-wire symbol on Karl-Heinz's left shoulder as he and his men had swept into her town to rescue her from the imminent tomb of Siberia. Within a mere few hours that morning, however, she saw it, vastly magnified—like sharp black lightning on a plain of red and white—greet Waldheim from the hill top. It waved to her merrily from the roof of Jasch's house where it had been fastened to the chimney with such haste that the stork nest lay tumbled below. The strange reflection shivered and trembled in the clear waters of the pond behind his house. By noon, she saw the sign displayed in every shining, sparkling window along the street. Like magic it appeared in the fists of little children. Before her very eyes she saw it multiplied a thousand times that sunny, windswept autumn day, floating majestically on top of this grey, steel-helmeted, determined wedge of certainty that now pushed past her house in an easterly direction, its tip well fortified with iron and steel and confidence to spare, so that never again, from this day to the very edge of eternity, would terror be permitted in her land!

She stood and watched and dared not breathe before this vast display of worldly might, an awesome silence in her heart before the sounds of victory and righteous vengeance flooding Waldheim's streets. And in her feelings she most surely was not alone, for she could see that in the shade of the acorn avenues beyond, there stood family after Mennonite family, weeping

113

from feelings so profound that they surpassed all emotions that had lacerated their lives for so many grief-stricken, blood-soaked, tormented years. This was deeper than life, much deeper than death, more powerful and pure than anything they had known themselves capable of feeling—this wave of utter gratitude and awe that now attached itself to the uncompromising, pitch-black sign which—they were told—was set to vanquish Europe.

Not for a moment did Katya doubt that this prediction would come true by virtue of the sheer magic inherent in this symbol. Of such power and conviction was its pull that she could feel it sweep David right out of her kitchen and into the path of the marching formation which kept on pushing past her house. To the end of her days, Katya knew, the memories of these sights, these sounds would be with her to be cherished, as column after column of singing soldiers now marched by. Their song came to her in intoxicating gusts borne by the crystal-clear air:

"Es zittern die morschen Knochen
Der Welt vor dem grossen Krieg.
Wir haben den Schrecken gebrochen,
Fuer uns war's ein grosser Sieg . . . "

She estimated that the formation of marching, singing German men must stretch past the outskirts of her town, and still there came more around the corner, and more yet, and more! And now, in their wake, a number of vehicles began to roll: automobiles and tanks and motorcycles, small armored cars among horse-pulled goulash cannons, packed to the brim with utensils for daily living—pots and pans, containers with water, bundles of dried bread and meat, here and there a covered wagon displaying the well-known merciful Red Cross, gleaming in the sunshine. And if one could believe the much disheveled, sputtering Jasch, who now joined her on her steps, this was only the beginning, for in the days to come, more than six thousand vehicles were scheduled to pass by—a chain, he told her, stretching from her house to the very waters of the Dnieper, moving steadily toward the east.

114

The soldiers' helmets glittered in the sun. Their faces, covered with the dust of their journey, were fixed in concentrated solemnity, softening with youthful pleasure now and then as flower after flower was thrown into their paths. For it seemed that Waldheim all but came apart at the seam from the effort of trying to welcome and accommodate this current of strength and determination—this flood of field-grey German ardor which marched on stoically, as heroes should, behind them a single smoke cloud like a giant mushroom in the air, in front of them this multitude of waving flags which led the way. The earth all but groaned from their tread. " . . . we will be marching on, should everything shatter to pieces . . . for today our homeland listens, but tomorrow the whole wide world . . . "

Yet not a single bomb had fallen from the sky!

People would later recall that a grenade had loosened a few shingles in an isolated village and the resulting air pressure had cracked a window here and there, but all in all, it was so evident that righteous vengeance was the German soldiers' mission that they could simply follow the clouds of dust stirred up by the panicky fleeing tormentors. They had entered the Ukraine like archangels sent straight from the hand of the Lord, dispatched with orders of uncanny speed to rescue the last, mortally decimated, beleaguered Russian Mennonites.

"Jasch!" cried Katya, alternately laughing and weeping, "Just look! Look at them! Just look! Aren't they beautiful, these men?"

"Indeed," he replied, eagerly waving his hands at the formation. "Indeed they are, our German boys!"

In her elation she could not help nudging him slightly with her elbow:

"Whatever happened to your communistic views?"

"Katya," he said, gripping her arm. "Now, Katyushka! Don't you talk nonsense now. I always knew it to be a mere matter of time until the Hitler Army would find and rescue us. Haven't I always prophesied the Hitler Army would come?"

"The Hitler Army?"

115

"The National Socialist Army," he informed her solemnly, "led by our *Fuehrer* in Berlin."

Berlin! The *Fuehrer!* The National Socialist Army! Her tongue, in the exhilarating weeks to come, would always stumble a little from unaccustomed reverence when giving a name to this miracle of helmets and flags and boots and steel, a part of which could now be seen detaching itself to hoist up a number of tents along the tree-lined streets of her village.

Very early each morning, Katya would pull away her kitchen curtains to make sure with a quick glance that her protectors were still there. Before breakfast, she and her family would watch in silent respect their ritual of saluting the *Fuehrer* and the flag. Then most of the soldiers would disappear, dispatched with secret orders, and only the officers would stay behind to study a map spread out over a long, makeshift table, and after a while, David would climb onto a tree to verify from above that a row of neatly color-coded pins moved steadily each day a little farther to the east.

David had brought home a picture of the *Fuehrer* the very first week of the German occupation. Katya had set aside for herself a quiet twilight hour of solitude to study the features of this man who, by a mere frown of his face, was capable of arranging and rearranging whole armies along strategic lines to ever greater efficiency so that, in due time, every hurt inflicted upon innocent integrity would be avenged. She had studied him intently, for she knew that she owed him her very existence on this earth. She thought him to be a very stern and lonely man, with his arms crossed on his chest. But it was easy to see how this man could declare with such confident assurance:

"Give me ten years, and you won't recognize the world."

Katya, who had come to know how fragile life could be, found such unbending certainty to be more than she could comfortably bear. With a sigh, she had given the picture back to David, who had driven a strong, straight nail into the wall above his bed to have his idol near for all his friends to see.

This same kind of inner certainty, however, made

116

comprehensible by credulity and youth, illuminated every German soldier's face. Katya never tired of secretly studying the faces of these *landser* as they sat on the steps of her house on their off-duty days, drawn there by Liestje's gentleness and Sara's teasing, laughing voice.

One could see at a glance that these young, alien warriors were very different from any youths that she herself had ever known. They looked different. They walked differently—with square, precise steps that shook her house from end to end. They spoke important words, intertwined with rolling, gutteral "r' s" deep down in their throats as if to underscore the weightiness of what they had to say.

"Our dearest homeland," they would say, "stands united in its assertion that the Treaty of Versailles was treason of the highest order, striking at the very heart of Germany . . . "

" . . . it's up to us to change our shame into sweeping, certain victory . . . "

" . . . once again, a German child can study the map of the world without flinching . . . "

" . . . our arms-spiked *Vaterland,* fearsome and powerful, right in the middle of the world . . . "

Such fervent words would always send a chill upon her spine—she would tremble with reverent regard.

But then, again, they might call out to her laughingly, light-heartedly: " . . . not the slightest doubt about the outcome of this war . . . " swinging the squealing Karin by her arms, tossing her high into the air and catching her with strong secure arms. " . . . of course we are winning, aren't we, sweet?"

"Of course!" Karin would shout, braids flying. "Of course. Of course!"

"Naturally!" they would repeat, tossing her back and forth.

"Naturally!" the child unfailingly responded, straining hard to imitate precisely the intonation of High German sounds.

"No doubt about it!"

"No doubt at all!"

117

Every tenth word, it seemed to Katya, was a glowing, sweeping affirmation.

"Imagine our surprise," they might say, "at finding in this backward Slavic country village after village of people of pure German ancestry, speaking the language of our *Vaterland* as clearly as we do!"

Then Katya herself would join them on the steps, always hungry to be told again how Karl-Heinz and his men had come to her rescue without looking left or right—Poland had all but exploded like an overripe watermelon when kicked aside by the impatient tips of their boots!

Of course one should shake one's head at such exaggeration. Those were tall tales, to be sure—rousing, thrilling, heart-swelling tales, with more than just a tiny touch of boastfulness. But what of that? Had she ever troubled herself to understand things of a political nature? But she loved to listen to them nevertheless, the way one would patiently listen to exuberant, lovable, somewhat pretentious children openly delighting in their youthful vigor.

Not all of these new times were loud and boisterous, however. In fact, discounting the songs and the thud of the drums which periodically shook the streets of her town, there was now a disciplined silence about the land that was to last for days and weeks on end.

The Mennonite plow started turning the land very early the following year, because the air outside, by early March, was as transparent as if an angel had taken a fluffy cloud and wiped clean the windows of the sky. Dead leaves from last year's storms were blown into oblivion by the vigorous gusts of spring air coming from this flawless horizon, and those that were left in corners and niches were quickly raked away by the diligent children. Flights of wild geese appeared beneath billowing clouds, and overnight the lilacs started to swell. In the very early morning hours, the earth was still crusted with ice here and there, but the days at noon were warm enough to moisten the soil so that the plowing could begin.

The communist holidays, always offensive to Katya, could simply be crossed out of existence with a gleeful sweep of one's pen. The twentieth of April, instead, now deserved to be encircled with red on her calendar, for it signified the birthday of the *Fuehrer* in Berlin.

Berlin had always appeared to be a sacred, somewhat fictitious city, much as Jerusalem and Bethlehem were. But one day, encouraged by the friendliness of the soldiers in the streets, someone had dared to write a timid petition:

"Do we have license now to worship our Lord?"

A letter came promptly. Christian teachings, the message read amid an array of swastika seals, were gladly permitted, as long as such worship did not interfere with the training of the young. For it was the young boys and girls that the *Vaterland* needed. The promising future about to descend demanded every drop of youthful, willing, unpolluted German blood. But yes, of course, the old might worship as they pleased.

Thus, miracle anew, the church gates were wide open.

The much expected change for esoteric human betterment that pulsated in the very spring-scented air became most forcefully apparent in young David. Katya, somewhat to her proud consternation, found herself one day to be the mother of a dedicated Hitler Youth. Well, not quite a full-fledged Hitler Youth as yet, much to David's impatient distress, for he was still too young to be admitted to full standing in the mystical cohort that seemed to have spiritual life of its own.

"But soon, Mother! But soon!"

At first, she had thought it to be child's play, no more, as she had smilingly watched him practice clicking his heels for hours in grim imitation of the admired salute. Was it not only yesterday when he, a little boy of ten, had shyly stroked the rifle that Karl-Heinz had once left leaning in a corner, and had sniffed with rapture the strange faint smell of gun powder on its muzzle? She had taken his hot little hand and had led him out of the room. Yes, that was but yesterday.

Now, suddenly, he was a child no more. He grew very

rapidly the following two years. His brown, lean body systematically soaked up the summer sun as he prepared and hardened himself with daily strenuous exercises. He spent days and weeks of hiking in the woods, sleeping under the clear, crisp sky, filling his canteen with the water from the valleys, walking with bare, sensitive feet through the ripening fields of the land, feeling with a disciplined purpose, almost a predestination, that there was sacred meaning everywhere these days. A certain simple arrogance took hold of him, as if he who thought pure and dizzying thoughts had earned his sacred place in the bond of knighthood.

He would stand in silence on top of the hill, watching with rapture how in the darkening valley below, fire after fire would spring to life beneath the trees—all comrades of his, surely, removed by a span of a few miserly years! He would stand awed, watching the forest begin to glow with autumnal rapture—first yellow, then golden, then orange, here and there a blazing red. He knew himself special and chosen. He was waiting for his hour to be called and be counted. He became irrevocably credulous that year, believing deeply and passionately from the purity of his twelve-year-old heart.

It was little Karin's turn now to be drawn out of Katya's kitchen, out of her very hands by the sweep of the ominous drums. Much to David's haughty distress, she would follow them along street after street, gasping from the effort of keeping up with the fast-paced marching formation. A breathless trot would barely bring her to the steps of Jasch's house, dizzy from excitement and heady exertion.

"Walter," she would yell, beating her fists on the door. "Come quick! Look! See? The flag bearer up front is my own Uncle David!"

"Oh, what a brat!" David would think, setting his heels to sharp clicking, looking neither left nor right.

Walter Kovalsky was only a little older than she, but already he seemed filled with dignity and calm.

"I know, Karin. I can see that for myself."

Karl-Heinz, Karin knew, was very fond of the sensible boy, calling him an unlikely sprout of the ostentatious Jasch. That was a mouthful, to be sure! Karin had carefully tucked away this ornamental expression, to be examined and dissected at a later, more suitable time. She always hoarded words, phrases, passages she did not, as yet, understand. A wealth of precious words, real gems, had come with the young German *landser*. There would be a time, Karin knew, when luxurious words would come in handy. Right now she had one at her fingertips, to be savored on her tongue with relish:

"He has already been initiated. Initiated, you see? You have to wait for another four years. To be initiated." So there! She now had that one under control.

"I know that, too, Karin. You told me yesterday."

The children sat down on the steps, sighing deeply to underscore their heartfelt, childish longing. Oh, to be old enough to be swept up and away as part of the glamor of the times! The booted, field-grey soldiers in their streets had marched straight off the pages of a fairytale book—knights come alive, with voices that all but shook the world expressing their mysterious callings.

Karin, long before she could have put these feelings into words, knew somehow with unfailing instinct that the young warriors seemed to draw their strength from songs and rituals as weighty as black lead, risen straight from the heart of their ancestral past—strange, heavy, powerful songs, songs about willingness to die for a cause but dimly explained, about death that was life, life always terminating in valiant purposeful dying. There was an undertone of threat if one listened closely, much akin to the threat that could be found between the pages of the Holy Book. A call for bitter burdens, Karin knew, for loyalty beyond a doubt, for blind sacrifice and for unquestioning obedience—that brand of obedience, she would recall with a shiver, that had forced the slaughtering knife into Abraham's unwilling hands when God had willed it that he sacrifice his only son.

121

But even Katya, for all of her concrete, solemn austerity, understood what was meant by these songs. She understood it fully and comprehensively on an intensely intimate, personal, emotional level. It was an understanding she could never have put into the proper words—how could she, a simple woman, talk of that which was so powerfully visible each day? She could only compare it to those teachings that she knew, and if compare she did at all, this is what she must have seen:

Mennonite children, too, were raised to live by the highest standards of obedience, of utter loyalty beyond a question and a doubt. She was familiar with the terms of honor and of glory. From earliest childhood on, she had seen them lifted directly from the Scriptures, to be passed on to future generations unstained and unbroken. Now she found them suddenly made visible, reachable, immediate, as personal and as steady as her own glad heartbeat in her chest as she waved behind the curtain to her young, flag-bearing son. It fit. It made sense. It took no effort at all to seduce her hungry, abused, weakened, credulous, order-craving Mennonite heart.

"*Lebensraum*," Karl-Heinz had once explained, "is what we need, above all else."

This, too, she understood. Mennonites, too, had always firmly pushed toward the east for land and yet more land to plow and sow and reap. He had explained to her with stark logic:

"In order to gain access to such wealth, one needs the fire and the sword."

Within herself she felt a mellowness these days such as had never before been hers save for the swift sweetness of her now dimly remembered youth. She would sit by the window for hours on end, all but enfolded in safety and peace, with thread and needle and thimble in her hands, her glasses balancing precariously on the tip of her nose. Fastening buttons and mending ripped seams, she felt privileged indeed to hold a German uniform in her lap to be repaired by caring hands.

Jasch was often teasing her these days that she—a somber woman—had witlessly fallen in love with Karl-Heinz. She

122

admitted to herself that she would wait with impatience for the *landser's* hard, crisp steps on her porch, for his whistling in the hall, for the piercing moment when the back door would fly open and Karin would shoot by, wrapping herself around the soldier's legs with incoherent shouts of joy. Hurriedly, Katya would smooth her hair and tie a clean apron around her waist and open the door with anticipation, just in time to see him hang his helmet on the wall in Sara's room. He would come to her smilingly and put his hands around her back and rock her gently back and forth in boyish, endearing affection:

"How good you smell, Oma dear," he would say. "What have you baked tonight? German *Apfelstrudel? Zwieback? Portzeltje?*" She couldn't help smiling at his awkward attempts at Low German, and for a brief, sweet moment, she would permit herself to put her white head on his young, strong, comforting chest.

One day, she put a trembling hand to the emblem on his sleeve and asked shyly:

"Will the Army go as far as Siberia?"

"Of course."

"Please look out for my husband . . . He may be weakened from hunger . . . " She hesitated, afraid to give away the name she was to keep to herself.

She had shown him a picture of Gerhard so that he would recognize him at once, should he come upon exiled slave laborers on his victorious way to the east. Two tears had rolled down her cheeks. He had brushed across her lids with gentle, warm fingers: "Now . . . now, Omalein."

The house seemed hollow, seemed dark on the days soldierly duty kept him away.

It was inevitable that her inner Mennonite feel for right and wrong would shift a little in response to such convincing pressure from all sides. She would catch herself smiling in tolerance at the worldly vanity creeping up on her young, for the change looked so natural, so rejuvenating, so healthy, saturated with the glow of deepest dedication to a powerful ideal. Sara's heavy braids had fallen to the sharp cut of the scissors; her braid bands lay forgotten somewhere in a drawer. Her hair was very short and stylish now, trimmed closely to flatter her radiant face, and made glossy by highlights of red bleached into its tips by weeks and weeks in the sun. Her narrow hips were accented by a short, spartanly cut skirt, her neck healthily suntanned against the white, faultlessly ironed blouse held together by a pin the shape of a wheat stalk. It did not surprise Katya at all that one morning her beautiful child swept into her kitchen and closed the door behind her firmly and put her arms around her mother's waist to confess in a soft, happy whisper:

"I am pregnant, Mother, with a German soldier's child. As soon as this war has been won . . . "

It was a dream. One did not question, analyze, scrutinize a dream. The incomprehensible seemed natural; the most unusual, matter-of-fact. Katya did not in the least feel compelled to remind her child of this man Franz—what, now, had been his last name?—who might still be alive and one day return. No, not in the least did she feel called upon to give advice, feel worried about the outcome of this new love-struck fancy of her foolish, superficial child. The baby that was born in due time was a lovely child—blond, blue-eyed, exquisitely fine-boned— teasingly named Lily Marlene after a haunting High German love song sung in the streets.

Jasch Kovalsky had deftly secured for himself an important assignment—the smooth streamlining of a Slavic work force to be put to useful purpose in the *Vaterland's* victorious behalf. He now sat, firmly entrenched, behind a heavy mahogany desk, to his right a life-size picture of the *Fuehrer* on the wall, and saw to it that at all times there was a deep, respectful silence in his presence. To Katya he would hint at awesome responsibilities now resting on his shoulders. She would see him stride by in the morning without as much as a glance at Ivan, who stood amid a cluster of frightened peasants against the walls of her cow shed,

124

talking out his fear in a low and frightened voice. Yes, Jasch was a man in charge and control of vast, important matters!

Always keenly attuned to gossip, he was therefore the first to notice the tiniest tinge of apprehensive hope among the whispered Ukrainian jealousies—that this city and that one had now been recaptured by the Red Army front. Such rumors came back to him from the east with the trucks dispatched by his personal orders and filled with sullen men to assist with the dugouts and trenches designed to trap the Russian panzer, should there be temporary setbacks, as could be expected in any war. These people, he knew, had reason to be unhappy. Therefore, it was to their advantage to plant rumors here and there—unfounded talk about disastrous German losses.

The Russian Army, it was openly said, had now begun to push back the insolent German invaders.

For weeks, to be sure, a steady dull thunder hung low on the horizon. At night, the eastern sky would flare now and then with the sparks of faraway rockets. Majestic bombers flew westward each day, carrying behind them a whitish, ominous tail. Suspiciously, he squinted at them against the brilliance of the autumnal sky. It almost looked as if he were winking.

"My windows have shaken for weeks, Katya," he finally voiced his concern. "The front is coming closer. I feel it in my bones."

"Oh, be quiet, Jasch. You and your oracles of doom." When had he not delighted in scaring her out of her wits?

"The German administration is sitting on a powder keg," he added, watching her face.

"Well, she replied, unimpressed, "You would be the first one to know. Why are you still here? Why aren't you fleeing?"

"Perhaps I should," he wondered aloud.

He looked at her with smoldering eyes. She could be such an exasperating trial to a man's frayed nerves. His own packed baggage sat in the hall near his office, ever since the curfew had been declared in the last days of September, ready to be snatched

125

on short notice. How very much like a gullible woman—to ignore such telling developments!

All his instincts seemed magnified these days. He had advised her only last night to make it a habit to sniff the air each morning—for did he not become more convinced by the day that the strong smell in his nostrils was the odor of the nearing front? He was a prudent, troubled man—so troubled, in fact, he felt compelled to inform her right now, that in all likelihood he would not be able to sleep a cat's wink the following night!

Having convinced himself by his own words, he could not, as a matter of fact, fall asleep. He tossed and turned. Anxiety churned in his veins.

Groggy from unresolved fear, he dressed very quietly at daybreak to leave the house on tiptoes in hope of some morsels of clarifying news. He was in dire need of news of some kind that would help him make an expedient decision, should worst come to worst. Should he, perhaps, visit the Hitler Youth building first? And then, in a rush, the railroad station? And on his way back, perhaps, the Army Headquarters as well?

Had worst come to worst?

He saw at a glance that the building was deserted. He found only David in one of the back rooms, burning stacks of documents in a fireplace.

"What in the name of common sense . . . ?"

"Shhh," replied David, impatiently. "Step out of my way, Uncle Jasch."

"Those are important lists," protested Jasch. "They represent weeks of effort and screening."

"We are retreating in a few days," said David, tersely. "Orders from above, Uncle Jasch. From the highest command." He dumped a new load in front of Jasch's feet. "We are evacuating temporarily. Within a week we have to be out." He carried files, documents, and books, and threw them on the floor. He emptied drawers and boxes, and then he paused briefly, saluted the flag, and took it from the wall, burning it as well.

What else to do but to beat a hasty retreat? Jasch felt himself perspiring. Where was the irresponsible conductor who had been instructed weeks ago to give him timely notice in the event of imminent flight? He peered left and right and left again and—reassured that no one was there to see him behave in such a silly, undignified manner—he fell into an urgent trot, heading for the railroad tracks.

Not a soul was to be seen!

Tools and supplies lay strewn over the fields. The area was a no man's land. He peered into the waiting room and saw that it, too, was deserted. All doors stood wide open. Two windows were broken and the glass was scattered about. Pieces of paper, straw, old bottles lay on the floor. A single bulb swayed forlornly and spread a sickly light. There was a freight wagon sitting outside on one of the rails, and in passing, he saw that someone had furnished it for flight: there was a bed, a table, and half a dozen boxes, all filled with food and supplies.

If haste was what mattered, then haste it should be! Quite out of breath when passing Katya's homestead, he spotted Karin sitting on top of the gate. His boy, of course, was at her side. It was a more than irritating sight! He would have to do something to put a wedge between the two unlike, inseparable children. The bright-eyed girl was an impertinent imp, too quick to see through a man's necessary life-saving pretenses. She had come upon him two years ago as he had stood behind his fence trying to paint new slogans over the old, rain-washed ones of the Soviets. She had asked him, eyes unwavering: "Why are you no longer a communist, Uncle Jasch?" That's what the Germans had wanted to know, too. It had almost cost him his head. It was only thanks to Katya who had spoken in his behalf and had told them about his futile, valiant efforts to save the German elder Gerhard Wall that they had reluctantly begun to trust him again.

"Tell your grandmother we have to flee," he now yelled, waving his hands for emphasis. "Tell Oma! The Russians have broken through the German lines and are advancing this side of

127

the Dnieper. I heard it on the radio. Tell her to get ready, but quick! Walter, come on!"

Was Katya, however, a woman to panic for nothing? She knew some people who would. Jasch's own wife, his Volga-wife, she knew, had just last night torn her drapes from the window and had thrown them in a heap on the floor. Katya had seen it with her very own eyes as she had gone to her house to borrow a pattern from which to make a dress. In the hall had been piles of boxes. A pail had stood in her path, with sausage ends sticking out of the lard. But that was Marusya and her disorderly, faint-hearted ways. Such doubt was alien to Katya, who had come to trust her protectors and friends. Only three days ago, Karl-Heinz had come to her house to give calm, reassuring advice:

"There will be plenty of time, Oma. More than enough time. Just leave things to me and my comrades."

Jasch's urgent message, however, followed her into her dreams. She was sure she was dreaming when someone shook her shoulder—when someone cried in an urgent, hushed voice:

"Mother. Mother, wake up! We have to flee. The Russian panzer . . . "

Sara's face, white and frightened, hung over her bed.

Blindly, Katya searched for her dress in the dark, trembling from sleep and incomprehension.

"The Russian panzer are advancing . . . "

With bare feet, she hastened to the window. She could see that David had already harnessed the horses to the wagon and was now tying a cow to the back. She grabbed the sleeping, tousled Karin by the arm, jerked her from out of her covers, searching for her shoes, stumbling into the fog-shrouded night.

Karl-Heinz stood by the gate. She heard him say, his voice tight but steady:

"You know about our scorched earth policy."

She looked at him, dumbly.

"I am truly sorry, Oma dear," he said with pity in his voice.

Taking Karin firmly by the hand, she asked:

"How much time is there left?"

128

"To mid-morning, at least," he said, putting his hand now on Karin's dishevelled head.

Katya went into the shed and scooped up a bundle of straw.

"Turn the animals loose, Karin," she said to the child at her side. She lit a match. The straw in her hand ignited.

The fire leaped wildly out of the windows, the doors, the chimney. In seconds, it turned the night into day. There was a dull, howling, sucking sound as the heat exploded window panes and blew wide open the doors of the threshing shed. Reddish-yellow licking tongues devoured in minutes what ancestral diligence had built in fifteen decades, what generations had cherished, had proudly preserved for the future to come. Katya stood and watched, Karin's moist little hand in her own. When the rafters broke and sent a scattering cloud of sparks into the air, she turned her back on the place from which her life had sprung.

She could now hear the sounds of the eastern front most distinctly.

She walked along the path to the summer kitchen, past the bench where she and Gerhard had been happy in their youth.

She searched her heart for a sign as to what to do next.

Somewhere, behind that burning sky, there was Gerhard, if he had not yet perished. She did not know if she would ever see him again, but the man who had been the life of her life became a blurred face at this moment. There were bigger issues at stake here than a single, humble destiny. Between her and the inferno, there stood the German Army, trying to stem the horror that was about to overtake them again. Above her, somewhere, there was God. In the west, there was the *Vaterland*. She turned her face toward the west.

With Karin's hand in her own, she walked along the side path, knowing now that she would never walk here again. It was a moment of keenest, sharpest recognition.

"Let's go," she said to the silent child. "Let's hurry and catch up."

Beyond the gate stood Ivan. She had rarely spoken to him

129

these past two years, for like a fearful animal he had retreated into a little hut by the railroad when the German *landser* had advanced. He was suspicious by nature and did not like their ways. When Katya had tried to reassure him that the soldiers had come as good friends, he had replied darkly: "Can you judge the depth of a well by the length of its handle?" Now she heard him say in bitter contempt:

"When they arrived, we stood at the gates and greeted them with strawberries and fresh milk. How foolish we were! They came, and they darkened our skies with their warfare, and ruined our fields with their panzer, and took our sons and our daughters, and confused and upset our hearts. We should have known better than to trust such noisy strangers. And now their boots will crush us again. *Mamushka* Katya . . . "

Why would he call her *mamushka?*—he who was very senile now, bent, trembling from age and fright. She had no comfort to give in this hour of departing. It was she who longed to put her arms around him as she had done when she had been a child, to soak into her nostrils the smell of sunflower seeds and *machorka*. She searched his face for understanding. He was her servant and her dearest friend. He had led her across the even meadows of her childhood. He had teased her mercilessly when she grew up and fell in love with Gerhard Wall. He had stood convulsed with grief the day she married Gerhard, the day she buried her parents, her brothers, her youth. He had helped her feed her young children in the lean, silent years, and had buried the ones who had died.

"Come with us," she said, overwhelmed by his eyes.

"What for?" he asked her sadly. "You know I have rarely left my gate. You go on, *mamushka*. You take your family and go on."

She walked past the summer kitchen, remembering the twins who had sat here on mellow summer nights and argued their hearts out regarding the virtues of Germandom.

She had to tell the child.

Where were the words, at this hour, to tell of the generous

leisure of life when their homesteads had lain stoutly in wide waves of blossoms, tucked into orchards that moved gently with the breezes of the spring and stood pregnant with rich fruit at harvest time—orchards so wide that the late summer air could pause in its branches and absorb the scent of the ripening fruit?

Her mind groped with the momentous fate that had once again been cast upon her people. She saw that the sky in the east was paling from the dust that rose under the hoofs of hundreds of horses that now began to trot toward the west.

" . . . Schoendorf lies over there, half an hour to the north of our village . . . My grandfather lived there, and my mother's family, and several of my uncles. How we loved to go and visit them as children . . . Over there, behind the acorn trees, is Altona, and farther north lie Muensterberg and Tiegenhagen..."

Karin walked quietly by her side, listening attentively to her grandmother's urgent, incomprehensible tale—never, never to be forgotten for its weight that made it sink like lead into her childish heart:

" . . . the first of our people came in 1789, more than a hundred years ago. They settled to the right of the Dniepr River, in a place where the waters embraced an island of breath-taking beauty. Fifteen years later, another trek arrived, among them your ancestors, Karin. Village after village sprang up along the little river Molochnaya with names brought along from Germany, reflecting our forefathers' longings . . . Friedenstal. Liebenau. Hoffnungstal. Gluecksfeld. Gnadenheim. Hope. Love. Peace. Benediction. Happiness. Those were the simple values that they sought . . . "

Like an anguished, pleading, hopeless prayer to stave off heaven's renewed, heaven's imminent wrath, Katya's intense yet monotonous voice flowed over Karin:

" . . . always our faces were turned toward the east. No distance was too far, too cumbersome for our farmers—to the Trakt, into Samara, to the Crimean Peninsula, even into the Caucasus and into Siberia and Turkestan and Central Asia, as far away as the Persian borders . . . " Karin's fingers now gripped her grandmother's hand. " . . . we were ever greedy for land. Our land! Our land! Our daughter colonies spread out all over the Ukraine . . . Roof after red-bricked roof, in an ocean of billowy cherry trees . . . There was house after house pointing its gables toward the streets, barns and sheds and living quarters under one enormous roof built in a horseshoe fashion, immaculately kept and proudly preserved for generations . . . And we had fences, whitewashed each spring and straight as a line. We had sidewalks swept clean with brushwood that the young fellows, when they came on Saturday nights to visit their girls, would pick on their way in the steppe . . . " Katya's voice, at first a moan, now died to a tormented whisper:

"For a hundred and fifty years," she explained to the tremulous child, "pacifist Mennonites have plowed these fields—to Russia's advantage, God's glory, and their own well-being. This now has come to an end. Now we go westward, from where we came. With the thunder of war in our ears and the flare of rockets at our backs . . . "

Karin stared at her grandmother's glistening face. In the distance, someone started to sing, in a clear, ringing, vibrantly pulsating voice. It must be her own Uncle David, who loved to sing. Yes, wasn't that David's favorite song?

> *"Vor uns marschieren*
> *mit sturmzerfetzten Fahnen*
> *die toten Helden der jungen Nation*
> *und ueber uns*
> *die Heldenahnen*
> *Deutschland, Vaterland, wir kommen schon."*

Vaterland, we are returning! It was, by now, a familiar song. They had often sung it during the months when the *landser* had first come and had brought with them the glamor of their Germany. Its powerful beat had captured the song-hungry ears of the Mennonite youth. Its melody now moved the child Karin.

132

To break the spell she hummed it quietly to herself. She climbed onto the wagon. The horses started to pull.

6

Her heartbeat in her throat, curiosity tingling in waves through her body into her very fingertips and toes, Karin absorbed into herself with all her seven-year-old might this most magnificent kaleidoscope of change: swaying landscapes, jarring emotions, suppressed, slow-rolling sounds along the edges of the horizon—sounds which, if ever released, might well fill the skies with a deafening roar. When the Great Trek started moving in early September, she was barely old enough, had times been right and orderly, to have had her first taste of disciplined schooling. As it turned out—if one were to add the days and weeks she attended school here and there on her long two-year's journey—she might have claimed a somewhat spotty, haphazard third-grade education by the time she became an adult.

Not that this grandchild of hers was in need of formal instruction, as far as Katya could see! She spoke three languages without any effort. She had taught herself to decipher the headlines of the Russian papers before she was five. Karl-Heinz had helped her with High German. She would have read Low German as well, had there been letters to go with its sounds. She knew one-third of the Bible stories by heart—including, Katya made sure, the moral lesson that went with each section. She needed to hear a song but once to recall its lyrics at will. And all the informal schooling Karin ever was to have took place within the confines of the slowly moving trek—and what a school of life it was!

Every inch of the road was filled to overflowing with refugees carrying their possessions on their backs and elbowing their way through innumerable clogs and obstructions. Hundreds and thousands sat at deserted railroad stations, waiting for trains that never came—cursing and crying and laughing and praying and spending endless nights around bonfires sending patriotic songs toward the stars.

The Mennonites tried to keep to themselves before such throbbing feverish living, but who could help being swept into gregariousness by such contagious fervor in the air? At times, far ahead, someone would wave a cap as a signal, and the whole procession would burst into a song. It seemed to Karin that people always sang—even Oma would join in at times, humming quietly to herself the heady melodies of war. David would walk by the side of the wheels, whistling loudly and marching to mysterious instruments which only he could hear. Sometimes a *landser* would play a harmonica to accompany Sara's clear, silken voice. Walter would clap the beat with his hands. Even the horses would walk briskly at such times, pulling stoutly at the wheels that crushed the road beneath. Karin would lean out of the wagon on such occasions and fling her braids to her back and shout along with fervent conviction: " . . . *Volk ans Gewehr! Volk ans Gewehr!*"

People to the guns!

High adventure indeed had gripped the imagination of the people on the trek. They felt it most keenly when they sat— shivering a little at times, for now it was late in the fall and the nights were already slightly cool—around the fires which were lit between bricks found somewhere along the way. The rhythmic battle songs gave them a feeling of a shared German past and the promise of a shared German future. Who would dare to complain about a little hardship in valiant times such as these? Hardships only toughened the faith of those who were chosen to be tested for the strength of their ethnic allegiance.

This was adventure at its piercing best! Many enviously remembered the story of a far more daring and adventurous exodus that had many years ago taken two entire Mennonite villages out of Russia in a bold and daring race across the frozen Amur River, somewhere between China and the great waters of the Eastern world. These people, Katya told Karin, now lived in a land where the sun shone so hot that one could fry an egg in the sand during Christmas time.

"In a country called Paraguay," Oma had said.

Karin's feet were never still. With Walter on her trail, she spent days exploring this wondrous world, concerned only to stay within reach of her grandmother's voice. No one watched her closely those days.

There was something powerfully fascinating in this caterpillar without tail. It seemed to her a monster of iron feet, of wheels and hoofs and rubber, pushing its way toward the west—across meadows at times, across planks thrown over ditches and creeks, across torn-up railroad tracks, circumventing broken bridges, dipping into yellowing forests and emerging after hours on the other side of the earth. Karin spent days in the field, walking happily alongside the slow-moving trek, picking the last autumn flowers and throwing them from bridges onto the whistling trains below, where hundreds of German *landser,* rolling to the battlefront, would throw kisses back at her and wave to her as far as she could see.

She slept soundly and dreamlessly at night, waking up like a spring to the adventures of the new day.

Even before breakfast, one could hear the roar of the aircraft overhead.

"That is the enemy," David had grimly explained to Karin.

She strained to recognize the tiny dots in the pale blue sky— humming steely mosquitoes menacing the air. Presently the German artillery at her back commenced its daily song, and its bellowing brought comfort and security to the trek. Its sound washed sleepy, unkempt figures out of cramped wagon space, stretching their limbs in the dewy chill, looking up toward the sky, then forward to search out the position of the field kitchen to secure a container of hot water for some breakfast tea.

Slowly, after a while, the trek began to move, flanked by monsters on chains whose steel reflected the morning sun and over whose motor hoods were draped the flaming flags of the *Vaterland*—the mere sight of such frightful persuasion that it

135

pushed the remnants of the panic-stricken Russian civilians ahead of them into the forests left and right. The open doors and windows gave testimony to the haste with which they had fled from the tank-pointed tip of the prodigious oddity that pushed in a westerly direction. Karin, at times, enticed Walter to walk with her on tiptoe through kitchens abandoned in such haste that the food still simmered on the stove. Yes, what truly fear-inspiring, omnipotent creatures these German panzer were! It was awesome to see them crunch through the soil with ferocious teeth, push their way across meadows, throw dirt and bushes and branches to the side, snap dozens of tender trees in passing. One was wise indeed to step aside and quietly let such a monster pass.

There was a delay in their flight lasting more than a year. Somewhere along the way in a grey, forbidding Russian city—temporarily, it was announced at first—the trek came to a halt. It was a trying, impatient, burdensome time, relieved only by rumors of an imminent German offensive. Katya was glad when the wheels started rolling again in late fall of the following year.

There was confident talk among many that the mysteriously delayed reinforcements would bring an easy turn of the tide. Rumors to that effect rippled along the trek—rumors of secret armies, powerful weapons, masterplans of strategy that would undo in the briefest time the miserly victories the enemy had accidentally gained. These rumors increased in intensity with the ever louder growling from the east. If one was foolish enough to listen to the few pessimists here and there, one could be worried out of one's wits by speculation that a storm was brewing whose eye was aiming straight at the trek of the Mennonites.

But for now, the skies were still washed clear of all menaces. The air was still warm, even though in early morning hours there hung a low, fine, chilly mist along the fringes of the creeping procession, and each day seemed to take a little longer to warm up.

This was a time that taught Karin fearlessness that was to last her for life. She was entirely on her own, for no one had time for her questions. She was free to explore the world beneath her busy feet. In front of the trek, there moved a weighty goulash cannon, jealously watched by a red-faced, jovial corporal who had become her benefactor and friend. One day she brought him an armful of dry kindling wood, and he placed a heavy, powerful hand on her shoulder:

"If you do that each morning, you can count on an extra helping."

Prestige followed her heels. She bullied Walter shamelessly. Before dawn, she would climb onto his wagon and shake him crudely by his shoulder out of his sleep:

"Let's get going. Let's go! The corporal is waiting."

To the corporal she said:

"Don't you dare let someone else help you as long as I have a breath of air in my lungs."

He grinned at her affectionately:

"Not as long as you and I control this trek."

He wielded true omnipotence, she noted with satisfaction. When his field kitchen pulled to the side, the entire trek would come to a halt. He was a most comforting, expedient friend. In his pockets, he carried bulging treasures: small sausages, bits of dried cheese, baked prunes, raisins, cookies that melted on one's tongue. Daily there now formed a line of hungry people. But she had privileges, did she not? She would stride right past them, chin up, stretching to peer into the giant kettle:

"Hmmm . . . does that smell good! Did you use onions, corporal? The front holds, right? Don't you agree?"

"Sure thing," he said confidently. "Hold this spoon for me, honey. The front holds. You can bet your last *pfennig,* dear."

It was a world without end, it seemed to her, held together only by a singleness of purpose that kept the trek's tip firmly pointed to the west.

Villages streamed by, bedded deep in valleys that had turned yellow from the autumn sun. There were Russian huts with sleek straw roofs, carefully tended potato fields, vast orchards bent with fruit, with no one left to pick the richness hanging to the ground. She climbed over railroad tracks that seemed twisted

137

out of shape by a giant angry hand. She slid down into the dusty depth of deep craters, feeling the racing earth along her bare stinging legs. She sat on top of dingy masses of cast-away steel and sang uproariously:

"... *denn heute da hoert uns Deutschland*
und morgen die ganze Welt ... '*

There were many peaceful rivers still, rivers that meandered and rivers that flowed straight, disciplined and purposeful. There were many little towns with people not yet panicky, forests flooded with the last sunshine of the year. There were hours of such peace that an ocean of yellow leaves could hum gently over Karin's head as she lay dreaming in the back of the wagon.

"Just stay away from the ammunition," Katya would caution the children.

They did not always pay heed, for love of danger was heavy in their veins.

One day they found an abandoned hand grenade lying dusty in a ditch. They stared at it, fascinated. They slid down the ravine, lifting it carefully, breathlessly.

"Let's get David," suggested Walter. "He knows how to detonate it."

"What for?" asked Karin, stung.

She had just added another birthday to her life. No one had remembered the important occasion. She had to assert her independence.

"You're scared," she observed with nonchalance.

_____

"Well, no ... " the boy said, reluctantly.

"Should I throw it?" she suggested.

For a moment, he held death tautly in his small, brown hand.

"Unscrew the end," she advised him. "Then pull the string."

His body grew tense from the effort. He swung his arm wide.

* " ... For today only Germany listens, but tomorrow the whole wide world ... "

138

"Crouch down, Karin!"

The detonation threw them back into the ditch, covered them with dirt and particles of rock, deafened them for a few seconds, made them lie flush to the earth by sheer split-second instinct. When Karin could open her eyes again and blink away the dust, she saw that Walter's chest was bleeding slightly from a dozen pin-pricked holes where the gun powder had penetrated his skin.

"You have been wounded in combat," she breathed in heartfelt admiration.

Subdued, they sneaked back to the trek, feeling strangely elated, as if they had drunk forbidden wine. At night, under the covers, they giggled.

"Feel my chest," the boy whispered proudly.

Her fingertips fluttered along his skinny ribs, sensing the bumps beneath the skin. Their hands clutched under the blankets. They shut out the world around them.

Those were spooky nights, calm and secretive, with a magic too vast and gripping for words. Long past bedtime, she and the boy would lie quietly, as still and as motionless as mice. There was something about those nights that placed a clamp on Karin's heart. It was as if she felt tensing in her own veins the growing tenseness of the trek. There was a momentous silence filtering down from the tip of the trees upon the sleeping people below. It lasted all night until dawn broke to bring the stirrings of the awakening east.

They had now reached the Romanian border, it was said.

"Beyond Romania is Poland, and Poland borders on Germany," Katya told Karin.

They tried to pick up speed.

The roads became more clogged by the day.

They found themselves immobilized for hours, for in the opposite direction there now began to flow a strong, replenishing current of men and supplies. One could always tell when new combat troops were coming, for the corporal ahead would curse so angrily that Katya would put her hands to her ears in shocked consternation and hastily pull her wagon to the side.

Thousands of soldiers would then pass by. Katya drew strength from the sight of them—young faces, solemn eyes, a firm purpose sketching the contours of their chins. They marched past the stream of refugees, looking neither left nor right. Every now and then, a train whisked by, moving in the opposite direction, filled to overflowing with wounded warriors from the front. Young Red Cross nurses stood on the ramps, grateful for pails of coffee from the refugees. Their faces were lined from nights without sleep, their blue and white striped uniforms limp. They were cold and hungry and exhausted. Yet they always smiled and did not complain.

"Our boys are fighting in exemplary fashion," they told the people on the road. "By the end of next month, at the latest..."

Such talk set David's cheeks aglow. Wherever there were *landser*, David could surely be found, as if drawn by a powerful magnet. He spent days away from the trek. Thanks to David's watchfulness, they were able to avoid the traps set in the woods by a handful of Romanian traitors. David's keen alertness filled his mother's heart with righteous pride. She tried to place a loving hand on his shoulder. At the touch, he had all but jumped out of his skin. She was startled by such a reaction. At night, with the fires flaring, she would watch him sit in the dark, knees drawn to his chin, his taut brown hand resting nonchalantly on the rifle at his side. Was this her young son still, or was he already a man on his own, beyond a mother's reach? She no longer knew for sure.

By late November the sky overhead, an impenetrable bluish-grey cover, bore heavily upon the trek, while from its mass a howling wind hurled icy sheets of wetness down upon the refugees. It was a needle-pointed, mean, embittered rain, relentless in its menace, determined to soak right into everyone's clammy, goose-pimpled, shivering skin. This morning, the trek had passed across a muddy river, and Katya had seen large chunks of ice drift by.

The horses, their flanks smoking from perspiration, began to skid and to slide. Time and again, she had to climb down from her seat and put her weight to the slipping wheels of her vehicle to counter the force of gravity and keep it from crashing down the ravine. Then again, she would have to push and pull until her knees trembled from the effort and her breath cut through her lungs in sharp, knifelike thrusts.

She was filthy to the roots of her hair, wet to her bones, so tired and taut that she shamefully lost her patience with Jasch and spoke to him sharply in an unloving manner. She should, instead, have felt some gratitude for him, for who but Jasch could have managed to trade a bag full of beans for a live mare when one of her horses had slipped in the rain and had broken a leg? Still, he had a way of burdening her tolerance severely. There was nothing more dispiriting than to have him walk beside her wagon, slushing through the mud, muttering ominously:

"We should have known better . . . whole armies have been whipped before . . . why, even Napoleon . . . "

"Oh hush, Jasch Kovalsky. Pull yourself together, for heaven's sake! You are not the only one who is uncomfortable."

His voice was squeaky with misery:

"Where are we going, Katya? Is this ever going to end?"

She did not answer. She felt sick with worry and fear. She heard Liestje coughing beneath the dripping piece of tent she had tied over the rainsoaked bedding—a rasping, hollow cough that cut into her throat.

"She should have a backrub," she thought, desperately. "Such a cold turns into pneumonia in no time at all . . . "

"The German front has fragmented like brittle glass," announced Jasch, wiping raindrops off his bluish lips. "Russian tanks, I heard this morning, are already squatting along the Vistula River, waiting for the waters to freeze over . . . "

She said nothing, her eyes on the ragged sparrows she could

141

see sitting in dark clusters along broken telephone lines, hunching against the winds.

"Commandos cover all bridges and blow them up in the wake of the fleeing civilians."

"What nonsense, Jasch!"

"Breslau has been turned into a hedgehog fortress. If only we can make it to the Oder! That river is still heavily secured. Do you think we can make it to the Oder, Katya?"

"I am sure you will, Uncle Jasch," David's passionate voice could be heard from behind. "Had it not been for the fact that you managed to get shot so conveniently in the calf by a stray bullet, you would have been drafted by now to fight on the front like a man. You wouldn't be here making us miserable with your oracles of doom . . ."

"David, hold your tongue," Katya felt forced to say, more from duty than conviction.

Last week, all men of the trek had been taken away except those too old or too sick to use a gun. How Jasch had managed to get wounded at such a critical moment was hard to explain. Were it not for the fact that she knew him to be so fainthearted when it came to suffering pain—but no! That couldn't be! Katya brushed the thought aside. But there he still was, a lone healthy man among frightened women and children, dramatically bandaged, feeling very sorry for himself, letting himself be swept along by the now badly disheveled trek, moaning and groaning at that!

Gone were the days when some hot water could still be had for a cup of spirit-lifting tea. No longer were fires permitted at night, for the glow, it was said, would make the trek an easy target for the enemy bombers invading the heavens of late. At night now, the stars hung glazed in the sky. White fog rose from the wagons each morning. People would call out to each other, at first in grim jest: "Everyone still alive out there?" for the air became brittle with chill before dawn.

As even the days became colder, they began a systematic search for hay barns so as to have a little shelter for the night. It

142

was on such an occasion that fate finally turned against Jasch. There were few on the trek, however, who truly felt sorry about his latest misfortune, for Marusya's untimely death was clearly brought on by her own inconsiderate actions. Had it not been for her ever so self-seeking ways, it was pointed out afterwards behind Jasch's back, she would surely not have died as she did.

Had they not, now, for weeks at a stretch, proceeded over endless muddy roads, counting their blessings aloud when they could spread their blankets and coats along the steps of drafty waiting rooms, or in the corners of abandoned cellars, or in the shelter of deserted barns and empty, unheated homes, or in a cow-shed behind an abandoned rickety hut? And was it not understood from wagon to wagon that in times such as these, one simply moved over and tried to keep one's elbows to one's sides and bravely swallowed one's complaints about the multiplying hardships and tried to keep aloof from acting selfishly?

For such was the spirit of war.

But how was Marusya to identify with such unwritten, considerate, sensible rules? Katya had often observed with misgivings how this woman strode by—a torn blanket bundled on her back, hungry-looking, uncourteous, morose—in search of some food and shelter. She was footsore, she complained loudly. She had not slept for days. "Why am I even fleeing?" she was heard to have muttered on one occasion. "This is not my war at all!"

Life on the trek, Katya could clearly perceive, had finally brought out her hidden overweening personality, despite her stubborn, ill-fated attempts to change into a proper Mennonite. The thin veneer of respectability she had acquired by her marriage to Jasch most certainly could not withstand these rains! Katya had often shaken her head and passed on to Liestje sidelong glances of stern disapproval. "Like a witch," Liestje had whispered back, "she sits there on her wagon, throwing darting glances left and right!" And Katya had nodded to that and

143

replied: "And why, in the name of common decency, does she not tie her hair in a bun and look proper?"

Why not, indeed! She had remained a stranger in a body of ethnic cohesion. One afternoon, she had resolutely parked her wagon to the wind-sheltered side of a hay stack and had refused to budge, fierceness in her voice and venom in her words. Did she not know that such a place must be relinquished to those who needed warmth the most—the old, the sick, and the youngest? She had burrowed herself and her boy in the straw, keeping people away with her bellowing. They were forced to walk around her and pluck and pull the straw to get a little warmth for their own wet, shivering children. The stack had finally tumbled. They had taken their time helping her out, meaning to teach her a lesson. They had pulled the white-faced Walter out of the hay, but when they drew the mother out, they saw that she had died from fright.

Those who had known her in life pulled to the side to lay her to her final rest. It was difficult to dig a grave, for the upper layer of the soil was already frozen. They had to hurry, as the days were getting short. By four o'clock it was already darkest night.

Jasch, henceforth, wore a black band on his sleeve. Katya, matter-of-factly, inherited Walter for life. She had long ago taken to feeding and washing the boy and putting him occasionally between herself and the much affronted Karin, who grudged him the cozy spot at her back during nights when the cold drew them together for comfort. The boy was so skinny and gaunt!

And as for Jasch—well, Katya had to admit with reluctance that a man was useful when wheels broke down or a new horse had to be obtained by someone who knew how to bargain. She was beginning to feel helplessly caught in this thoughtless, heedless flight, pushed onward against her will by the increasing flares in the sky—she and her family tiny specks of quivering life in this gigantic wave of human misery, fleeing with the knowledge of the enemy behind them and the icy days of winter just ahead.

Again and again, new smaller treks merged with the ominous chained procession, coming from north and south, pushing with great urgency toward the Polish border. A stream of household goods and discarded items began to mark the path of their flight: bedspreads, pillows, pots and pans, furniture, wall clocks still ticking, books of irreplaceable value, children's toys, here and there a sack filled with edible goods that someone had abandoned.

Massive, ragged clouds tore across the sky.

People began to leave their wagons and tried to flee on foot to escape the congestion of the roads—across meadows, across irrigation ditches, through soggy rain-drenched forests, past dead horses and abandoned kitchen utensils, past broken-down and stripped wagons, past a freshly cut grave here and there. The air bore the sounds of infants crying from hunger. It seemed to Katya that any hardship would be bearable if only she could fill the baby with some warm milk. Lily Marlene, in Liestje's lap, whimpered and shriveled. Sara spent hours searching for food, but no one was willing to sell, or trade, or give away some nourishment that Lily's weakened intestines could endure.

When Katya could no longer bear to see the child's innocent anguish, she gave a stern order:

"Get me some carrots, Karin, from the fields over there."

At that, she valiantly smothered her conscience. Had she set a child to theft? And if so, what about the Lord and His justice? But what was she to do? She gritted her teeth. What did it matter? This was a time of war. Many things were known to happen during war that peace time would never permit. Could one be concerned about the Lord's commandments when one's own life was a never-ending stretch of wet, clammy, chilly misery? A very great impatience had gotten hold of her. David had told her that people were beginning to loot the homes along the way. Would God be so petty as to hold her accountable for a miserable carrot? The fields were deserted anyway, scarred and

145

criss-crossed by deep panzer tracks, the harvest trampled into the ground. Gone were the people who could have reaped what little there was to be had. If she did not take what was in her way, someone else behind her would take it for sure. Lily Marlene, beneath the soggy blankets, was a wheezing, dying bundle. She would explain to the Lord at a later, more suitable time. She could not talk to Him now anyway, with her chattering teeth. It seemed too disrespectful.

She set her jaws against the bomb craters blocking her way with stale puddles of brackish water, the leaves of a departing fall floating limply on the surface. Biting gusts of wintry air pushed her forward, bringing along the faint scent of gun powder and smoke. Each bridge she crossed gave her a brief feeling of security. Bridges could be made into strongholds, could they not? The wheels moved ever more clumsily. There was no shelter for the animals at night, little food to strengthen them for yet another day. The shortage of fodder was frightening indeed. Katya's heart contracted every time she looked at their hollow flanks. This was the one thing that could move her to enraged tears—to see how herds of cattle and horses were driven by with their rib-cages visible beneath their skin, with dull, apathetic eyes, with hoofs so worn that the creatures left bloody footprints on the road.

She and Jasch now rode together in one wagon, having harnessed their horses and vehicles to each other so as to be able to take turns with the reins. Jasch's leg was badly infected. His face was grey from pain.

Like a giant reptile, the trek kept creeping toward the Polish border, spanning a length now close to a hundred kilometers. From time to time, rows of military trucks, moving in the opposite direction, would force them off the road in great impatience, and would cause wheels to be broken and carts to be tumbled into ditches and wasteful delays for hours at a time.

Cryptic messages streamed over the broadcast channels— hints about miracle weapons, strategic cunning, victory always a mere hair's width away. In order to conserve strength for the counter-offensive that was to come soon, an insignificant part of the eastern territory had had to be abandoned. "We have never been," came the firm message, "as strong and as confident as now."

David told Katya one night that he had witnessed how a deserter had been shot. This louse, he told her, choked with emotion, had been caught hiding in the rain-dripping forest and had been placed with his back to the wall to die a shameful, bullet-riddled death.

Katya replied in sympathy:

"Maybe he panicked, poor boy? So many of our *landser* are mere children."

David said harshly:

"He was bound by his word of honor. It served him right."

"Don't be so merciless, son," said Katya, mechanically.

But in her heart, she could not help agreeing just a tiny bit with her son. Who did not fight discouragement these days? But one kept such thoughts to oneself so as not to weaken the spirit of the trek. How could they survive unless they believed in the invincibility of the Army, unless they supported each other in word and in deed in times of such utter distress? Even the most steadfast morale would otherwise be washed out of one's heart by these drenching rains.

The refugees lay deep in the soggy straw, under soaked pillows and blankets, with tent panels tied over them to break the force of the winds. Every once in a while, the clouds above them threw fistfuls of snow upon the trek, which kept on snailing along the bombed-out roads, over this rickety bridge and that one, through his little town and that. The trek slid down hills and broke wheels and lost horses by the score. The ones that remained pulled listlessly—their bones sticking out of their emaciated bodies, their eyes lusterless from hunger and fatigue.

At night, patrols would walk along the trek, holding their rifles at the ready, tensing imperceptibly each time the trek would wind itself into yet another darkening, dripping forest.

Had they ever sung happy, confident songs? Nothing could

147

be heard for hours on end but the sounds of the squeaking discs as they slid along the way, and Liestje's wracking coughing from beyond.

No one had a map. Someone up front, presumably, was leading the way. Perhaps it was not even necessary to know which way to travel. All that was needed was to keep the ever louder sounds of battle squarely at one's back.

Could a night as dreary, as murky as this rightfully claim to be the birthday of the Savior who had been sent to comfort frightened souls? Katya took her obstinate heart in both of her hands. She no longer talked directly to her Lord. She would think of Christmas in her own good time, but not now, not at this bleak, dripping hour, not with the knowledge in her heart that Liestje, in the back of the wagon, was dying.

She had guided the horses into the wind shelter of an abandoned train and had tried to tie the reins to a post.

"Walter," she now called out, as she climbed down stiffly from the wagon. "Try to find some fodder for the horses, will you, dear? Liestje, can you manage, child? How your face is burning! Do you feel very ill?"

"Not really." Liestje's voice was rasping. Her eyes were fever-shot, her eyelids swollen from unhealthy fluid. How difficult it was to keep from trembling!

"Sara, get going! Find us a dry place for the night. Don't ask. Go. Just go!" There was raw panic in Katya's command.

With reluctance, Sara peeled herself out from under the soggy covers.

"All right. Just stay here, so I can find you again."

She hunched her shoulders against the wind. She walked along the drafty railroad station ramp, looking desperately about. A train roared by. The gust of air blew her hard against the wall of the poorly-lit waiting room. She peered through the window. No, there would be no use—it was filled to the walls, she could see. All the world, it seemed to her of late, was

148

sleeping on tables, on chairs, on the steps of abandoned buildings, like sardines packed side to side on the floor. No way to squeeze in!

She leaned against the door frame for a moment, trying to catch her breath. Another train pulled in. Apathetically, she watched the passengers ready themselves for farewells. A grey-haired woman was weeping against a young soldier's braided shoulder seams. A young *landser* bent over a tiny blue-and-white striped nurse, burying his face in her hair. At the sight, she felt a stab of longing for Karl-Heinz. He was doing duty at the eastern front. She had not heard from him for more than a year, though she had the address of his parents in her pocket. She was to find them in Germany and stay with them until he could come and claim her the moment the Russians' defeat was assured. In his loving letter he had explained to her carefully that they lived on a farm near the outskirts of Berlin.

People poured back and forth. She heard them shuffle and hurry and call out impatiently. A radio was blaring its cheerful message:

" . . . the enemy, spreading his unfounded lies . . . "

She sighed, hugging herself for additional warmth.

" . . . thousands back home believe in our mission . . . the kind of loyalty that has helped our *landser* to burrow into the Slavic eastern soil will now once more . . . "

She knew the message by heart. She had heard it repeated a thousand times—on paper, in the air, on the screen during the pauses in their flight. It was a message that no one would dream of contradicting, a message that no power could distort—it came through loud and clear and full of certainty as she stood there, small and forlorn, hunched against the wind: " . . . to the last drop of loyal German blood . . . " She sighed again, thinking of the swarm of Russian aircraft that had harassed them all day. Single artillery sparks, occasionally visible along the horizon, had tightened into a roaring inferno in early morning, accompanied by a deafening sound of furor so overwhelming that it had swept the rest of the hesitating civilians out of their

149

beds and into this heedless, panicky scramble now clogging the already overburdened roads.

The train conductor whistled sharply. The wheels started to move again, turning faster now, becoming spinning discs, creating a sharp suction that whirled dried, crumbled leaves onto her feet. She closed her eyes against the draft. Her knees felt like butter.

"Are you all right?"

She stirred reluctantly. A German officer leaned over her. She could see that he wore the epaulets of a colonel. A long warm coat fell over his shiny, spotless boots, held narrowly to his waist by a wide firm belt. The hand against her face was very warm. She gazed into his serious, sympathetic eyes and felt her own fill with sudden tears.

He took her by the arm. "Did you see someone off? Your husband?"

She shook her head. "No. It's just that . . . that it's Christmas." She swallowed.

"I have an air raid shelter," he said. He steered her gently along the slippery ramp. "There are nine of us, but if you have no one, I'm sure we can manage to make room for you as well. A tiny pretty thing like you."

"I have a wagon full of people," she said with a sigh. "I have a child who's a baby still and a brother who is a Hitler Youth. And my sister Liestje is very, very ill. And then there's Karin, my daughter. And Walter, a stray whose mother died on the trek." She quickly omitted Jasch—let him fend for himself! But she added with loyalty: "And Oma." How she longed for some warmth! She looked at the officer pleadingly: "We have come such a long, long way. From Russia. We have walked almost the entire stretch—more than a thousand kilometers."

"You came from Russia? On foot?"

She nodded emphatically.

"You have a grandmother with you?" he asked softly. "And three children?"

Would he leave her now? She grasped him by the sleeve.

"All right," he said, smiling down at her. "What's Christmas without children, anyway? And what's Christmas without one's Oma?" He pressed her fingers with his large warm hand. "I have three little ones of my own at home in Duesseldorf. I am Horst Goericke, in charge of this Godforsaken Polish town."

"Where are we?"

"Near Hohensalza," explained the soldier. "And who are you?"

"My family calls me Sara." She added hastily: "I just come from a clan that's fond of the Bible."

"I see," he smiled.

"And your hand is so warm I don't ever want to let go of it again. I have traveled the face of this earth, but now I am going home into the *Vaterland*. And never have I celebrated Christmas yet the real German way."

"Follow me, madam," he said, grandly. "Celebrate you shall!"

Was it really true that there was still a night of wonder—at the very gates of Germany? Indeed yes and yes again! They were sitting in a bunker so warm and comforting that for once they could be oblivious to the blasts that came rhythmically from the east and shook the floor and made the kerosene lamp sway gently back and forth with each explosion.

Katya looked about to verify this miracle. Liestje, still shivering from time to time, sat near the fire, her cheeks alight with warmth. David could be heard insisting: "I know how to fling a grenade! Each morning, I measure my height against a wall. I will be fourteen soon!"

"Hurry up," smiled the *landser* and put a comrade's hand upon the boy's right knee.

"Sheer insolence will do," said David loudly, in turn putting his fist squarely upon the *landser's* knuckles. "If we keep our guns visible at the doors of our vehicles, the enemy will run like the rabbit from the hound."

"David," warned Katya gently, to let him know she thought him boisterous.

151

The candles flickered softly. The baby was asleep. Karin sat cradled in the arms of a *landser* who talked to her in whispers of his hometown in the Austrian mountains. Katya could make out fragments of his hushed, poetic tale:

"Loaded with presents, shoppers will hurry along the street, strangers calling out to strangers: 'And a very merry Christmas to you.' Young children, knocking on house after house, sing ancient songs of a Teutonic past when candles would come alight in every hut, from the gentle waters of the Danube to the harsh waves of the Northern Sea . . . If nature is willing and in a good mood, there is snow on each post and each fence. Tiny, fluffy caps that children, walking by, will wipe off playfully with warmly gloved hands . . . " He rocked Karin gently back and forth on his knees, holding her cheek against his face. " . . . huge piles of firewood, Karin, can be found in front of every home. And smoke rises from chimneys, scented with the smell of baked apples . . . "

Karin snuggled close to him, enchanted to glowing warmth by the spell cast with High German words. So as not to wake Lily Marlene the soldiers now started to sing very softly, giving way to their own homesick longing: *"Heimat, deine Sterne . . . "* Homeland and your myriad stars. Silent greetings, standing in far distances, sent to me gently by my own dear love.

Katya sat on a couch, her legs and shoulders wrapped generously with a heavy *landser* blanket, feeling in herself a comfort so deep that it soothed the marrow of her bones. Why should the outside world matter on a night such as this? This very morning, another warning had come over the broadcast that along the Vistula River, Russian cannons were already pointing threateningly across the waters of the winter-sluggish stream. Any moment now, it would be frozen over for the onslaught of the horror that would try to roll across the ice. To her immense relief, she now learned about a counter-offensive with the aid of the infantry that would once and for all bring a reversal of the tide. In her opinion, it was high time for such a reversal indeed! The past weeks had taught her most convincingly that every shrub could mean ambush; that every darkened window might spell treason. Just last week, David had come to her with a fistful of lies that had been thrown from the sky. The flyers had slanderously spoken of a bled-out Germany, a land more than ready for surrender, a weakened, dispirited army bracing itself for impending defeat.

"How can that be?" she now thought, looking about. "How can the Western Allies be so blind to right and wrong that they would fear the straight, tall, knightly German soldier more than the creeping slit-eyed danger from the East?"

A tiny Christmas tree stood in the very center of the bunker, decorated with silver threads and ornaments and slender stars made artfully from straw. A cup of hot coffee steamed in Katya's hand. What riches! There were nuts in a bowl on the table, mixed with candy and dry, scented fruit. Above the door hung a tiny angel, moving its golden wings most gently in the air. The spewing little iron stove held half a dozen apples on its plate. The room was crowded, to be sure. The soldiers stretched their long legs all over the place; one could barely set one's feet down without stepping on a *landser's* toes.

A giant cake was placed in front of her, a miracle of baking skill, as far as she could judge. Horst Goericke, with grand ceremony, sharpened his pocket knife on the window sill till it gleamed:

"My mother sent me this beauty," he explained, proudly. "She saved up for it for three months, dear good soul! Do you know how strictly our people at home are rationed now? Cut big pieces, Oma dear. It's Christmas only once a year."

"Gladly," replied Katya, feeling a surge of love and gratitude fill her heart.

They talked, of course, about the war.

She listened quietly, enveloped in warmth.

" . . . Sooner or later, we'll grab the Russky by the neck! Can the Soviets tolerate the kinds of losses we inflict . . . "

" . . . they tried to get us from behind, the cowards. Three times they tried. Three times we threw them back . . . "

153

" . . . What do they know about camouflage? Their cannons reflect the sun's rays like a mirror . . . "

" . . . And then we shook the living daylights out of them! Our bombs were right on target, man!"

" . . . We surprised them by building a horseshoe formation and took the outposts by overwhelming the unsuspecting guards . . . "

"Poor devils. And their air cover from the ground? A joke! That's all I can say. A joke!"

Here was a sample of Germany's sons. This was the personification of Germany's pride, admired and feared, as well they should be, as ever dedicated to eradicating the ills of the world. She could picture them so well, with their chin straps tightly around their jaws, with their hand grenades on their belts—loyal friends and fierce protectors of German women and children! Her eyes, her ears could never have their fill. No one could put into his voice such confidence, such utter devotion, such iron discipline, were it not for this certainty of the rightness and righteousness of his beliefs. These boys had trained themselves to hold images of flight, of defeat, of disintegration at bay. They had trained themselves to uphold images of heroism, beliefs of serving a historical purpose, of being the unbroken shield against the barbarism from the East. She could not, of course, have put these thoughts into such pompous words. She could only sit and marvel about the source of this unbending certainty and pride, and she could say to herself:

"Surely they must know of tightly guarded secrets that will bring about a turn of this disastrous war."

Silently she watched David's glowing face. The boy was truly entranced. Single-handedly, these *landser* had pushed back a threatening flank of the Byelorussian Army at the very hour his trek had passed a targeted city, thus aiding the civilians' flight and freeing the territory for the decisive battle about to begin. There were so many tricks to the trade. There was so much to learn. One could block roads, set outposts, threaten with bombs and firing squads and spine-tingling fear. One could set fire to

154

one side of a stronghold in order to surprise the enemy's flanks at the other. Shiver after shiver trickled down David's spine. Every fiber of his being understood the dedication illuminating those shining, confident eyes. He felt the power and dedication behind those sweeping statements. An invisible force pulled him to his feet to stand at awed attention as now Horst Goericke began to draw on words—heavy, leaden, almost drunken words, reaching deep into the pagan darkness of their time-dimmed past, transforming the little fir tree into a symbol of feelings too vast, too sacred to be fully expressed before such solemn, irrevocable duty as was placed once more into the *landsers'* hands:

"... the *Vaterland's* valiant warriors steel their hearts to storm a vicious fiend ..."

David's young face was glistening with unashamed tears. The floor beneath his feet shook faintly, rhythmically, and predictably with each new dull rumbling detonation. Soft, fragrant wax continued to drip gently onto the prickly needles of the tree.

The clouds overhead were gathering again, a grey merciless mass firmly tying horizon to horizon. It was as if heaven and earth had united to enfold those who had tried to roll toward the west. The air became thicker as daylight retreated. It was not yet three o'clock in the afternoon, but already it was difficult to make out the wagons and horses a mere stone's throw away.

It snowed all night, gently and relentlessly. When dawn broke, a sharp wind tore apart the clouds and briefly revealed a pale sky devoid of any pity.

The day ahead seemed an arctic blanket of glittering icicles.

And still, the trek kept swelling.

Lucky indeed was Katya, who still owned two horses, though one of them limped pitifully. Many people now had to go on foot, moving their children and their possessions over the slippery road on an overturned table or chair pulled by a rope.

Part of the morning they pushed through the shelter of a

forest which somehow broke the force of the wind, where trees hung heavy with snow, their branches bent toward the earth. But by late afternoon they reached the plains again and felt themselves sucked right into gusts of arctic air sweeping horizontally across wide stretches of bare land. As far as the eye could see, there were dunes and hills and valleys of snow—it was a mass of swirling, choking, virgin white disaster.

The road in front of them stretched like an icy ribbon into the distance.

People staggered alongside their wagons, their breath tiny clouds of vapor in the air. Many would sink to their knees, and double up, and die with their backs to the howling wind, which kept on heaping snowdrift after snowdrift into their path. The struggling figures would hardly merit a glance from those who staggered on. The storm blinded them viciously by blowing needles of ice into their smarting, tearing eyes. The wind drove them on, froze the breath on their lips, froze the pity out of their hearts, pushed them full force into another endless arctic night. The blizzard tore the blankets and coverings off the wagons and whirled them high into the air and into the darkness from which they could not be retrieved. Never had they been so cold in all their lives as they tried to huddle together against the whipping winds. They clung to each other in a cluster. Liestje held Karin in her arms, her trembling body pressed tightly against the sobbing child. Behind her lay David, clinging to her in gasps. Between Katya and herself, there was a baby—no longer crying, shrinking to still lifelessness. It was a miracle they did not smother it to death in their desperate attempts to find and give a little warmth. Time turned into eternity that night. Above them, the stars kept blinking. They could hear most clearly the groaning of the front.

Jasch disappeared that night. Katya had last seen him at dusk. He held wrapped around himself a piece of old *landser* tent, frozen into a board. Out of his boots stuck wads of shredded newspapers.

"This is the end," he had moaned, staggering on.

156

"Oh, hush," she had cried, almost sobbing. "Will you be quiet, for heaven's sake?"

"This morning," he said, stumbling alongside the horses, "Stalin's troops have been launched across the Vistula River and are now fanning out in all directions. Zhukov's Army is pushing west after having pierced Warsaw from both north and south. Allenstein, Tannenburg, Posen have fallen. The Russians stand at the gates of Breslau. Let's stop. Let's hide. Oh, my leg! I cannot stand this pain! Let's stop somewhere, Katyushka!"

"He ought to be shot," came David's muffled voice from behind. "For treason."

He spoke straight from Katya's heart.

There was no feeling any more in the tips of her fingers and toes; there had not been for more than a day. Her teeth had bitten through her numb, whitish lips. Snow and frozen dirt stuck to the wheels. There was clearly no more strength in the horses. They stumbled along, their flanks wet despite the cold. Their sunken sides heaved and fell. They snorted with the effort. When she could hold the reins no longer with her heavy, dead hands, she had fastened them to the wagon and had slumped against the wind. The ice made the horses set their hoofs very cautiously now. Every once in a while, she took a deep breath, gritted her teeth, and let the whip come swishing down. The horses' heads dropped. Sweat shone on their flanks, solidified the moment the droplets appeared. Fine shivers rippled over their skins.

"Liestje is going to die on me," thought Katya in wild panic. "She cannot last another night."

"Get down from the wagon," she told Sara. "You too, David."

The place beneath the blankets clearly belonged to her sick child who could no longer walk. The horses were too weak to pull all of them. She tied Karin and Walter with a rope to the planks as best she could while powdered snow was thrown at her in fistfuls from an embittered, uncompromising, merciless sky. The tiny figures slid along, fell to their knees, struggled up, kept

157

on walking. The wind picked up speed again, started to howl. Choking snow fell and blew and drifted over the endless procession in blankets of whirling whiteness. The blizzard moved with howling speed. It had gathered great strength and fury by now; it could well afford to push the last living refugees along the icy, slippery road.

Liestje, in the back of the wagon, fought wave after wave of nausea. Sooner or later, she knew, it would make her spit up blood again as she had done yesterday behind a bush. The snow had reddened. She had seen it almost with relief. All night, she had felt her bones being consumed by a slow-burning fire. Beneath the planks of the wagon she had lain doubled up, staring at the glittering band of the Milky Way girdling the sky. Tremor after tremor had swept over her. Now she crouched in the back of the vehicle. She felt her forehead wet with perspiration despite the cold. Her eyes were luminous with the fevor in her veins. Hot knives seared along her ribcage every once in a while. She was too miserable to care about the added pain. She held her hot face buried in her deadened hands. Behind her closed eyes there swayed a wild array of fever dreams. The jolts of the wagon threw her head from side to side. The wheels beneath squeaked. In the approaching darkness she saw her mother's body huddled against the wind.

If only the wind would stop!

Her tongue moved over her parched lips. She lifted her face with an effort.

"Let Karin and Walter ride for a while, Mother. Maybe walking will help a little. I feel somewhat better now. Let me walk for a while so the blood in my toes will circulate again."

"Do that, child," mumbled Katya. "Just be sure not to lose us in this wind."

What she would give for a hot bath to soak the deadly illness out of her child's weakened limbs! Terror contracted Katya's chest. So many had died of pneumonia since the fall—first the old ones, then the little children, later, here and there, a man in his prime, a woman not yet forty. Bomb craters had come in handy. One could leave one's dead there so as not to clog the roads with those who had succumbed. They had left them by the side of the road, in deserted barns, behind shacks, in abandoned wagons, covered with newspapers proclaiming great German victories at the front. Many little ones were simply left in ditches, their lids frozen shut. Was Lily still alive? Yes, there was still a faint stirring.

"Liestje?" called Katya, straining to see past the blanket of whirling flakes. "Are you all right, child?"

"Yes," said Liestje, forcibly. A spray of stars danced in front of her watering eyes. Melted snow slushed in her shoes. She stumbled alongside the trek, coughing violently from time to time. She heard Karin whimpering beneath the covers. She heard Katya say: "Give me your other hand. And stop howling. I know it hurts. But it will hurt more if I let it be. Do you want to lose your fingers? Walter, hold her feet. Another fifteen minutes, Karin, that's all. I promise! Just a little while, all right?"

And still it snowed.

It came down vertically now, as the winds subsided for a while, sheets and sheets of whitest damnation. The flakes were soft and fluffy and fell onto the moving trek and most persistently stuck tightly to every surface.

Liestje clutched onto her scarf that she had tied around her neck. There now began a whistling in her ears. She fell. She struggled to her feet, trying to keep the storm at her back. She tried to call out Katya's name, but the gurgling sound was wiped right off her lips.

Now she was walking through nothingness. There was no substance, no matter where she stepped. Her feet slid by themselves along the slippery road. She still grasped the back post of the wagon, letting herself be dragged along. Suddenly she felt a most sinful, terrible craving. She all but gasped from desire. She had tried smoking for the first time in her life in the bunker at Christmas Eve. Oma had sorely disapproved. Remembering, she searched her pockets with numb hands. She managed to strike a tiny flame. Its light illuminated her bluish face, found a brief reflection in her fever-shot eyes. The unaccustomed taste of the cigarette smoke gave her a brief illusion of warmth.

She whispered:

"If I can stand it another hour or so . . . "

The sole of her right shoe had loosened, but she no longer felt the ice and gravel of the road cut into her foot. The whistling in her ears had turned to humming. There was a hollow softness beneath her knee caps. Her lips were blistering now. She looked up to the darkening sky. Huge ragged clouds raced across a meager slice of a moon.

"Oh, dearest God in heaven," she moaned softly.

She let go of the sideboard to which she had clung. Stepping to the side, she felt the next wagon pass by. She could barely see the horses. Suddenly, a feeling of euphoria flooded her veins. It must have been the cigarette smoke which now transformed the world. The hollowness in her bones disappeared. Beneath her feet, now, she felt the unevenness of plowed land.

She knew the direction of the trek; all she had to do was to follow the path that lay before her in the dusk.

"Lietsje . . . " called Katya, from very far away, "I think Karin has regained the feeling in her hands . . . "

"Good," she muttered.

She stood for a while and listened to the sound of the disappearing wagons. The tip of her foot felt its way across a ditch. It was almost fun now to walk in a world made of cotton. Her shoe hit something hard and round. Mechanically, she bent down. Her numb fingers felt the obstacle.

"Why, a sack of potatoes," she said, utterly surprised. "Now, what idiot would have . . . " Just for a moment she would sit on it and contemplate. There was food here for weeks! But how could she move it the distance to the road? What riches! And right here in the snow, not belonging to a soul! She would drag it to her family after she had taken two or three seconds to close her eyes so as to gather the necessary strength.

Katya would later recall that this was just like Lietsje—to

close her eyes quietly and never open them again, lest it be to the glory of a better world. David, sent out to look for his sister, recognized her by the neck scarf that stuck out of the drift which had started to pile around her body. He tried to lift her onto his shoulders and put her by the wayside, but she was too stiff and unyielding, and he was too weak from the hunger and cold, and so he went back and took Katya by the arm, and together they stood and waited until the snow had finally covered Liestje's pinched face before he led his mother away.

When they returned, the horses had fallen to the ground. Someone had pushed the wagon to the side and had tumbled it over so that the trek could move on.

They dug the children out. And then they simply walked into the night. They walked to keep from freezing on the spot. They simply walked straight into the whiteness, no, the blackness ahead—dazed, tearless, all but frozen alive already. They walked until before them, suddenly, there appeared an obstacle, a barricade, made of boxcars and wheels and rows of yellow lights. Katya leaned her face against an iron door, feeling her life give way. She could no longer make out the Red Cross painted generously across the railroad wagon, reaching majestically from edge to frozen edge.

"A hospital train," whispered David.

She fell to the ground as someone pushed open the heavy door. Someone said: "My God, there are some children outside, frozen to the rails."

Someone reached out into the night. Someone pried Lily Marlene out of David's clutching hands, dragged Karin by the arms into the train, helped the stumbling, gasping Walter. Someone helped Katya to her knees, to her feet, pushing her forcibly into a place brimming over with warmth and animated talk. There was a numbness around her still. She was, in fact, as good as dead already. All of her senses were gone except for her ability to hear—she heard most clearly the enormous trembling sound that went like a giant ripple along the floor of the train. She heard the throaty breathing of the locomotive. Now she

161

even felt the push beneath her feet as iron wheels began to spin. Someone wrapped a blanket around the legs that were so clearly no longer her own. Someone pushed her onto a chair near a sputtering iron oven. She could hear huge sliding doors fall shut, closing off an island of warmth, locking in a paradise of comfort. After a while, miraculously, a dim vision of sorts returned, for as she managed to focus her eyes on the little frozen-over window, she saw pole after pole speed by. And as the train went around a bend and slowed temporarily, she could catch its own reflection in the window. Every snowed-in box car had its little chimney. Smoke rose up toward a meager slice of a moon hanging distant, lean, and unperturbed, pouring a dim last light over the white frozen land.

7

They were to become a nation of steel—as hard and as pure as the Krupp material which steadily fueled their war, bound to each other in death as in life, smelted to purposeful unity by the fires of world persecution. Katya would sit and listen to this daily broadcast message, her own jaws like fire from the effort of trying to suppress her own selfish sorrow for her poor, frozen child. With all the strength at her command, she willed herself to keep from weeping, for there were greater issues now than an old woman's lonely grief. There was a purpose now to dying—a purpose more sanctifying than life could have granted. By dying as a victim of this war, this gentlest of her children had secured for herself a victory noble and chaste. Still, could she as a mother be blamed if once in a while sheets of fog drifted across her soul—intangible, clammy, chilling her to the very marrow of her bones? She felt of late as if she stood within a transparent shell, conscious of a deadening of her sensibilities—a creeping, hollow, having-been-cast-out-of-everything self that once had had the power to sustain her deepest beliefs. Why this should be,

162

she did not know, for a besieged *Vaterland* it was, to be sure, into which she had come, yet a Germany invincible. Katya felt it most keenly each time she listened to the broadcast from Berlin as she sat close to the window to take full advantage of the fading light of the day.

A feeling of great urgency was in the air, for the enemy had grown surprisingly strong—much stronger than had been anticipated in the beginning. The world papers falsely proclaimed that the political sky was ominously darkening for Germany, since defeat after defeat continued to weaken a embittered, valiantly resisting combat front. Just this morning, while waiting for her weekly rations at the corner grocery store, she had overheard bits and pieces of this erroneous dribble of lies:

" . . . the *Fuehrer* is preparing to escape by means of a forged passport and a false beard . . . "

" . . . and three of his ministers are said to have swallowed poison . . . "

" . . . and Goering is supposed to be hiding in the mountains, waiting for the inevitable clash between the East and the West . . . "

As she went home, she thought about what she had heard.

In the West, it was said, there was serious talk about peace. There was even talk about a humbling appeal for Allied understanding. For weeks, the air had all but vibrated with rumors—rumors of approaching American panzer divisions, rumors of meetings between powerful heads of state, confident talk that a personal confrontation would clear up any tragic misunderstandings between Germany and the incomprehensibly ignorant West. Just a few weeks were needed to wait out the American realization of the imminent collapse of the civilized world, should the inconceivable happen and the eastern front give way.

"And yet, despite all evidence," thought Katya, "Western awareness seems mysteriously blunted."

Two months ago, in February, Dresden had perished in a single night and day.

Dresden had no strategic importance at all—it was a city filled to the seams with weakened, hungry, helpless refugees, a city of women and children, a place removed from the tremors of combat, a city known to the world for its exquisite beauty and grace. There was no reason to reduce Dresden to ashes but for the baseness of an uninformed vindictive West. The flags of the *Vaterland* had flown half-mast for three days to give people time to come to terms with such grief as was now asked of each German man and woman and child. The smoldering ruins of Dresden appeared on screen after screen, and people sat stone-faced, looking at such utterly senseless destruction. Never would they forget! From now on, was there reprieve or return? The hate-spewing voice found a thousand willing echoes in the farthest corners of the land.

Sara, after some effort, had located the parents of Karl-Heinz, who had welcomed her with genuine warmth. She and her family, she had explained to the farmers, were to wait here until there was a lull in the war that would permit Karl-Heinz to come home on furlough and find them a more suitable place of their own. However, even she could see that it would be impossible to stay for more than a few days, for the farm buildings were overflowing with refugees en route to Berlin. Trains kept on bringing people, pouring them by the thousands into the crammed space that was left of Germany. Katya, not having anything better to do, would often watch them arrive, hoping for a familiar Mennonite face. The tired, bombed-out refugees hung in clusters outside the windows and doors, rode on the bumpers, clung to the chimneys of the box car roofs. Hallways, sheds, barns became their habitat for weeks to come. However, Germany—although harshly besieged—was still a place of meticulous order and miraculous means. Efficient hands took over, registered each refugee in proper detail, put food rations in his hands, gave him a bundle of clean, used clothing, some bedding, an address to look up where he

164

could wash off the grime of the trek, and to sleep off some of the horror that he had witnessed. It was amazing how regenerative a solid night of sleep could be! Katya found herself assigned to a second story room and a tiny, immaculate kitchen in a little town nearby where she was told that they could stay until such time as was still needed to push the enemy to headlong flight once more.

"Maybe we would be safer in Berlin," Sara would sometimes suggest. "Berlin is a strong, fortified city."

But Katya shook her head.

"Let's wait," she said. "Now we have safety. And warmth. And food. And a measure of comfort." Every week, Karl-Heinz's parents would send her a basket full of fruit, or a bag of potatoes, or a jugful of creamy milk for the fast-growing, recovering baby. Karin and Walter would often help with the animals and with the work in the kitchen, and would in turn be invited to share the farmers' meals. Sara had volunteered for duty as a Red Cross nurse and was gone most of the week. David's time was taken up with his Hitler Youth training. "What soothing silence," Katya would think, "is suddenly mine to come to terms with my grief."

As she sat by the window, letting her gaze sweep over the acres beyond—at times absentmindedly counting the many dugouts and trenches—she told herself in bitter irony that now she truly belonged. She had paid her price and more in precious coin; she could rightfully claim to be part of her *Vaterland* for today and next year and forever. Yes, a child of hers had been taken, but who was she to grieve when now her homeland, in sorrow, was forced to count by the hundreds of thousands the names of her fallen young sons? Was not she, Katya Wall, still truly blessed when in very early spring there was a knock on her door, and Karl-Heinz stood there smiling in full soldierly stature, putting two strong, firm arms around her back? Well, not two whole arms, to be exact, for he was wounded rather badly. His left arm and part of his shoulder were still in a cast. But he was full of confidence and humor, glad to be home for a change, sitting in her kitchen, his feet in soapy water to soak out the frostbite he had acquired by accident and out of carelessness as he had come an incredible distance to be with them for three days. He described the journey to a breathless audience: On his back, the heavy pack, hand grenades on his belt, his pockets bulging with ammunition—through swamps and forests and rivers! He rapped his cast impatiently:

"Our entire army is on the alert," he explained. "And a silly thing like this has to happen to me!"

"Have you actually seen the Russians?"

"Oh, yes. Yes, indeed! We can see them very well standing there across the river, with their thickly padded coats, with their woolen hoods pulled deep over their eyes, stocky feet in felt boots . . . How we hate their smugness, when we stand there, teeth chattering . . . Constantly these monsters try to overrun the river. We have our hands full trying to keep them at bay."

"Is that possible?"

"I beg your pardon?"

"Will you keep them at bay?"

"Why, Oma! Our people stand at Seelow, barricaded to the utmost, armed to their teeth. I don't want you to worry, Oma dear. Nothing will happen to my family as long as there is but one soldier carrying a handful of cartridges on his belt. I'll see to that. I promise!"

To harbor persistent doubts would surely be treason before such glowing confidence. On days such as this, Katya, too, found it easy to believe in the miracle that was now expected by the hour—that many felt to be vibrating in the very spring-scented air. Somewhere there was an explanation for the puzzling fact that cities were lost and retaken and lost again to an enemy that should have been finished off long ago. There was an explanation that she in her nearsightedness somehow could not clearly perceive.

"All we need is a week of concentrated military effort," she heard Karl-Heinz assert.

"Do you really believe that, my boy?"

"Oma," he replied, shocked. "What kinds of doubts are

166

those?" He put his arm around her shoulder. "There is no question that the upcoming battle will turn the tide. Never for a moment do we question final victory."

She sighed.

He gave her a look that made her blush in shame. Gently she stroked the sleeve of his shirt.

"Just take care of yourself, my boy."

"Of course," he answered, impatiently. "We still have secret weapons. We have new jets that will sweep the heavens clean of the enemy. We have supplies and ammunition to spare. And we have a united country, Oma, determined to stand together as one man."

"It's just that so many have died already. And so much territory is daily being taken. Let's agree on one thing, Karl-Heinz. If worst comes to worst . . ."

"Oma," said her soldier, "you silly rabbit heart! If beans start falling from the skies, you go to the farm. I will try to be there to shield you."

"Let's make that a promise," said Katya. "On your word of honor, Karl-Heinz."

"*Mein Ehrenwort,*" he promised, his eyes crinkling merrily.

Who wouldn't be comforted by his confidence? Katya berated herself severely. Who was she to doubt this land—she who now lived among her German people as one of their own? She belonged to them totally and fully—she was part of these people, who since the days when Razin had put the torch to the Ukraine had rescued her and fed her and reached out with their hands a thousand times and more in truest loyal brotherhood.

Thus life, once again, took on a gentle tinge of beauty.

Sara, as everyone could see, was truly lovely, clad in her immaculate blue-and-white striped uniform, as slim and as vibrant as a seventeen-year-old girl, though she was, Katya had to remind herself every once in a while, in age now nearing thirty. Full of patriotic eagerness, burning with pity and hardworking dedication for the wounded *landser* arriving by the thousands from the front—that was Sara! She had enlisted for

167

double duty to help the *Vaterland* as best she could. The children could safely be left to Katya's care. Karin and Walter were now old enough to fend for themselves, though Karin grew up to be a very headstrong child, badly in need of a consistent hand to guide and discipline her. Sara sighed when reminded of her inconvenient parenthood. But Lily Marlene, she told herself quickly, was steadily recovering from her anemic infancy, was starting now to speak, to walk, to turn into a very pretty smiling little doll. Her limbs were becoming much stronger, thanks to Providence and the care of Karl-Heinz's doting parents.

David, of course, was Oma's constant worry. David was so very impatient with the progress of the war. He was gone for days at a time, unwilling to account to her for his hours. Katya longed to have him near. She told him so every time he pleaded to be enlisted, every time he begged her to let him falsify his age, to let him bribe his way into the ranks of the valiantly fighting men at the embattled eastern front. He begrudged every *landser* the privilege of fighting. A hundred times and more, he told her, his voice choked with emotion, these men had been thrown into combat. Over and over again, they had withstood the onslaught of the enemy. How much longer was he to remain tied to his mother's apron strings? Wasn't he almost as tall as a man?

"You are only fourteen," Katya would say.

Nothing could antagonize him more than to be reminded of such a shameful fact.

One afternoon he marched into her kitchen, took off his cap, loosened his neckerchief, sat down by her table, and announced in his casual, nonchalant way:

"Guess what, Mother."

"What?"

"Uncle Jasch is in town, minus one leg."

"Really?"

"Yes. Now he won't be drafted, that's for sure. How some people manage to avoid their share of the burdens of our *Heimatland* is beyond my comprehension."

"Oh, David," cried Katya. "Come on, now! Don't be so

168

judgmental, son." She was genuinely glad to find out that Jasch was still alive, though she was sure that if anyone had managed to escape the terrors of the trek, it had to be Jasch! But yes, she was happy to learn that he was well enough to be in charge of a refugee center, that he would come and visit her soon. She had not heard of him for many months, although she had thought of him often and had felt guilty for having been impatient, especially now that she learned his leg had been truly infected to the point of requiring amputation.

She was so glad about his arrival, in fact, that she decided to save her flour and sugar rations for a week so she could bake him a cake as a welcoming present. She badly missed her people. He was almost as good as one of her own. She did not know how many of the Mennonites, if anyone at all, had survived.

"Mennonites?" her ignorant neighbors would ask, blank looks on their faces.

Thus it was a genuine welcome that awaited Jasch in Katya's tiny kitchen. Walter had grown so much! His father looked at him with pride. "Be sure to mind your Aunt Katya," he would admonish him time and again. "Were it not for your good, dear Aunt Katya, we would have lost you on the trek." Oh, those times on the trek! Together, they relived every moment, shared experiences, exchanged hopes, wondered aloud about the chances of soon terminating this slow, dragging, incomprehensible war. Before Jasch left, he planted two solid kisses on Katya's cheeks, right in front of the grinning, grimacing children:

"Take care, Katyushka," he advised her solemnly. "I have this funny warning feeling of late . . . "

She smiled as she pushed him out of the door.

"None of your oracles of doom, now, Jasch," she told him gently.

She watched him limp around the corner awkwardly with his artificial leg. He, too, had paid his price. She stood outside on her doorstep for a while, wondering if at home the cherry trees had yet begun to bloom. She sat down on the steps with a sigh, feeling the breeze die down. She could hear faint radio music drift through the silken air. She became conscious all at once that the night seemed far too quiet. It was a quietness of utmost intensity, a quietness that stood like an exclamation mark amid the musky scent on the horizon. All day, she now remembered, there had been black smoke clouds in the sky which had drifted across the fields and had made the farmers lift their faces in vague concern.

A voice began to broadcast now:

" . . . during this moment in military history, when it seems that all the forces of hate and destruction from the east, west, south, and north are storming against our front, I am addressing the German people on the eve of our *Fuehrer's* birthday . . ."

As she took her hands from her eyes, she saw that to the northwest the sky was so red that it seemed someone had dipped the clouds over Berlin into a giant pot of blood.

"It must be from the smoke," she thought. "The sun's rays are caught in the clouds at this hour of the day . . . "

" . . . that Germany is still alive; that Europe—and with Europe, the civilized West—has not yet been swallowed by a gaping abyss—in due to our *Fuehrer*. For he is going to be the man of the century . . . "

"Sara," she called. "Come here. Listen."

Sara joined her on the doorsteps, her face aglow.

"I hope David is listening," she whispered in awe.

"...as the lonely and mighty leader of a valiant people..."

"He should be home by now," worried Katya. "He has been on duty for three days in a row."

" . . . we follow unquestioningly and loyally, without excuses and doubts, without weakness and hesitation . . . trusting the good star in spite of the fact that this star is temporarily dimmed by darkest clouds . . . "

"There's David now," cried Katya, relieved. "I heard the front gate."

" . . . this war is coming to an end! The madness brought down upon humanity by the enemy's forces has already reached

170

its zenith. The head of a conspiracy has been shattered by fate . . . "

The air was pregnant with the scent of freshly plowed soil.

" . . . He is the core of resistance against universal disintegration! He is Germany's most valiant heart, and its people's most glowing will . . . It must be affirmed tonight: that our nation still breathes, that there is still a solution to the deadly serious danger . . . We stand in awe: in deep unshakeable trust, defiant and invincible . . . Never shall history claim that a people deserted their *Fuehrer,* or a *Fuehrer* his people. That alone is true victory."

The door flew open. David stood in the light, his eyes blazing, his cap sideways on his blond, tousled hair. His boots were heavy with dried mud, his uniform dirty and torn. His face seemed illuminated:

"Mother! I am going into combat. This very night." He clasped her around the waist, kissing her noisily on the cheek.

"Oh, no. No, David."

"Oh yes! Yes, indeed!"

"I cannot let you go. You are my last one, my only son left."

"Mother! The People's Army is readying itself for battle. We will be part of the defense. We have been given rifles . . . We are ready, Mother."

"You are just a child, son."

"I will be fifteen before December," he cried, impatiently. "I have been in training for years! I know exactly what to do. Our leader has given us precise instructions." He held her eyes, unwavering. "We are to hold the Richterstrasse. Do you know that the enemy is already pressing the outskirts of Berlin?" He buckled his belt. "Mother! Don't look at me like that!"

She could not say a word; she only stared at him and shook her head, and felt her knees give way. What she perceived, she knew to be beyond control. Who was she to touch on that which was profoundest in his life? She saw him before her—credulous, shaken, craving the ultimate sacrifice.

" . . . we are to assemble in half an hour. We have been told that by holding the Richterstrasse, we are really defending the Goetheplatz, strategically a very important position . . . "

He was gone. She did not hear the gate; he must have jumped the fence in his impatience.

"So many times," she thought, "a part of me has died."

She counted her dead mechanically, a habit she had acquired of late. Her parents. The twins. Then Benjamin. The little ones—faces which, to her distress, were already beginning to fade from her memory. Then Peter. And then Liestje, the one closest to her inner essence. Her eyes filled with tears. Life could never be the same when burdened by such grief. But it could, she felt to her surprise as she stood there listening to the whistling of her son, still be surprisingly poignant and sweet.

"This one will not die," she said firmly, thankful for the gentle breeze to dry her cheeks. "This one, after all, has a good cause."

With a sigh, she rose after a while, readying herself to put the children to bed. Just as she stepped over the threshold, a giant iron train, it seemed, roared across the sky with a sound so deafening that Karin, by the table, put her hands to her ears with a whimper. A glowing shell seared across the room, shearing the flower pot off the window sill.

For two seconds, the world shook.

A gust of hot air came through the door torn open by the blast. Katya felt glass splinters in her face and the taste of mortar and chalk on her lips. Swaying, she groped her way to the window, just in time to see a white-hot bolt of fire soar toward the sky, on its heels a giant blackish mushroom, boiling, swelling, darkening the lights, choking the breath out of her lungs in a suction of fire and smoke, pushing myriads of sparks over a flattened heap of rubble where there had been a majestic building only a moment before.

She trembled, not comprehending.

Down below, she saw two children, live torches, in the middle of the street, shrieking in terror and agony. A woman, holding a baby's bleeding body, stood swaying for a moment in a

172

doorway before sinking to her knees, bending over, burying the child beneath herself.

She heard Karin whisper in a thin voice:

"Oma . . . Oma, we have to take cover."

She looked at the child blankly. Lily Marlene started to sob in fright. Walter leaned weakly against the sofa, bleeding from the forehead. Sara emerged from under the table. Karin began to cough violently. Katya heard window after window crack under the intense heat that was building up outside.

"We've got to get out of here," stammered Karin.

With Lily Marlene in her arms, Katya stumbled down the stairs onto the street. Huge buildings to the left and right collapsed groaning, giving way to convulsions of smoke and ashes that darkened the few remaining lights. The sounds of a world gone mad now came into focus. From the vicinity of the Bremerstrasse, the artillery began to hammer. The howls of a Russian *chayka* answered from the east. Somewhere in the distance, a *Stalinorgel* shrieked. A Hitler Youth, dashing by, yelled hysterically that the Russian flag was already pinned to the pole of a neighboring church.

Sara stammered:

"We have to try to make it to the farm. We will be safer in the country."

"I know a short-cut," gasped Karin. "It's out in the fields. To our right . . ."

Dazed, they hastened along the sidewalk. In front of them, the pompous poplar avenue looked as if a giant hand had beheaded the trees in one solitary stroke. In a ditch, in passing, they saw a twitching child, its legs torn to shreds. Ahead of them, a grenade blew a truck into oblivion. The sky above them, it seemed, had melted.

In the shelter of a fragmented house, they paused, inspecting each other, half blinded. Lily Marlene was bleeding from the ear. Someone handed Karin a wet towel; she pressed it greedily against her smarting eyes. Smoke clouds enveloped them, almost choking them. A chunk of debris hit Walter on the head. Along the street, small precise mushrooms of smoke rose up, leaving disaster and death and hell.

Across the street, the post office was now being ripped in half by an invisible fury. Flakes of soot and ashes flew in their direction. The ground beneath their feet heaved in convulsions. Avalanches of brick hindered their way. They climbed over ruins and blown-out army trucks, trying to circumvent the battle which raged, they now realized, in every street they were trying to cross. Machine gun bullets whizzed past their heads. Smoldering ammunition dumps ignited into shattering explosions. The world was enveloped in flames which leaped toward a sky illuminated to whitish brilliance by blast after blast after blast.

"Try the Schillerstrasse!" yelled a *landser,* hiding behind a wall, madly emptying his gun into the smoke. "It might still be passable."

Katya struggled against the smoke, tightly clutching the child who was, by now, a kicking, sobbing bundle of terror. Perspiration matted her hair to her forehead as she steeled herself to throw herself into this incredible pool of uncontrolled madness, for hell's gates were opened to flood the world with lightning after lightning, boom after eardrum-ripping boom.

In front of her now, a house was crushed into rubble. She reeled, instinctively crouching over Lily Marlene. A shower of dust, glass, and broken pieces of bricks fell into her hair and onto her back. When she could see again, she realized that the crumbling walls had blocked the street, cutting her off from her family. She called out their names, but there was no answer anywhere. But she still had the child. Yes, Lily was still unhurt. She flung the toddler over her shoulder and ran.

Sara coughed violently, spitting out the bits of dust and mortar she had swallowed. Now she leaned weakly against a wall, making a rapid calculation as to what she would do next. Karin and the boy surely could fend for themselves, agile creatures that they were! Oma, most likely, still had Lily Marlene. Oma would never panic and let go of the baby, though it seemed to Sara that at this moment, panic was certainly rampant everywhere. Everyone was scrambling for cover. People leaped into bunkers: soldiers, civilians, Hitler Youth—everyone ran and stumbled and fell and yelled and pushed. She herself ducked involuntarily as she saw a detonation on the opposite side of the street lift a woman off her feet and squash her against the walls of a church. Its front was already blown away, but its tower stood tall and uncompromising in the bullet-riddled air.

She realized after a while that the *landser* were trying to wrest certain streets from the enemy, creating a protective curtain of bullets for panicky people like herself. Eyes half closed, she took a deep breath, fastened her sandals tightly to her ankles and let herself be sucked along. She knew a path that led into the country. Half by intuition she let herself be swept along, through streets that were lost and retaken and abandoned again within minutes. It seemed to her that any moment now, if she did not watch out, she herself would have her limbs torn live from her body. Her eyes watered as she ran along. Her heart beat like a rapid hammer in her chest. As she wiped the perspiration off her face, she realized her lashes were seared off her lids.

She seized a *landser* by the arm:

"Which way?" she gasped. "I am trying to reach . . . "

"I don't know," he shouted, covering her with his body. "Now will you hurry up, girl? Hurry now! Get out of my way."

"But which way?" she repeated, almost sobbing.

"Try the street to your left," he yelled. "I don't know if it's still open. We have lost contact with our commands."

A troop of Hitler Youth swept by, their faces blackened by the soot, their eyes drunk with fury. Was David among them? She thought she had seen him, though she could not be sure.

She tried to get a grip on herself. Was she to be frightened all that easily? she asked herself severely. She paused, assessing her chances to reach the farm by means of the Birkenallee, since she could now clearly make out the Russian tanks approaching from the east. Yes, it was better to turn to the left.

She slid around the corner and gasped.

This, most certainly, could not be true! She blinked rapidly, careful not to lose cover behind the wall. For in the street just in front of her, walking stoically and most unhurriedly, were a dozen or so Red Army troops. She saw them clearly. Speechless from shock, she watched them move across the street toward the opposite building. It seemed to be a deserted warehouse, out of whose windows there now fluttered, so help her God, two huge white bedsheets in the wind!

Her eyes grew dark with disbelief. She whispered in outraged patriotism: "Never in all my life have I seen such impertinence . . . " Was it not well understood from border to border across Germany that wherever the flag of surrender appeared, the people were to punish such cowardice at once? She stared and blinked and could not understand.

Around the corner, she observed, there rolled a Russian panzer, loaded with clusters of slit-eyed men, firing languidly a mighty blast into the walls and windows of the opposite house. Her quick glances took in the number of Red soldiers which seemed now to multiply: behind every crumbled wall, out of every bush, out of doors and out of windows and from under parked vehicles they climbed, grinning or glowering, swarming over the street, climbing over fences, jumping out of cellars, appearing behind barricades—the world was filled with Red troops, all wearing the detested hammer and sickle emblem on their ugly furry caps. And out of the door of the warehouse, there now marched straight toward the guns of the grinning Red enemy a group of German people, holding in front of them a broomstick to which an embroidered white tablecloth had been hastily fastened.

What nerve! And what outrageous insolence! Sara quivered

with anger and humiliation. There was Dresden. There was Stalingrad. There were six years of bitterest war. There were heroes' cemeteries all over Germany. And here now, before her eyes, surrender?

She took a deep, calculated breath of air and did without hesitation what the *Vaterland* and the *Fuehrer* would demand on such a provocative occasion. She squared her shoulders and walked directly in front of the cowardly people.

"Aren't you ashamed of yourselves?" she demanded sharply.

The Red soldier next to her reached out for her with a grin.

Her nerves gave way. She couldn't help it; she gave a strangled sob and ran. Her heels clicked on the asphalt. Her blue-and-white striped Red Cross uniform was a visible target in an otherwise blackened, crazy, smoke-filled world. She had the feeling she was stumbling right into a nightmare—this couldn't be anything else but a nightmare, she thought wildly. She was sure she was dreaming. This couldn't be real, nothing like this could ever be real! She saw Red troops everywhere; there were six, twelve, twenty, fifty. She shook them off, sobbing. She felt her uniform rip from seam to seam. She fell. She felt a sharp rock bite into her shoulder blades as she was pinned under the weight of man after man after man. If one let go of her, another was there, rolling on top of her, gasping over her, giving way to the next and the next. They smelled of onions and vodka and *machorka*. She gagged. A fist hit her face. Before she lost consciousness, she saw, red and flashing, the swastika sway by, wrapped over the hood of a dazedly moving truck.

Karin told Walter, holding him tightly by the arm:

"Let's take the River path to the Alley and from there to the bridge and from there to the little side street to the right. And if the Schillerstrasse is still open . . . " Walter was bleeding badly now from a cut on the forehead. Her own leg showed a blister across her calf as wide as the palm of her hand. She was dizzy with pain, but she gave him an impatient push.

177

"Let's go. Let's get going. It's only a little while longer. Oma is probably at the farm already, waiting for us, wondering where we have been . . . "

The boy's face was damp. His cheeks were smeared with tears and blood, his nostrils blackened from smoke. It was easy to see that she would have to take charge if they were to find their way out of this deafening commotion and noise.

"Hold onto me," she said, energetically pushing him ahead of herself.

It seemed a sensible thing to do, for the river path, she knew from past experience, was always free of traffic at this hour. But when she reached the waters of the little river, she saw that even here shells ripped across the surface and disappeared, swishing into ripples. Instinctively she turned toward the left, trying to climb over insurmountable piles of rubble, sliding into craters, scrambling out, and running as fast as she could. She paused as a *landser* who was driving an old army truck, spotted the children, stopped, and waved his arms: "Jump up in the back, quick. Hurry, will you?"

They lay on the floor in the back of the vehicle, their faces buried in their arms, their fists over their ears. After a while, Karin gathered her courage to lift the cover off the side of the truck:

"Walter! Look! Isn't that the grocer Paulsen?"

The children shuddered.

Someone had hanged him with his own belt in the window of his store. A sign was pinned to his chest. Karin strained to make out the words: "I am hanging here because I am a coward. I disobeyed my *Fuehrer*. I would not fight."

"He must have refused the People's Army," whispered Karin. "He had bad rheumatism in his back."

The *landser* behind the wheel seemed to have taken leave of his senses, for like a madman he tried to take his truck through mortar and shells. Coughing, spitting blood, weeping at times, running over a man in his way, he finally gasped:

" . . . Why would I want to pick up these children . . . I am

178

running out of gas . . . Have I lost my way? . . . is that supposed to be the post office over there, for Christ's sake. . . . " He stepped on the brakes so suddenly that the children were sent flying forward. He grabbed them by the legs and jerked them off the platform: "Just run along, will you, now . . . Just run, for Christ's sake! Find someone else. Get out of my way! Run! See the park over there? Just try to make it through. Find someone else. Run!"

The main traffic artery was crammed with truck after truck, vehicle after vehicle. *Landser* picked them up, covered them with their bodies, held their faces in the dust, put giant hands over their ears to keep them from exploding.

How could they have stayed alive?

Surely they must have run during the pauses in the heaviest bombardment; they must have ducked in split-second escapes a thousand times or more. Brakes had screamed. It had rained shingles and mortar and dust and shells and bricks and iron and smoke. Overhead the fighter planes had roared, blowing up fountains of dust left and right and in front of them and behind. It was a cataract of madness.

It took more than a night and a day before they finally managed to break free of the sucking shell fire that was about to swallow them alive. They inspected each other, half blinded. Their faces were bleeding, their lips bitten. Where were they? They strained to see. They had reached an open park. The noise, suddenly, subsided.

"Over there is the Richterstrasse," stammered Karin.

Many years later she was to read in a scholarly book that Germany's death convulsion took place in the inferno of the Greifenhain Forest where the enemy's thrust for the city of Berlin broke out on the eve of the *Fuehrer's* birthday and lasted until the lilacs had ceased to bloom.

At one point, Walter whispered:

"A Russian tank. See over there?"

A heavy enemy panzer pushed its barrel across the street.

179

They ducked behind a wall. After it had disappeared, they resumed their running.

At dusk, dizzy with hunger and fatigue, they finally reached the farm. The building was still there, miraculously. Karin pushed open the heavy iron gate. She swallowed. By the barn, she could see, lay two bodies—the mother and father of Karl-Heinz. She hesitated for a moment, but then, with resolution, she jumped over the grotesquely hunched body of a warrior sprawled across the front steps. She opened the heavy oak door and stepped carefully into the dark narrow hall.

"Heil Hitler," said Karin, staring into a Red soldier's face.

Karl-Heinz lay in a pool of blood, crouched against the wall of the dark, drafty entrance to the farmhouse. Outside, darkness had come several hours before. Katya had had to light a candle she had found in the kitchen so that he could see she was near.

"Oma?" he asked.

"I am here," she said. "I won't leave."

She cared for nothing else. She held his clammy hand in both of her own, sitting quietly, waiting for his face to become still. She would wait. She would sit here all night if need be. It seemed to her that never again would she be able to look anyone else in the eye if she let herself be frightened away from this man.

Her eyes held his face. He shivered from time to time from loss of life. She bent closer, trying to read his lips. It was very important to her to understand. She struggled to grasp the entirety of this darkest of all nights. She surmised for the first time the vastness of trust and belief that had fueled this man, that had propelled him to a deep and unfailing commitment.

"He was like a child with a knife," she thought, "fascinated by its glitter and the power that it wielded. He knew that if he waved it, worlds would fall, and borders would change, and the swastika would rattle in the wind. And when it was taken away from him, he could not let go. Like a child, he held onto the blade with his bare hands, struggling to have his way, oblivious

180

to the pain in his palms, confidently waiting for the turn of the battle's tide that had been promised him."

Her eyes wide open, she waited for his to close, thinking sadly how indestructible Germany had seemed in its time.

"I am a simple woman," she thought. "How can I understand?"

How, indeed, could she ever come close to understanding the enormity of a people's ideology gone astray? But she felt that, perhaps, if she tried hard, she would comprehend enough—she who had also been raised in beliefs of loyalty and obedience to a higher order not always clearly explained. When first she had put her arms around the shoulders of this man when he had come to rescue her from the Bolshevik terror, he had outlined for her in preciest terms his code of honor. It was as sharp and as certain and as uncompromising as her own. Then, she had so clearly understood. Why was it now so difficult?

Could it have been that the burning question of *Lebensraum* for Germany should never have been asked? She searched his face. Was he to blame? It couldn't be. Where, then, lay the fault? Was there deception at the source which had given rise and fuel to his brand of dedication? She felt chilled to the marrow of her life. Such thoughts were desecration, she was sure.

Perhaps she could attempt to understand by looking at herself? Could she not parallel this man's belief to the divine guidance that had given strength and direction to her life in times of grief, that she knew worked steadily from the very core of her being? As she and her people had done, this young soldier had followed a compelling sense of duty, so compelling that it became an all-consuming urge: to join forces with one's comrades, to bury differences of opinion, to discard the doubting voice within one's inner self, to be victorious or die proudly and in dignity. He had believed in his *Fuehrer* with a fanatical certainty, much the same as she herself believed in the omnipotence of her God. And this belief had sanctified his cause. He had fastened his eyes to his doctrine and it had made him a fearless warrior committed to the ultimate consequence; it had

181

caused him to raise his weapons, time and again, sure of the sanctity inherent in his deeds.

At the end of the hall stood a Red soldier, shifting his weight from leg to leg, staring at her with smoldering eyes.

She paid him no heed. She had wrestled a blanket away from him so she could warm a little the mangled body at her feet. Now her eyes held him at bay.

This was a night fit to feel oneself drenched in purest white-hot hate. It gave her satisfaction to savor this emotion not accessible to her in sane times. She knew that she hated the enemy with all the strength at her command, as one was compelled to hate the evil in this world.

Only fleetingly did she remember Sara, now struggling in the hands of the drunken men. Lily Marlene had finally sobbed herself to sleep on the couch. Karin, she knew, sat outside on the doorstep, a vacant look on her face. Walter sat quietly by the window, trembling violently from time to time.

"Are our panzer coming?" whispered Karl-Heinz. "Oma? Can you hear them?"

"You have asked that question a dozen times since dusk," she said gently. "No, my boy. Not yet."

"I hear them," he insisted.

"Mein Junge. Try to sleep. Those are not our tanks."

He strained against the pain in his loins.

"The relief has to come," he moaned.

"Of course."

"We were promised relief. On highest orders."

"I know."

"I read the letter myself; it had the seal of the *Fuehrer's* headquarters."

There were questions to be answered, she felt with strong conviction. She would try, though she knew she lacked the means of clear communication. Words had never come easily to her and her kind, though language was easier in joy than in an hour of such grief. But she would try.

"Is nearsightedness equal to vice?" she asked herself. "Does youth not count? And ardor? And gullibility?" Since his tenderest years, she knew, this *landser* had learned to equate failure with cowardice and treason. "How was he prepared to deal wisely with what he was taught?" she asked of the night. "He who was raised on slogans designed to make him immune to any other thought but victory?" She listened to his stammering for affirmation:

"I disagreed with . . . I told them the relief had to break through the Grunewald and sweep around the Birkenalle . . . Strategically, it would have been . . . " He struggled to sit up. His voice shook.

"They will come," said Katya, calmly. "It is just a matter of time, Karl-Heinz."

"There they are now," he called.

She, too, felt the trembling of the earth.

"They are not our tanks," she said again.

Long ago, she had become adept at distinguishing the war sounds of the East from those of the West. The sound that now convulsed the earth beneath her feet, she knew, was the horror creeping over the freshly plowed acres of the Niederlausitz, pushing relentlessly toward the center of Berlin, toward the very core of German life.

She would force herself to listen to what he had to say:

" . . . had we tried to stop the Russian Army from the south . . . Had we made connections with . . . Our right flank should have been covered . . . Why, our *Fuehrer* would never . . . " His head rolled from side to side. She had to steady it. She would hold his temples and let some of her own strength flow through her finger tips into his eyes. The Red soldier stirred impatiently. He was tired; he wanted to get some rest. One bullet was all that was needed.

She asked herself severely:

"Why should he have doubted? He who knew nothing of the past, who was raised in a present swept into frenzy by flags and slogans and songs, who never learned the way we did that slogans can be used by both sides with great effectiveness? He

183

who had daily listened to a voice capable of welding to great new strength whole armies of weak, battle-fatigued, tired men, weld them together to high-pitched aggression to shed rivers of blood on which the Bolshevik evil would rightfully choke? He, a farmer's son, who had so deeply believed in the redistribution of the earth, whereby the diligent, and no one else, would get their due? Who grew up on drums that were as heavy and as heady as sweet wine?" She thought, stroking his hand:

"It is worthy to die for an ideal if one can't live to see it to its conclusion. What is life, anyway, but living out one's deepest convictions and beliefs?"

No, this end was not defeat. This was far, far deeper than that. Not even death would erase what had powered this life. And she thought further:

"What was it that he might have done in youthful ardor compared to what will now be done to Germany?"

He stirred again. His hand felt moist in her palm.

"My boy," she said softly, for the hundredth time, "what can I do for you? Is there anything at all that I can do?"

"Yes," he struggled. "I . . . I can't stand it any more. Oma . . . would you . . . could you . . . "

She bent her face to his lips, uncomprehending. "What is it?" she asked again. Suddenly she understood. "Oh my God! Why didn't you tell me? I am an old woman. There's no need to be ashamed." She hurried into the kitchen and snatched a jar from the cupboard, feeling hot tears of pity and grief and rage sting her eyes. She returned and unbuttoned his pants. She gritted her teeth, trying to keep the shock from her face. She felt his blood sticky on her fingertips as she helped him. "I will try not to hurt you, my son."

The quart jar filled to the brim. She felt it warm in her hands. "Can you hold a while, son, till I empty it?" He nodded. She poured the container from the window, returned, helped him again. It almost filled a second time. Gently, she pulled the blanket over his loins.

184

His face became peaceful after that. She stroked his hands. He was very weak now. The earth convulsed faintly.

"Are they coming?" he kept asking. But the urgency was gone.

She could bear it no longer. She bent down to him, and spoke the first and only premeditated lie of her life. She said with as much assurance as she could muster:

"They are coming. I can hear them in the distance now."

He died at daybreak, quietly. She sat for a while, conscious of nothing but the wasteland in her heart. Then she reached into his shirt and took out the identification plate she knew a *landser* was to wear at all times around his neck. She broke it in half, trying to read what was written:

"Karl-Heinz Krause, born on July 14, 1920, in the Teutonic City of Stettin." A perforation ran across the oblong platelet; the lower part bore an added inscription: "Fallen for the *Fuehrer* and the *Vaterland.*"

She held the metal tightly in her hand as she walked by the yawning Red soldier. She said to him in passing:

"He was as decent a boy as any mother could have wished for. He died for something of great meaning. Will anyone remember what it was?"

The Red soldier shook his head:

"Nichevo. Nyemets kaput?"

She nodded: *"Nyemets kaput."*

She walked past him to the kitchen and sat down at the table, burying her head in her hands. She sat like this for a very long time. Then she rose and took an apron from the nail, tying it around her waist, letting the identification plate slide into her pocket. She opened the cupboard and looked for some pots and pans. There was a box of matches on the window sill. She would build a fire in the stove.

All morning, Katya walked the pockmarked, shell-torn fields covered with helmets, torn-off wheels, ammunition, canisters, and dead, twisted bodies, her dress hem heavy with the dew of the night. She forced herself on, though she was nauseated with fatigue and the sight of death at its ugliest. She took a shirt off a fallen soldier and fastened it around her waist, tying knots in the sleeves to make two narrow sacks. They swung against her knees now as she walked, the many broken platelets inside giving a metallic sound as they swung back and forth rhythmically with each step. The weight around her waist became heavier as time and again she bent down to pick up yet another identification plate and break it in half along the perforated ridge.

At the edge of a wheat field she came upon a *landser* still breathing in shallow gasps. She knelt down, lifting his head with both of her hands, trying to speak into his unfocusing eyes:

"Can I try to move you?" she asked. "It will hurt you badly, I am afraid."

He did not reply. She looked about for something to wrap around his head. She would have to drag him by his legs. Under a burnt-out vehicle she found an old blanket. She tried to fasten it beneath his head by tying the ends under his armpits.

"Hold still," she said. "You just have to hold still."

He was unconscious by the time she arrived with him at the farmhouse. His arms dragged behind in the dirt. His head rolled from side to side, grotesquely. Karin, sitting on the steps, silently moved to the side to let them pass.

"Get me some firewood, quickly," said Katya. "No, better still, you come with me. Lift his head over the threshold. Hurry, open the kitchen door."

Karin pushed open the door for her grandmother. While doing so, she ducked away from the window and kept herself to the wall.

"Take this sheet," said Katya. "Rip it into strips. Like this." She took the cloth off the kitchen table. "We have to improvise," she explained. "We have no medication and no bandages. Perhaps we could boil some soapy water . . . go see if there's soap in the bathroom, child."

186

Cautiously, Karin looked around. She felt drugged. She could not believe this silence now; she could not trust it. For a night and a day, the noise had been deafening. She pressed her hands to her ears. The silence was encroaching upon her now. She tried to hold the monster at bay that she had seen falling upon her town to crunch it down its fiery throat, spewing glowing dust while doing so. The sparks had settled in her hair. She still felt its breath on her neck. Right and left the shells had struck around her. She had jumped and fallen and coughed and been swept along by a crazy current of fire and smoke. A soldier had reached out for her at one corner, trying to lift her onto a truck, moments before a shell fragment had sliced away half of his face and his hands had had to let go of the child. Here and there, the asphalt under her feet had bubbled from the heat. She shivered.

"In the back room, the enemy is sending messages in Russian," said Walter from the door.

Karin listened to the detonations in her head. The noise had reached from one end of the world to the other. Lightning had shot out of cannons. Smoke had seared her lungs. The earth's belly had ripped open right before her very feet.

"Inside the back room, they are torturing an officer," said Walter. "They put his fingers in the door slit."

"Shhhh," she whispered, impatiently.

She glared at him. He was too noisy. Caution was all that mattered. One had to be small, invisible, humble. Body against convulsing earth, face to the dust, that was the only way! Any moment now, another detonation would rip open the sky, would trigger a chain reaction of deafening madness, would send fistfuls of sparks into her face. One had to be prepared at all times. Her eyes turned cautiously toward the stone entrance.

"They are all dead," said Walter, following her glance. "There must be forty or fifty of them. They have piled them up to clog the gate from the outside."

She exhaled carefully.

"First they torture them inside and then they shoot them in

187

the head behind the house," said the boy. He trembled. "All officers."

She put her arms around him after a while. Still, she did not reply. She could bear now to look at the motionless pile by the gate. What a mess of arms and legs and torsos—bled-out, twisted, unbearably ugly! She swallowed hard. A Russian guard stood at a little distance, languidly puffing a cigar. Her glance swept to the garden beyond. There was a dead pig under the lilac bush, its belly bloated from shell fragments. She grimaced.

Oma's kitchen, meanwhile, became impassable, blocked with dozens of wounded men. Oma's face, and Oma's voice, and Oma's hands, and nothing else, it seemed to Karin, had the power to bring the world into focus again. Oma moved ceaselessly among the *landser:*

"Walter, help me lift this boy. Be careful; hold his head. Karin, child, hand me a wet towel. Hold still, my boy. I know it hurts. But I have to clean your face." She moved swiftly and with purpose. "Take this plate, Walter. I am putting you in charge of the fire on the stove. Stir the soup now and then; don't let it settle and burn. Look around you, child. There's so much to do. Take towels. Take the sheets off the beds. Karin, help your mother; don't be underfoot."

Early this morning, Sara had appeared. Karin had seen Oma drop the pail she held in her hand and put strong arms around her trembling mother. She had seen the feelings in Oma's face spread across the faces of the wounded men on the floor. Karin had felt her blood thicken in her fingertips.

"Are the children all right?" Sara had finally stammered.

"Yes. Lily is all right, just glass cuts in her face. Karin's . . . Karin's leg is badly burned, and I fear she is in shock. Walter has a cut on his forehead and a broken toe. They arrived here late last night, all by themselves."

Sara started to weep.

"There were thirty or forty of them," she stammered. "And they . . . they took . . . turns . . . "

"I know," said Katya.

"And they . . . "

"Shhhh."

"They were drunk . . . "

"Be quiet, child. It is over now. We will not talk about it any more."

"And when they finally finished . . ."

"Take this handkerchief. Blow your nose. There's some oil on the shelf. Salt is to your right. We will have to do without pepper. Stir the peeled potatoes over there."

"Mother, listen to me . . . "

"Be quiet, child."

"Mother . . . "

"I need some help," said Katya, harshly. She took two towels from the wall. "Someone has to dry the dishes. Have a cup of coffee, daughter. And pull yourself together. This very minute!"

Katya looked around. Those who needed help had been helped by now. Those for whom help was too late had died. She could see with a glance that three of the *landser* had died since this morning. She would have to have them moved out to make room for the others. For the time being she would put them beneath the cherry tree at a little distance from the pile of dead men at the gate. She felt they deserved a special place. She had known them by their names. Briefly, each of them had meant more to her than just another pair of vacant eyes."

She said to Karin:

"Watch this boy for me, will you? He's in fever, he thrashes about. I don't want him to loosen the bandages." She stepped to the door, calling over her shoulder:

"Now, would you believe this, child? Isn't that Jasch, over there?"

Jasch gesticulated wildly to the Red soldier, pointing to his little hand wagon that he had pushed through the gate. It was carefully covered with a tent which was fastened to its edges with four giant safety pins. The guard lifted one corner and peered underneath. He snorted contemptuously, but then stepped back, apparently deciding to let Jasch pass.

189

Jasch presented a pitiful sight indeed. His clothing was torn, his body covered with dust. His face was greenish with fear and fatigue. Carefully, he pulled his load up to Katya, who had stepped outside, narrowing her eyes in disbelief. Her cheeks colored a furious red.

"The world might fall into pieces—trust Jasch to find something to salvage," she said bitterly.

His face was sticky with perspiration.

"Katya," he stammered, weakly. He sank to the stairs at her feet. He wiped his face with the back of his hand.

"Is Walter . . . is my boy all right?"

Curtly, she replied, "Yes. He's inside."

"And your girls?"

"They are fine."

"David . . . " he said.

She turned her face away. "Get out of my way, Jasch. I am busy. Go inside and let Sara give you a cup of coffee. Then perhaps you can try to give me a hand."

She gave the wagon an impatient push. He jumped up and steadied it with his hands. He pulled it with care into the shade of a tree. Then he followed her, limping, into the kitchen.

"We have some 25 wounded soldiers inside," she explained to him. "We found them everywhere. Below the bridge. In corn fields. In ditches. Underneath burnt-out vehicles. In other houses." She looked at him. "I am sure there must be many still alive that we haven't yet found. After you have had something to eat, you come with me, Jasch. Unload your plunder. We need your wagon. These men are too heavy to drag."

He did not reply; he just looked at her and turned the cup of coffee in his hands.

She blew the fire beneath the kettle to sparking life. She took a rag and moistened it and carefully wiped a bloody stain off the window sill. "Many are dead," she told him, without turning. "Those who are dead, are dead. There's just so much I can do. This house is filled to its seams with hurting, bleeding, dying misery. We have no food; we have only a little sugar left and

190

four jars of canned fruit. What do you have in your hand-wagon, Jasch? You will have to give it to me if it is something we can use."

He stared into her face out of tired, red-rimmed eyes.

"Don't you have any heart at all?" she asked him, trembling now. "Don't you care? About anything? About anything or anybody besides yourself?"

"Katyushka," he replied, slowly. "I brought . . . I have . . . I think it's David. It must be David, by the looks of his hair."

8

A brisk wind came from the west and blew for an entire week. It swept away the smoke and the smell of the battle. It broke open the lilac buds overnight. Ladybugs appeared in scores out of the blue. One could look at the sky and fear nothing.

Once again, for hours at a stretch, Karin and Walter would roam the countryside—the only children, it seemed, left alive in the whole wide world. Now and then they encountered Russian guards who came to know the children well. It happened not infrequently that a Red trooper would wave at them and yell:

"*Kartoshky?* Potatoes? In the cellar, honey. Beans? Flour? Wine? *Deutschland kaput, nyet?*"

"*Deutschland kaput,*" they replied seriously, loading their little wagons with treasures to bring home.

The Russians were boastful, noisy, powerful people who good-naturedly stepped aside to let the children pass. Karin thought them silly with their greed for watches, radios, and jewelry. But she was not afraid of them—not really! Once she had come upon a Red soldier holding a gun to a young, blond woman who—clinging to his arm—pleaded with him in a high-pitched, terrified voice. Karin saw him seize the woman and throw her brutally on the asphalt. She stood and watched, somewhat puzzled, not comprehending the woman's hysterical

191

sobs under the heaving, convulsing, uniformed bulk. But she backed away as he emptied his gun and carelessly stepped over the blood-spouting body at his feet. The five-pointed star had sparkled merrily.

Bloody death, however, had become a fact of daily life. Not infrequently, she would stop and would gaze thoughtfully at the drawn features of a fallen youth. So many of them still lay in the fields. However, wheat and barley and corn began to sprout rapidly. The moonflowers started to bloom, swaying their dainty, fragile heads, quietly helping disguise the sight of the ravished acres—marred and criss-crossed with wide panzer tracks, strewn with ammunition, helmets, canisters, and heavy, bulging, torn-off rubber tires. The world, overnight, turned a luscious, deep green. Yet she never lingered, for she knew that as soon as the sun sank low, Katya would stand outside and watch worriedly for her, shading her face against the pale, fading light.

Walter slept soundly again; it was an easy thing to do after Oma had tucked him in and had whispered: "Be sure to say your prayers, son." But Karin just lay there in the dark, her eyes fastened on the stars outside. These nights, it seemed to her, would last forever. She was made to go to bed at dusk, for all power lines hung limp. But she could not sleep, could not relax, could not untie this knot in her stomach. She dreaded the darkness with a dread too vast for words, but by now she had learned to keep this dread to herself. There was an end, after all, to a night. Early in the morning, she knew, a fire would bristle beneath the huge pot of coffee on the stove, and Oma would stand straight and tall, busily stirring a giant pot of soup with a wooden spoon. In the morning, there would be safety and comfort in Oma's sun-flooded kitchen.

The farmhouse was nearly bursting with the casualties of war. The *landser* lay beneath the tables, along the hall, in the bedroom, outside on the porch—everywhere! Katya moved between them silently to bandage a leg or an arm, to wipe the perspiration off a face, to give comfort with a smile, a pat on the shoulder, or a moment of quiet conversation. There was no room for Karin to set her feet as she tried to close the windows for the night. She always insisted that windows should be closed. She could not bear to have them open, though Katya longed for the coolness of the night air. Windows must be shut, Karin insisted hysterically. At such times, her grandmother's hand would briefly pass across her hair, and Oma would sigh as if carrying a burden too heavy for an ordinary human heart.

"How long have we been here, Oma?" asked one of the *landser* one morning.

"I am not sure," replied Katya. "Two weeks? Or has it been three?"

They looked at each other.

"Now it must be almost the middle of May."

What had happened to the war? They did not know. There was no German broadcast any more. No living soul had passed by their farm for weeks. Perhaps no living soul was left to pass by.

But then, around noon the next day, Katya happened to look out the window. Her hand flew to her lips.

"War prisoners," she whispered, aghast. "There must be hundreds . . . "

She watched them approach the house, thinking frantically: "Oh, what am I to do?" She looked around wildly. She rushed outside, facing the approaching formation, hands to her sides, her face determined:

"No one is here," she said loudly, blocking the entrance. "No soldier. No *Nyemets*. All dead. All *kaput*. No good for anything."

The first ones had reached her steps by now. They looked at her with pity. The *landser* uniforms, across their backs, were caked with dried blood. Some leaned heavily on sticks and crutches. Their heads were shaved bald. One of them, she could see, had bloody blotches where his fingernails should be. Their faces clearly held the knowledge of what was now to come. Half a dozen Red soldiers were guarding them closely.

193

"Aside, *Babushka!*" one of them now yelled, elbowing her crudely out of the way. "We know you have them here. We take them off your hands. We take care of the *Nyemets* from now on."

"No one is here," she repeated with a sob.

There was a Ukrainian tinge to his halting German. His face was wide with glee. "I work for years for German war. Now *Nyemets* work for me. In Siberia." He grinned. "Guns broken. Hands up. *Nyemets kaput. Nyet, Babushka?*"

One of the *landser* put his face against hers for a moment. His wounded foot left a bloody print on the threshold as he was pushed out of the door. Jasch struggled past her, his face ashen, a Russian gun in his back. The others followed, helped along with curses and kicks and the hollow, sickening sounds of rifle butts falling on rib-cages and shoulder blades. Karin leaned white-faced against the door, looking at torn shoes, blood-soaked limbs, uniforms with the emblems ripped off. Katya held onto the gate for comfort, watching the sun as it tinged the clouds once more a fiery red beyond.

" . . . to save our homeland," she thought irrelevantly, blinking.

Once these words had had a ring to them that made them meaningful, that gave them fire and power and glow. Where had these feelings gone? What seemed to have happened to Germany was so far beyond all human comprehension that Katya—who had more than once tasted the bitterness of death—now knew that hollowness of feeling was much worse.

"I think they are still bombing Berlin," she said to Sara, mechanically. "Look at the crimson sky!"

Sara did not answer.

"There is no use thinking about it now!" said Katya. And for the hundredth time she said to her foolishly trembling child:

"Pull yourself together, daughter. This very minute!"

Sara struggled for words.

"What is it?" asked Katya swiftly, gripping her by the arm.

194

"They are going to . . . to shoot us tonight," said Sara in a small voice. "I heard them through the wall."

Many a time, these past few weeks, Karin had seen her mother rub dirt and grime into her lovely face and dress in old and ragged clothes so as not to tempt the lust of the Red troops, as Oma had coolly explained. There were horror-filled moments when the door would fly open and Sara would rise and silently walk away with The Enemy, as white and as lifeless as a sheet. Only once, in the beginning, had she resisted, but a Russian fist had landed in her face and had sent her reeling past the children. Since then, she responded promptly to the short, consistent command:

"*Frau, komm!*"

Why would she now wash her face by the sink in the kitchen? Karin watched her mother straighten her skirt and smooth her hair back from her forehead in an almost gentle gesture, and bite her lips to make them glow a deep full red. Sara's short, determined steps echoed from the walls of the old farmhouse. She knocked on the Russian commandant's door at the back of the hall. Her grey eyes were glistening and very, very wide.

"Vanya," she said to the startled Red soldier, smiling sweetly as she walked up to him, "I want to be your girl."

Through the door which was left wide open, Karin saw the spectacle from beginning to end.

The Enemy gave a surprised grunt. Sara put her arms around him like a gracious kitten. Her voice was teasing, as if she were sharing a secret with him, sure that he would understand.

"I am your girl," she repeated, as she settled herself in his lap.

"What in the world . . . " said the Red soldier, immensely pleased. "You speak Russian? You no *Nyemka?* Who are you? What are you doing here? Are you a Russian woman?"

"Does it matter?" she smiled. "I can translate for you. I can help you with the interrogation of the German officers. Make them talk. Yes?"

Karin did not have to strain to watch her mother bend over The Enemy to put her lips to his fat, perspiring, beaming face.

She overheard her grandmother later, behind a locked door, her voice breaking with anguish. She heard Sara's reply—calm, sober words of great determination:

" . . . seven, eight, ten brutes used me every day. Now it's only one. And we have shelter. And food. And protection. Don't talk to me about honor, Mother. What's honor? Where are our boys who believed in honor? Where's my dearest brother David? Has honor helped Karl-Heinz? Has honor helped us? Ever? And does it matter, anyhow? Does anything matter now?"

The war was over.

News had come over the air waves in Vanya's room this afternoon. The war was over, and Germany had lost. It was as undramatic as that. And it truly mattered little now in retrospect that honor had ended for Sara an hour earlier than it had ended for Germany. She had deliberately deserted The Cause. She had betrayed her destiny, and that seemed to her a perfectly natural, sensible thing to do. The bits and pieces that had led up to her desertion she could never quite sort out for herself. Nor did she try, being Sara—the beautiful, the light-hearted, the vain. She knew that she lived, and that her children lived, and that her dearest white-haired mother had been spared being shot to death in a ditch like a dog. But to the end of her days, matters of conscience were always a little confusing for Sara.

Thus the Enemy took charge and command. The Enemy was everywhere. His roaring, hearty voice set Red soldiers to running, kept the constant threat of rape at bay, put food on their table, bolted doors at night, cleaned up and buried the dead around their farm. It was true that his big, hairy hands were all over Sara, who tolerated his crude jokes, his childish pranks, his quickly aroused amorous overtures, with a patient smile and a shrug. It was, after all, one man's exhaustible love demands against indiscriminate, unchecked, unleashed Asian gluttony. It was one pair of hands instead of many. All she needed to do was to step out of range ox Vanya's protection to know that her decision had been right. His salacious remarks that caused lewd laughter among his men were an annoyance, to be sure, but not an intolerable burden by any means. And Katya's grief would have to be endured. Sara had long ago resigned herself to the realization that no one could tackle, and win against, Katya's stubborn, unreasonable, unyielding brand of conviction.

"That filthy, obscene, odious communist pig!" Katya would say between her teeth, not even conscious of her language.

"He's not as bad as all that," replied Sara, lightly.

"I could kill him with my own bare hands," cried Katya, forgetting her pacifist tradition.

"And then what?" Sara wanted to know.

Then what, indeed! They were at the mercy of this man. They were trapped inside the farmhouse with guards on the alert to protect the elaborate radio equipment installed for Vanya's convenience so he could arrogantly dispatch his resounding orders across the devastated land. Katya could hear his voice in the farthest corner of her kitchen. He seemed to be in sole charge of an intertwined network of communications spitefully designed to squeeze the last living drop of blood out of her bled-out Germany. From his back room, with Sara in his lap, he appeared to be in control of the entire systematic dismantling of her precious *Vaterland.* Persistently she turned her back to him whenever he was near. She for one would not give him the time of the day. Not that her resistance mattered even one iota to this man, who seemed quite fond of her in his pretentious, boisterous way, who smiled at her beamingly and slapped her shoulders left and right in genuine affection until they stung like fire from the force of his hands.

It was late summer when he stalked into her kitchen, nudged her with his elbow in passing, and announced casually:

197

"You come back with me, *Babushka*. To Russia. Next week. Repatriation is a good thing for loyal Russian citizens."

Katya felt a chill at his words—a chill that was to spread and grow and deaden any other feeling, any other thought. Flight! They had to flee. They had to flee, and soon! Repatriation. Russia. Siberia. The end.

"We have to flee tonight!" she whispered to Sara, grasping her by the arm.

"It is too dangerous!" cried Sara. "The area is mined. They have guards everywhere. They have powerful search lights on the hill. Berlin is more than two hours away. They have . . . "

"There is no other way!"

There was no other way. Even Sara knew it all too well. In urgent haste, they threw into a knapsack a few necessities. A blanket for Lily. Some money. Their documents. A map stolen from Vanya's desk marked with a number of red arrows.

"Sara, you carry Lily. I'll take the backpack. Walter, take this billfold. Don't lose it."

"Oma, what about the guards outside our house?"

"Karin can distract them. She has done it before."

They waited until it was dark, too tense to eat supper. Then they closed the door behind them quietly, stepping out into the night. A dog barked viciously. They froze and felt their hearts beat in their throats. After a while, they stole along the shade of the house, along the street, crouching from bush to bush, gliding from wall to wall, listening. But then the tarred road stretched before them, and moonlight lay across it as clear and as straight as a silvery stream.

"We will never make it," faltered Sara.

The searchlight lifted itself from the horizon, pointing an evil, yellow finger across the land—gripping them for a terrifying moment, leaving them, moving along the edge of the road.

Between search light beams they ran. Gasping. Struggling. Falling. Panting. The light was upon them, freezing them, exposing them. Then it moved on, and they ran, and crouched, and crept, and ran again. An hour had passed. Two hours. There was a forest now where they could catch their breath, form a chain of perspiring hands. There was no end in sight. Was it now almost dawn? What were the lights over there? They ducked. And crept. And slouched. They now had reached a stretch of bare, plowed acres. Was this the infamous no man's land—tightly patrolled by guards, barbed-wired, mined, flooded every thirty seconds by the jaundiced searchlight from the hill?

They drew together, hugging, steeling themselves for the run of their lives.

"Now!" whispered Katya.

The night erupted like a boil. Shots rang in the air. The yellow finger stopped as if steadied by an almighty hand.

"They've caught us!" moaned Sara.

"Karin, run!" cried Katya—wildly, loudly, piercingly. "Take Lily and run!"

This was it. Perhaps she could, with her body, stop the guards long enough to permit the children to reach safety. She knelt and waited for the bullet that was to put an end to her life. She heard her children scream, and heard the screams silenced by shots, and put her fists to her ears with a moan. Through her knuckles many voices penetrated—intermingled German and Russian words, Russian curses, to be sure, and Russian obscenities, frenzied pleas for mercy stopped in mid-stream by yet more shots. Was that still Sara's voice? Was Sara not silenced yet? Sara cried and cried and cried.

"Oma!" cried Sara. "Oma! Oma! They don't mean us! My God, they've caught someone else. A family, apparently. They will be busy for a while. Let's run! Let's run!"

Staggering, Katya rose to her feet. This was a nightmare, but she ran, as one was compelled to run. There was a light, over there, at the end of the long poplar avenue, and somehow, as in a dream, she knew that she had to reach it, and she strained to reach it, and she would reach it, no matter what, and now it became larger and larger, and she stumbled into the brightness and fell to the ground, struggling for air to fill her lungs.

Someone swept up the gasping, weeping, hysterical children. Someone cried, jubilantly:

"They've made it! They've made it across! With three young children! Unharmed . . . "

There were German voices around her, and German faces, bending over her with concern, German hands patting her shoulders, gripping her under her armpits so that she could not help rising shakily, and putting her arms around the neck of a stranger, who stroked her shoulders over and over and murmured soothingly:

"Now . . . now . . . mother. Don't cry. You are safe. You are safe now. Don't cry, mother. You are in the American sector of Berlin."

Karin awoke from the morning sun tickling her nose. She fought against a voluptuous sneeze as she lay there, covered with a quilt that smelled of mothballs and fresh, sweet-scented soap. Carefully she moved her toes against newly starched bedsheets. From outside through the open window came the smell of coffee and fried bacon. She opened her eyes wide. On the opposite wall, in a wooden frame, there hung an embroidered decal—two clasping hands, framed by rose-colored, carefully cross-stitched words:

"Mennonite Central Committee—In the name of Christ."

"Oma," she called, bewildered.

Katya entered the room, carrying a tray in her hands.

"Child," she explained, smiling all over her wrinkled face, "we have found our people. Late last night."

She sat down by the bedside. Karin held her breath. Oma looked brand new to the roots of her scrubbed fingernails. Oma wore a long, clean, heavy, dark brown skirt and a black blouse with wide silken sleeves. Every single strand of her white hair was tightly combed into place. And Oma spoke Low German:

"Our brethren in Canada and the United States have come to our rescue, child. They have rented this house here to find and assemble our people. We are safe and secure, thanks to our dearest Lord." Her hands stroked the quilt on Karin's knee; she could feel them tremble with emotion.

One need only look outside to know that there was peace once more in heaven and on earth. Outside, it was Indian summer, past the beginning tinge of early fall. A giant oak tree, a dome of glossy sunshine, leaned its branches, it seemed, almost clear across her bed. She could see that birds were tucked in its leaves. Oma put the tray on her chair, and on it, Karin saw, were treasures—golden buttered toast, a glass of milk, a little dish of jam, two apples, and a chocolate bar!

"Say your prayers," commanded Oma grandly, and Karin complied speedily, lest this mirage disappear.

"After you have finished, take your shoes in your hand and come downstairs to wash your face, but be sure to make no noise. It is Sunday today, and there are services in the large hall to the back of the house."

Karin went to look for her mother. She found Sara on the steps in the sunshine. She, too, was wearing a long, dark skirt with many swinging folds. Sara seemed like a stranger to Karin, and yet, familiar once more in a piercingly beautiful way. For not even this somber attire could hide the fact that Sara looked young once again, and clean, and carefree, and very, very pretty, with her raven hair flowing freely down her back. Karin immediately attached herself to her shadow, as always bewitched by her mother's appeal. Sara now stood, aglow with genuine pleasure, in the doorway of the massive, grim, shell-marked house, to greet perfect strangers with her warmest, loveliest smile:

"Good morning. Welcome to the House of the Mennonites. Do you speak Low German? Welcome to our midst."

Even the Lord was in charge once again. For more than two years, God had covered His face from the horror that had ravished the land, but now Katya had found Him again, now she could pray again, talk to her Lord in emotional outpourings that took her more than an hour each night and left her purged and relieved. It was so comforting now to once again have access to the Lord. Through this and that and more than one inferno she had been swept, and not one hair had been touched on the heads of her innocent children—Karin and Lily and Walter! If that was not a miracle straight from the hands of her generous Lord, what was?

Each night she made very sure that Karin would fold her hands in humility. There was so much to be done now to soothe this grandchild's shaggy, unruly, obstinate soul. Katya came to understand quite early that it would be her task alone to drain off the damage of this war by much the same laborious means by which Germany was now beginning to clear itself of the rubble—step by step, brick by brick, piece by broken piece, stone by stone, with the help, perhaps, of pail and shovel and broom, but little more than bare hands and sheer force of grim determination. Yes, let Berlin and its dogged, taciturn people be her model and measure of what must be done with this child and other young, rescued souls. From her window she watched so as to be guided.

Only a handful at first had appeared to dig their devastated city out of its grave. But in a few short days a chain of human bodies had been linked together in a staunch, silent formation. Kitchen pails moved from hand to hand, from street to street, around this corner and that one, empty and full, full and empty, diminishing mountains of rubble by pouring them into the craters and cellars of Berlin. No one had ordered these people into the streets after work, but they stood there and did what had to be done, night after night, all summer long, far into the chilly autumn days. So, too, Katya knew, the inner destruction of this war would have to be drained off in children of Karin's disposition—step by step, in bits and pieces— patiently, carefully, steadily. Relentlessly. It was always Karin now who was on her mind.

Sometimes it seemed to Katya that if only she could bathe the child in enough prayers, she could wash away the sights and the sounds of this madness that still set the girl to wild, incoherent screaming many a night. Lily Marlene was too small, and

Walter—thank God—!—too sensible to have been so damaged, but with Karin it was different. There was a white-hot, uncompromising intensity about Karin that would put a clamp on Katya's heart and would, she was sure, destroy the child in time, were it not for God's help and her own time-proven Mennonite determination.

"The children should go to school," Sara would vaguely suggest once in a while. "Karin can barely read."

"What for?" asked Katya, instantly armed. "She reads all right! She learned it somehow; she reads much better than I do. And don't we have right here in our midst our own very good Bible school?"

Once again, it was so easy to distinguish right from wrong. From her window, she observed how slowly the streets of Berlin came alive. People, having risen from the depths of the cellars— haggard, yellow-faced, morose—now hurried about, carrying their suitcases and bedding on their backs, or rumbled along the road on bicycles held together by wires and strings and large, rusty bolts. People looked old now, preoccupied, tense, unfriendly. They ducked and whispered. Germany, here and there, began to show a devious face at last. It was an ugliness that shocked Katya deeply—an ugliness that she had never perceived during all of the cruelest hours of war. People elbowed each other off the sidewalk. No longer would strangers bid each other good day.

In Berlin's ruins, the winter winds began to howl. People began, it was said, to eat the bark off the trees of the Lindenallee. Long human chains stood in front of the bakery at four o'clock in the morning, waiting for meager rations of stale bread. People starved miserably in the drab, windy streets of Berlin. Stores were ransacked each night, flour and sugar and lard were carried away. Nothing could be bought these days: no rice, no soap, no fuel. There was horrid whispered talk about lost children being slaughtered and sold as sausage across black market counters. These rumors did not die. They sprang up everywhere with stark persistence.

"Stay here with me," Katya fearfully cautioned the children.

Could one be surprised at the sight of such spiritual disintegration in a country without a mere foot's width of soil to call its own? The Germany she had loved was dead—slain by the hammer and sickle in the East and the stupendous indifference of the supposedly civilized West. She shook her head. She listened to no radio. Never again would she touch a worldly paper in her life. She hardened her heart against the whispers in the streets that a tight, persistent net of communism was now growing all over eastern Europe. She locked and bolted her door at night against the sounds of the city of Berlin.

She did not know that Karin had secretly taken up her wanderings once more. Karin craved these explorations with insatiable greed. Whenever she could manage to escape, she would slip away from Katya's watchful eye and stray around the ruins of Berlin. She would smell the ashy taste of a burnt-out, glamorous era so as to feel invisible fingers stroking her spine. With burning eyes she would stare along the bullet-riddled walls. She spent days between ruins pockmarked by shells, blackened by smoke. She climbed over bricks and door frames and rock and walked with young, barefoot, sensitive feet over the shambles of this violent, heart-piercing war. When she thought herself alone, she hummed to herself the vigorous old battle songs—melodies that had somehow, like so much else, been shot off the face of this earth. She wondered about it sometimes—why it should be that songs as well as people should be murdered.

One day, by chance, she stumbled upon a school. She had to bend down to find her way through the door that led to a basement which had been converted into a makeshift shelter for two dozen silent children.

She sat there quietly all morning in the farthest corner of a back row.

A young girl, apparently the teacher, read a story to the youngsters.

Afterwards, moved by the thirst in Karin's eyes, she handed her a book, a little reluctantly.

"It's called the *Odyssey*," she said. "You may keep it if you wish."

Powerful feelings sprang up to her from those pages. A strange, voluptuous pain would make her mouth go dry. She felt shaken by the beauty of the words. She felt her soul on fire. On a strong impulse, feeling profoundly guilty, she hid her treasure under her pillow. She had never hidden anything from Oma before.

She turned ten that year.

This fever in Karin would have been a sore worry to Katya, had it not been for the fact that for once she, as the head of the family, was engrossed in a consuming concern of her own. For she was given a letter one morning that was to change the course of her life."

"It's for you, Oma."

"For me?" asked Katya, only mildly curious at first. "From Paraguay? Whom do I know in Paraguay?"

Vaguely she remembered that she had once before heard of this country. Was that not the place to which the sled-driven Amur Exodus had fled almost two decades ago? Undecided and a little fearful, she held the envelope in her hand, opening it finally with some reluctance.

"Oh! Oh dearest! It's from my oldest brother Hein. The one who went to Canada. Why would he be in Paraguay?"

She read the letter once, and then she sat down and clutched the table for support and read it again with silently moving lips, and then she gave it to Karin to read aloud to the others:

"Dearest Sister," wrote Hein. "News of your rescue arrived. Our colony closed its schools so all of us could assemble and read its message together. For over fifteen years, no word had come to us from any of you dear ones over there in Russia. Yours was the first letter that told us that anyone had survived this most terrible of all wars. Dear Katyushka! You and your family are as welcome here in our homes as we would be in

205

yours, were our fates reversed. Our colony is waiting for our refugees. Paraguay is a quiet, sun-drenched land, and though we have no riches, we have our peace and freedom to worship our Lord."

Similar letters followed—letters that told of willing money, letters of support, assurances of kinship, assurances of willingness to share. Each letter brought a divine plan more sharply into focus. For in this country named Paraguay there could be had—for nothing but the mere asking!—a simple life of order and tranquility, an old-fashioned Mennonite life tucked safely away beneath the warmth of the tropical sun.

"Paraguay will take us all?" they asked, incredulously. All but a mere handful of them had vanished forever. But this handful of them, now huddling together in the *Vaterland's* windswept ruins, still breathed to live out God's inscrutable will. Katya sat amid her kin and listened in reverence to somber, God-fearing men sent from across the great waters to help steady the shattered remnants of the last of her people. And just as in trying times past—when it seemed that the world had come to an end—a door was opening to simple and honest and straightforward living.

"Article One guarantees freedom from religious interference."

"Article Two makes sure that no alcoholic beverages will be sold within the limits of the Paraguayan colonies."

"Article Three exempts the Mennonites for ten years from all taxation."

"No present and future law shall hinder the entrance of Mennonites into Paraguay for reasons of age or physical or mental incapacity."

"And never again shall a gun be forced into a Mennonite youth's hands."

Was it still possible that such a miracle of sane worldly government could exist?

And so it happened that in no time at all they found themselves packed and baggaged—with a brand-new passport in their hands—en route to a new continent on the other side of the earth, as far away as one could possibly go without coming close once more to those places from which they had fled.

Shortly before Christmas a ship pushed off from the shores of Germany—a little lopsided, it seemed, for two thousand Russian Mennonites stood weeping on its starboard and watched the homeland of their ancestry sink slowly into the sea.

Book Three
Karin
[1946—1957]

9

It could be seen on a map that Paraguay was as large as Germany had been before the war: a land-locked country, in the very heart of South America, divided into two equal parts by a river of like name. The eastern part, it was said, was bold in colors and very picturesque—with lazy rivers rolling through hills and flatlands of luscious dense forests, and with a populace that lived pleasantly in little towns along its shores. Visitors from foreign countries would be enchanted by the still and even quality of life along broad sandy streets, held in deep languor save for a wandering goose or goat or young, naked, sun-tanned children, playing quietly in the shade of bitter orange trees.

The western part, however, had remained unpopulated since ancient times, for it was said to be a land of utter ferocity. But the refugees looked at it and saw that it was far away from the cities, and they said:

"It is a place to find refuge from the world. We are a sifted people. God willing, we shall be worthy to blaze a trail of civilization in this savage land."

As they embarked, each with a number on cardboard to be worn around the neck, an unkind post-war editorial had proclaimed:

"Religious fanaticism leading into nowhere . . . Women and children, and the old and the crippled, to be swallowed by an obscure, boiling vermin-infested land . . . "

They knew better. For was it not clearly written in Amos five, verse eleven: "I have overthrown some of you as God overthrew Sodom and Gomorrah, and ye were as a firebrand plucked from out of the burning, yet have ye not returned unto me, saith the Lord . . . "? Had they not been rescued straight from the Devil's throat—a mere handful of them, where there had been hundreds of thousands of them before? Now those who were left grasped the Holy Book and held it in their trembling hand and vowed they would never let go of it again. And they said:

"Instead of building our faith in God, we have flirted with worldly knowledge and longed for riches and power and been bewitched by the swastika flag. Only after God's wrath struck us down and all but annihilated us in its fury, would we consent to bow to His divine will."

On the planks of the Dutch passenger ship *Volendam*—given their ancestral roots, was that not a sign in itself?—more than two hundred of their young knelt in humility before the Lord to receive the holy baptism, as behind them there disappeared on the horizon a whirlpool of madness that had swept them across Europe and halfway around God's ravished earth.

Three times that very first week they gathered around the Lord's table. More than three dozen young people had asked to start married life with the blessings of the *Gemeend,* and a sizable group of older ones had in humility pledged spiritual surrender. It had not surprised Katya at all to find Jasch Kovalsky among the newly converted. He had appeared on the *Volendam* at the very last minute, pallid and shaken, limping pitifully, but firm in his new-found conviction:

"Dear Lord, more than forty years You followed me. Let me now follow You for the rest of my life."

"See?" Katya could not resist pointing out, "The Lord slowed you down so that you would listen."

"Yes," agreed Jasch, chastised for once. "How right you were, dear Katyushka."

While still on the ship, Karin had chanced upon a book that described their future homeland. Now she sat cross-legged on her high berth, informing her family below:

" . . . swamps and forests, steaming in tropical heat . . . "

"How exciting," said Sara, with flushed cheeks.

" . . . a murderous climate, with extreme heat waves during summer and devastating. . . . "

"I'm sure it must rain sometimes," interrupted Sara.

" . . . devastating rainstorms whipping the land during

212

winter, creating rapid, muddy, tortuous rivers, to be sucked up in no time at all in the cracks of the grey dusty soil."

"See?" smiled her mother.

"How wise of our Lord," said Katya, "to let it rain when it is needed most."

"Endless, borderless flatlands," announced Karin. "A dreary waste of lagoons and marshes, thought to have been once a giant inland sea. Not a single natural rock can be found for hundreds and hundreds of miles! The land is as level as if a giant roller . . . "

"Just like the plains we used to know in Russia," said Katya with hopeful longing in her voice.

" . . . Trees are upheld by knotted, twisted creepers, as thick as the arms of a man. The timber is so hard and durable that it will sink in water like a rock. Dust storms ravage the dried-out deserts for months at a time . . . "

"How you like to toy with words," Katya had said in mild reproach. As they slowly moved up the Paraguayan River—all of them now crammed into a short-winded steamer—she looked with strong misgivings at the first palm trees she had ever seen: not tall and graceful and slender, as she had envisioned them, but ungainly monsters—thickset, with bulging trunks, prickly with forbidding spikes, wearing a dry, rattling, miserly crown, shaggy with last year's leaves.

Now they were here.

And even the heavens above seemed strange!

A hot, menacing sun—a yellow disk of tingling haze— hung overhead as their riverboat reached the shore around noon. Hot gusts of wind, coming in gulps from the north, blew clouds of dust into their smarting eyes. Their shadows were underfoot, shrunken and sharp at first, then stretching more and more in frightening, spiderlike fashion. And as the night approached, with such black suddenness that all but took their breaths away, they discovered that instead of the Big Dipper familiar to them from their many travels during the night, there flashed the Southern Cross amid a velvet sky. The

213

moon hung low and gigantic, its tilt askew and its shape upside down. It made them shake their heads in wonderment. This was a weird land indeed into which they had come in search of a purpose that had been all but lost in the years they were thrown around the war-torn landscapes of Europe.

Katya recognized her brother at once, even though more than a quarter of a century had passed into the sea of eternity since she had seen him last. Head to grey head, they kissed and hugged each other, devoid of words. Lena stood by his side. She had been a skinny, shy, grief-stricken girl, having lost three of her sons to the death knell of Razin and a newborn to the plague that came in his wake. Now she was huge with complacency and the weight of many years, soft like Mennonite *zwieback* dough, spreading to all sides with excitement and heartfelt hospitality, caressing Lily Marlene with shrieks of joy at such beauty in a child.

"Let's go," urged Ohm Hein, taking Karin by the hand. His grip almost crushed her fingers. He wore a huge, shaggy sombrero with perspiration-stained fringes that scratched his neck as he turned here and there to nod his welcome greetings. His bare feet were stuck in wooden sandals. His toes were swollen and red. From time to time, he rubbed them against each other. "Those nasty sand fleas," he complained. "They bury themselves right under one's toenails, between cuticle and skin, and you don't notice them until there's a bluish-white sack filled with eggs. That's when the itching begins. Our poor dogs almost tear off their toes in a futile effort to get rid of this itching. I have to show you how to take them out with a charcoal-heated needle to avoid a dangerous infection."

"Insects that eat into one's body?" thought Karin, revolted. "Surely that cannot be!"

Rows of ox carts were waiting to take them inland to their destination. Slowly they proceeded through stretches of densest bush for many hours on end. As far as the eye could see, timbered areas alternated with open camps and occasional swampy meadows, covered with a thick, green, reedy-looking grass.

Katya surveyed the landscape with pleasure and envisioned it to be perfect for grazing, but Ohm Hein, guessing her thoughts, said regretfully:

"Most grasses are bitter, and unfit for cattle to eat."

"How far is it from here to the colonies?"

"Three to five days in good weather," said he. "Six to eight weeks if it rains." His eyes followed the deeply-cut wagon tracks. "Not a living soul in this land," he said sweepingly, after a while, "save our people. Except for a handful of *estancieros*—cattle ranchers—like Don Bartolo, who lives near your future colony, there's not a living soul for days on end. There are the Indians, of course, an abomination in the eyes of the Lord with their laziness and their heathen ways of life. They are nomads, at the mercy of this land. They kill their young by choking them in hot sand, and they let their dogs suck off the milk of their women. Too many babies, they say, would slow them down as they drift about in search of survival."

"Who is Don Bartolo?" asked Karin, charmed by the strange-sounding name.

"He sold us the land," explained Ohm Hein. "There's rumor that he is part German, that his mother was a stray at the pier somewhere near the coast who forgot her honor at the sight of Paraguayan gold. It's hard to believe, though, that he's of German stock. For even though he's richer than our entire colony, his house has no walls, and one can enter his sleeping quarters from all sides. He has more cattle than he can count, but he sleeps far into the day. His son Carlitos, who comes and goes because he studies in the city, wears an embroidered scarf around his waist. No girl of ours would dare to walk the camp by herself when he is home on vacation, for he's a very brazen youth. He speaks a little German, too."

"What does he study?" asked Karin eagerly, her imagination beginning to gyrate at full speed.

"The border dispute," explained Ohm Hein. "This is a land so virgin that no one knows just where it ends. To us it always seems that it is stretching to the very edges of eternity."

215

"Then how would the border police know . . . ?"

"Police? We have no need of police. If we judge our own conduct, we prevent others from sitting in judgment over us. Strong arms can grab a sinner in the dark and help him to a lesson on his backside that is not easily forgotten. And did not our forefathers way back in Russia believe in just this kind of discipline?"

"Is Russia still that close to you?" asked Katya, smilingly. "After having left it more than twenty-five years ago for Canada? And why did you then leave Canada, Hein?"

And now, rolling along the Paraguayan plains, Katya learned in great dismay that Canada too, after initial friendliness, had reached out for the Manitoba Mennonites and had asked for their children, to turn them into alien Canadians with English customs, and English language, and English instruction in schools. Was that not equal to sacrificing one's children to the world? Would they not lose their German services as well, and with their German church their very souls? How could a Mennonite bear such hurt?

"What is wrong with our German language?" Hein asked accusingly. "Why English? And what about those privileges promised us?"

Katya could well understand how the ghost of Czarist Russia had begun to haunt the Manitoba settlers. When Czar Nicholas had demanded the closing of the German schools, that had been as good as the beginning of the end.

"We tried," explained Aunt Lena, her lips trembling with the remembered insult. "I myself went to evening school twice a week, even though, God knows, I had far saner things to do. But they wouldn't leave us be! Hans became 'John.' Maria changed to 'Mary.' Franz lost his tail 'z' and gained a useless 'k' instead. What for, I ask you? Why such nonsense?"

Like mushrooms, she explained to Katya, English words had popped up in the most unexpected places, poisoning the minds of their foolish, impressionable youth. It was obvious that there was something indecent about the English language, with its chewed

216

sounds and its soft and blubbery texture. "We were asked to put our tongue between our teeth," she cried, scornfully. "They made us sing: "God save the King!" Her bosom heaved; there were red blotches on her neck. "Were we going to permit a Canadian flag to be flown in our school yards? Were our children now to greet a worldly symbol? Have another cup of coffee, Katyushka. For the sake of Germandom . . . "

"For the sake of Germandom," echoed Katya's heart, silently.

For the sake of Germandom, Gerhard had vanished in the bleak Siberian night. For the sake of Germandom, her dearest child, her Liestje, had perished. For the sake of Germandom, David had been shot to death at age fourteen. She listened quietly and understood the price one had to pay.

Panic had taken hold of the Manitoba Mennonites. No compromise was possible, that much was clear from the beginning. It was as clear as the sun hung in the sky that German would not be surrendered. Was not one's very doctrine welded permanently to its sounds?

"Is there anything as frightening as a record of broken promises?" asked Hein. "Was there a choice except to take our *wanderstab* and search once again for a place in which to live in peace? We had no choice. Real estate brokers began to crowd our doors. Private homesteading farther up north? To be lost in the expanse of the unexplored Canadian land? Never. Loose leaves get scattered in the wind."

Two years were set aside to make sure the wary Manitoba Mennonites would not walk into another governmental trap. Delegates were hastily chosen and dispatched with great urgency to embark upon a search that was to cover many countries. The messengers took their plea with them after having memorized it: "Freedom to maintain and administer our schools. Freedom to teach our religion and language without interference. Freedom to worship our God in our own way as we have done for centuries . . . "

When they returned after having traveled abroad for many

months, there was almost a tinge of adventure swinging in their somber tales.

"The Lord led our messengers," explained Hein proudly, "to a country of great promise."

Paraguay was a young land, behaving like a child in many ways, forever getting involved in border disputes, looking glaringly and full of envy at its richer neighbors on all sides. But the President of Paraguay was a very well-informed and clever man, quite aware that even Canada had no better citizens than the Mennonites.

"All our requests were honored, assured with rubber stamp and seal, in exchange for nothing more than our diligence and our honesty. There was plenty of soil, virgin and waiting, far removed from noise and revolt, and a landed owner willing to sell it as cheap as a piece of unbuttered bread."

"So inexpensive," the delegates had exclaimed," that it will practically pay for itself, with the timber that grows in its forest. Two and a half acres can be paid for with the sale of a single full-grown tree."

Even the most skeptical of them had been sure that it was a sign from heaven. They sold their farms in haste and packed their belongings into huge coffers and trunks. Did it matter that there appeared in Canadian papers harsh words about ungratefulness and stubborn Mennonite skulls?

When they arrived in Asuncion, their riverboat lay deep in the silken waters, weighted down by the farm equipment and sturdy furniture and kitchen utensils that they had brought along. A crowd of cheering, waving people was waiting for them at the pier—shiny, dark-skinned faced, heads with hair as sleek as a horse's mane. The President of Paraguay in person walked up the narrow plank to shake their elder's hand.

Ohm Hein fell silent. He suddenly looked old and grey. Karin saw that his eyes were red-veined from the glare of the sun. Why, suddenly, had his voice turned unsteady?

"When we arrived here in the Chaco," said Ohm Hein, finally, "no one had heard of us or the land we were to occupy.

Don Bartolo himself was away on one of his trips, and had forgotten to leave his instructions. We were forced to stay and wait for months, housed in crude sheds near the river, without food, or medication, or any means of going back."

They had left their comfortable Canadian homes just as it was time to light the fires for the winter. Here it was summer, the hottest season of the year. Less than 900 feet away loomed the unknown threatening jungle. No one had warned them that danger was that close.

"Our daughter's baby toddled off the first week we were there," said Aunt Lena, remembering their sorrowful beginnings. "Before it could be found . . . " She swallowed. "It died of a sun stroke, it was said. Would God it were true. We found its skeleton after more than a week's search, gnawed clean by the ants . . . "

To the west, they were airily told, lay their land. It would take a while to have it surveyed. Nobody knew when Don Bartolo would be back.

Typhoid broke out the second week of their stay. The water they drank was dirty. The natives had never heard of soap.

Ohm Hein said heavily:

"We left two hundred graves behind when we set out upon the narrow ox cart trail which finally took us from the landing harbor through the bush to our new land. One-tenth of our expedition . . . Most of them were children, too young to know the grief they left in our hearts."

With axe and knife and raw determination Hein and Lena had cut their way into the bush. They built a shed of leaves and straw. They dug a hole in the ground and put a flattened tin can across it, leaving just enough room for the air to move through. On it, they cooked their monotonous meals. Plow after plow splintered to fragments, broken on the iron-hard roots of the jungle.

"Our harvests were pitiful at first. We lacked knowledge of the land and efficient means for farming it. The climate was murderous. Insects fell from the clouds that made the plagues described in the Old Testament seem child's play by comparison. Grasshoppers, locusts, caterpillars, fleas and flies and mosquitoes, plant lice and worms and ants, ants, ants! Hundreds of thousands of ravenous insects, all determined to live off the luscious cultivated plants rather than the meager vegetation of the bush."

"How hard we struggled," added Lena quietly, and Katya shivered a little in the heat.

"Whole settlements felt defeated from the beginning. Entire villages were literally driven out by ants. Some fainthearted settlers gave up and took the first riverboat back to the city to return to the pleasant and familiar sights of Manitoba—impoverished, humiliated, and defeated."

But the severity of the first decade of pioneering created a unity among the settlers that lay like a harness of protection around the colonies. " . . . Each able-bodied man signed up to help dig wells, cut roads, build bridges. Women and children gathered each morning to make bricks out of mud and cow manure and dry them in the sun . . . " By pooling their strength and their courage, humble but steady victories could be wrestled from the bush. " . . . Had it not been for our unity, we could not have survived." Slowly but persistently, village after Mennonite village thus sprang to life in the unyielding soil of the Gran Chaco.

"This is Waldheim," explained Ohm Jasch, spreading a map over his knees. "And this settlement is Kleefeld. This here is Friedensfeld. And Schoenwiese. And Friedensruh."

"Just like in Russia," said Katya. "My God!"

"Not quite," smiled her brother. "But almost like old home. In fact, we voted to call our colony Fernheim—'faraway home'—for we are indeed far away from anything we have ever known, dear Katyushka."

There was a sawmill in two of the villages. There was an oil press, a corn starch factory, a saddler's shop. A co-operative was flourishing by buying the settlers' commodities and selling them to the Indians and Don Bartolo's men for specified weeks of labor in return. The grass huts of the early years had largely disappeared. Sprawling, spotless homes could now be seen from an airplane through the dark foliage of the bitter orange trees.

"We built a makeshift church the very first year. Now we could sing and pray to our heart's content and feel much more secure in what we had set out to do. It is evident that we will never be given a burden we are not strong enough to bear." He paused, his eyes on the children. Then he said:

"We came, and we intended to remain. Life, for us, has never been easy. The fainthearted ones who left strengthened those who chose to remain, for dissatisfaction and doubt were weeded from our midst. Our harvest began to pay off. Our numbers tripled in some twenty-five years. Our children, without exception, are deeply God-fearing and willing to work. Not only did we survive. We won!"

"Over there, Katyushka, are our tents," said Aunt Lena. "You must be tired to the bone."

Katya shook her head, a thick lump in her throat.

Life here was complacent and calm. Not even a ripple of the world's aches and pains could reach these secluded settlements in the middle of the Paraguayan bush. No one would stop the Mennonite plow. Once again, there would be order and predictability. Once again, there would be self-control and cleanliness in the *Gemeend,* and weeks of well-planned work, and certainty in spiritual matters. Children would once again grow up in the fear of an omnipotent, uncompromising Lord, and would accept without blinking the expedient teachings of the past. New generations would grow up beneath low-thatched roofs that would look and behave exactly like the youth that she had known in her own young years before fire and death had shaken belief. And once again, there were aliens around her who needed the Mennonite example.

"Now we are here," said Katya, taking a deep, tremulous breath.

"Now you have come. It will not be easy. There are strange diseases that strike our cattle, and sudden illnesses that kill our young. We have had to relearn in very many ways. We have to be careful to sleep with our heads toward the north, for oxygen here seems to flow in a southerly direction. I have read it in a book that contains all there is to know about the physical world. We have to guard against the radio, which is a temptation to many of our young. We have had to get used to pigs with long, pointed snouts, straight-backed and high-legged and noisy day and night. Our work is spread over the cool tag-ends of the day so that we can rest for hours in the middle, for this land, around noon, competes with purgatory. We still have to build roads and dig wells and clear the land. The jungle is ever at our heels. But going back and losing our souls? Never in a million years."

No longer could worlds tumble and borders be shifted by capricious whim and human dignity be stomped underfoot. There was this, and there was that, and countless tears had been shed. But it was really quite simple. One could choose to look down and around and one would see shadows in every corner. Or one could look up and be comforted by a vast, glittering, incredibly beautiful sky.

A multitude of insects was drawn to the lights of their tents. A lightning bug, landing in Lily Marlene's fine hair, crawled over her forehead and along her little nose: a miniature train, it seemed, spreading a bluish-green light, with two red dots in front and two rows of greenish windows at each side. The sky above their tent was so brilliant and soft that Karin felt the urge to reach up and touch its texture with her hands. The child, giddy from emotions and drunk with sleep, strained hard to keep awake to soak into her every pore the momentous flavor of this day.

A silence settled down upon the refugees. And then, in a faraway tent, someone started to sing, with a strong, confident, full-ringing voice:

"A mighty fortress is our God,
A bulwark never failing,

. 222

Our helper He, amid the flood
Of mortal ills prevailing . . . "

For one thing they had salvaged indeed! Their hymns, which had wandered with them around the globe, now rose toward the sky in the vast loneliness of their new home. And what a powerful declaration of confidence and faith it now became!

"And though this world with devils filled
Should threaten to undo us
We will not fear, for God hath willed
His truth to triumph through us."

Yes, this was the hour indeed to savor to the fullest the comfort that came with time-proven songs. Had they not, one by one, gone through the fires of persecution, and had they not been tested by the agonies of warfare, famine, revolution, flight, and separation from loved ones whom they would never see again?

"For still our ancient foe
Doth seek to work us woe;
His craft and power are great,
And armed with cruel hate,
On earth is not his equal."

Katya wept openly as her voice joined the others in the rugged ancient German Reformation battle hymn:

"The Prince of Darkness grim
We tremble not for him
His rage we can endure
For lo, his doom is sure
One little word shall fell him . . . "

———————

Their colony was called Neuland, to give proper credence to the roots they were determined to grow in Paraguayan soil. Some had wanted to call it Hindenburg, or Neu-Berlin, or even Heimatland, but others had taken indifferently to these suggestions, for in this Godforsaken pocket of the world even the glamor of Germany would fade a little in the heat.

It was all but impossible to get a proper feel for seasons. At home, the resurrection of the Lord and the awakening of nature had duly coincided. Here, Katya was told, it would be autumn at Eastertime, when nature would reluctantly shed a few discolored leaves. Leaden skies would settle upon tree tops and rains would fall to all but drown out the world. At home, before Christmas, a certain tender, saddened light had spread across the land. But here, in early December, the foliage around them had bristled to a brownish color. The north wind, whipping along the street, carried air laden with heat, splitting the soil into millions of dusty cracks. The meager clouds that could be seen in the very early morning hours were soon dissolved by the broiling disc which hung for endless hours vertically in the sky with menacing persistence.

Katya would often recount in later times that no one could fully appreciate under what burdens they lived and labored during their first year in the Chaco. Farming with spade and hoe was an almost impossible race against the ferocious growth she tried in vain to clear away from her steps. To her joy, she observed that the seeds she had planted all but exploded to life, but try as she might to give the cultured plants a chance to grow, strangling rank weeds and underbrush grew back as fast as she tried to cut them away. Pestiferous insects, erupting into hideous clusters before her very eyes, continued to frustrate her to tears. The sound of axe blows surrounded her on all sides, as her own blade ate a little deeper into the bush every day. Perspiration drenched her body, soaked into the skin between her shoulder blades, roughened her armpits to burning discomfort, left dirty smudges on her cheeks. She could feel the granular salty drops of perspiration run between her breasts and trickle along her thighs. By ten o'clock it was so hot that the whole world, now and then, would blacken away from her eyes. There were moments when, much to her distress, her axe felt like a murderous instrument in her hands, which had become as callused as a man's.

Walter—barechested and grim—worked steadily with quiet persistence on the plot next to her own. His back had tanned as brown as the skin of the heathen. Ohm Jasch was always nearby, sitting on a tree stump, his wooden leg stretched out for comfort, supporting his young son's labor with ready advice:

"Cut here. Take that tree over there first. If you burn down the twisters . . . "

Every once in a while, Katya would put down her jungle knife and sit with the boy for a while, silently sharing with him a drink of lukewarm water.

"You shouldn't work so hard, Kastyushka," Jasch would vaguely protest.

To that, Katya never replied. Sara, fumbling and fainthearted, could not be trusted with an axe, and it was too much strain to put up with her sniffling protests. So Katya had put her in charge of the fire. The children were too young to help. Who else could do the work? She wiped the perspiration off her brow. Most trees were so hard that not even the most vigorous blow could make more than a shallow dent, although she had come across a few trunks of brittle, papery texture so soft that it was said in Fernheim they could be cut down with a pocket knife. Katya was deeply impressed. She took care to caution the girls not to swing on the vines that hung from certain trees, fearing they would give way and come down upon the intruders and crush the children beneath.

At first, she had wanted to leave a few stately *quebracho* trees on her land to give some shade during the day. They looked so pretty that she ached to keep them. But when she saw that swarms of parakeets would settle on their branches—green, screeching, gluttonous birds hanging in feathery clusters amid the dust-laden leaves—she realized that no grain, no bean, no seedling would be safe. The winged, shrieking little monsters would leave the foliage in perfect unison and with their greedy crooked beaks destroy in minutes weeks and weeks of strenuous work. No, the *quebrachos* had to go!

Oh, but what an untamed, crazy, sullen land!

At night, snakes as thick as a man's arm would crawl along the newly-cut path that connected her homestead with Ohm Jasch's. Indeed, there were more snakes than anyone had dreamed possible: they wriggled beneath leaves and hid beneath the boards in the horses' barn and lay like glittering exotic belts behind Sara's bed, and to Lily Marlene's tearful horror gulped down a number of Katya's newly-hatched chicks. The hideous reptiles would not even bother to disappear into the bushes at such times. Bloated and lazy, barely wriggling their tails, they would just lie there in the blistering sun and let the digestive juices do their work. Katya had cautioned the children severely never to step on one of these creatures, although Hein had reassured her that few snakes in this land were poisonous.

"They will disappear as soon as the great rains arrive," he had smiled. "They are more of a nuisance than a danger, Katyushka."

How much there was to learn!

But Katya, that very first year, discovered within herself a resourcefulness that must have been the result of centuries of Mennonite pioneering. She had built herself an oven that was the envy of the village, made from the shell of a giant ant hill on her land. The girls had helped her to burn the ants out of their nests. She had hollowed out the shell with a spatula, making an opening large enough for her baking sheets to pass through. Around it, she built a makeshift overhead shelter. She soaked strings in kerosene and hung her staples to the rafters: sugar, flour, soup, meat, anything she wanted safe from crawling insects.

The chickens were still a problem, though—clumsy creatures that they were, they would struggle through her kitchen with flapping wings, topple her dishes, and leave droppings on her table, and make a nuisance of themselves as only chickens could.

A drought hit the land soon thereafter. Walter, now fourteen but fully a man, would ride the range for days on end in search of dying calves too young to survive the severe lack of water. So often had he plunged his knife into the soft flesh of the dying creatures that he no longer bothered to wipe the blade before he put it in his belt. His hips were covered with blackened blood. His nails were torn and brittle.

He seldom smiled, but when he came home, he rode past Karin's homestead and whistled a sharp, fanciful tune. Karin would drop whatever she was doing and run to greet him and walk with him for a while. The village was sharp in condemning a girl not yet baptized who acted in such a foolish way. But Karin, flushing crimson at the sight of Walter, thought nothing of her behavior. Quick as she seemed in other ways, she was slower than most to learn that discipline in thought and deed was once again a goal to be aspired to in the Mennonite settlements.

Katya was grateful for having Walter near, for he was as dear to her as one of her own. He helped her in very many different ways, for he was of practical mind. It was Walter who constructed the frame of her hut. He assisted in filling a hole with stagnant water from the camp, and with his bare, mud-splattered feet he kneaded a mixture of finely chopped grass, dried leaves, and chunks of red soil to a doughy, elastic mass. He had a patient way with the girls, putting them to work with gentle words to carry hundreds of wads to be stuck between the braided twigs. He dispatched Sara with instructions to cut from the underbrush a number of heavy, even rafters, and he showed Katya how to push them neatly into the wall. When that was done, he took heavy twine and criss-crossed it from side to side, and then from left to right, and then obliquely from corner to corner.

"The girls can sleep on this," he said awkwardly. "They shouldn't sleep on the floor; it's too dangerous with the scorpions around." Scorpions! Katya hastily brushed some kerosene along the wall to keep away the horrid creatures, large as the palm of one's hand, with dozens of hairy legs, hiding in outhouses and beneath pots and pans and in shoes and behind her broom in the corner. But she was very proud of Walter's creation. As soon as she could stop and take a breath, she traded eight days of mending for a Fernheim family for an equal number of empty flour sacks, which she then carefully ripped and re-stitched into a sturdy mattress cover. She sent the girls to collect banana leaves from the Bartolo *estancia* and dried them in the sun. She stuffed the bag with this sweet-smelling filling, and over it all, she spread the cleanest blanket she could spare.

She soon perfected her skills for creating more built-in furniture: wide benches along the north wall, to be used for seating arrangements during meals and as beds for herself and Sara at night; several cupboards which held her staples and kept her dishes out of reach of the three dozen clucking hens which Lena had given her as a housewarming present the very first week of their arrival in this land.

Katya, always fastidious and tidy, now came to revere cleanliness more than anything else in her life. She would not even permit herself to have a cup of coffee in the morning unless she had first sprinkled and swept the floor with a giant broom of reedy twigs Sara had broken from the underbrush which covered the camp. Her floor was her pride and her joy. She had worked on it for an entire week, smoothing over the jungle soil beneath her roof with many layers of a specially prepared mixture of cow dung and moistened mud, mixed with a generous dose of ant poison. Anyone should be impressed with the results! The finely chewed grass residue in the manure was an excellent aid, binding the clay and preventing the floor from cracking. Once dry, such floors kept fresh and clean for weeks and would go a long way in keeping the ants at bay.

One night, to everyone's delight, a slight, mild rain had fallen, leaving the ashes in rivulets all over the fields. Karin, stepping carefully across the stumps and roots sticking out of the ground in search of some firewood for breakfast, noticed that a chalky white substance was left on her feet, feeling smooth to the touch and smelling sharp and clean. She took a handful of wet ashes and mixed it with some water in a dish.

"This is as good as chalk," she said to Katya.

With Walter's help, she painted the inside of their hut. Lily Marlene, not to be outdone, whitewashed the tree trunks around their home so that they looked, Katya said proudly smiling, exactly like the acorn trees back in Russia when Waldheim had readied itself for Pentecost.

From Lena she learned further that she could use the ashes of burnt-down trees to scour her footsoles and those of her children, for walking barefoot all day over the freshly cleared land left ingrained blackened ridges in their feet. Come Saturday night, she made sure and doubly sure that a thorough scrubbing took place behind a blanket securely fastened to the roof of her hut. Water became scarcer by the day, but water was not to be saved on a Saturday night. Not only one's hands and feet, but one's ears and scalp and neck and back were scrubbed clean of the soot and grime of the week, with such a force that the children's bodies tingled for hours from the thoroughness with which they were prepared for the day of the Lord.

Life went on once more—harsh and cruel, to be sure, but with a definite measure of order and certainty. And sometimes, in rare moments, life could be breathtakingly poignant again.

For there was always this moment of gripping satisfaction: when the match could be put to the slain enemy and the flames would leap wildly through the entanglement of crisp branches and dried, twisted roots. There was a definite art to jungle burning. One could not be impatient. The branches had to dry for weeks. It was important to have the trees fall tightly, one on top of another, to form an even mass. If they did not burn down to the ground in a single roaring inferno, one was forced the next day to untangle the half-charred grimy pieces—work more unpleasant and tedious than the clearing of the jungle itself.

Wherever one looked these days, smoke rose straight toward the sky. How rewarding to see the flames licking at the clouds, howling with ferocity. Karin, especially, loved this fiery spectacle; she loved it with a strange intensity that summoned sparks of madness into her eyes in moments when she felt sure no one was watching her closely. She would stand swaying in the glow, the odor of ashes and smoke in her nostrils, the never-quite-forgotten fear quivering in her heart. She would stay motionless, watching the smoke blacken the sky, drift over the village, hang in the tingling air for hours, veil the sun, then magnify and redden it and bring it very, very near.

"Every once in a while, she still fights terror," Katya would think. "The war has seared this child. There are times when she reminds me of . . . " With an effort, Katya would force herself to abandon her thoughts.

During those nights when fires all over the new colony would set the horizon ablaze with pioneer effort, a feeling of purpose would warm Katya's heart and spread through her veins like slow, gentle honey. She liked to sit on her doorstep, imagining the gleaming fires to be the lights of a far-away city. She was glad that cities were now far away. She did not want any part of the outside world, now that she was with her people again. She remembered how the Russian servants at home used to say: "It's always best where we are not." This could never be true of a Mennonite. The only place of comfort was where one could congregate with one's kind, no matter what the circumstances or surroundings.

On such nights Karin would come and sit quietly by her side, speaking little but moving restlessly from time to time. The girl was growing rapidly, becoming too tall and slender, hasty in her movements and very quick of speech. Katya never missed such moments to add substance to her soul.

"Once again," she would tell her grandchild somberly, "we can live on the essential fare of Bible and Bread."

Karin suppressed a smile in the dark. She knew of Oma's biggest grudge against her new homeland—that wheat could not be grown. This was why they had come! But such bread as they now had to eat was a disgrace to any housewife worth her salt. Katya's pride would smart sharply. Kaffir flour was just not nearly as good as home-grown wheat would have been. The dough stuck to her knuckles while kneading. It would flatten out on the baking sheets, and crumble after baking, and sour in a day or two. The girls preferred to go hungry rather than eat the bread gone sticky from heat. Katya herself could eat it with some difficulty, for she was now working harder than ever before in her life.

Had it not been for her deep, unshakable conviction that there was a purpose in all that happened, she could not have survived. Time and again, one could hear the settlers affirm that a purpose had brought them to Paraguay. Even so, there were times of such frustration that these words were all but lost.

Was there a chance now to pause and take a short gasp of breath and watch the growth of new, promising life? The creepers of her watermelons, Katya had discovered, were forming tiny buds. The beans had finished blooming. The tiny citrus trees, limp for so long, were sprouting tender tips. But then she heard a noise that sounded like the Indians gone crazy. She saw Ohm Hein's grown sons ride into the village, shouting wildly and pointing to the sky. A cloud pushed upward, spreading along the horizon, coming closer, stretching the length of some twenty miles, hanging overhead now, lowering itself onto the tree tops, breaking into fragments, falling, falling, blackening the earth. Locusts! The settlers working on their land grabbed whatever they could: pots and pans and lids and covers, banging them against each other, yelling and shouting and screaming and whistling, and then praying weakly for deliverance from such calamity.

By nightfall, locusts were everywhere! In every utensil, in shoes, beneath the sheets and blankets, falling from the roof in clusters and jumping up on one's legs from the ground. The next morning, after a horrible night, the girls took brooms and swept the insects out of their kitchen, where they had formed a slimy cover as thick as the palm of Katya's hand. The chickens walked dizzily, long grey legs hanging limply out of their beaks. Many birds began to die from gluttony the following day; the few that survived laid eggs that were inedible for weeks to come. Their village well, the only one containing water fit for cooking, was

231

ruined by the insects. No pail could cut through the odious slime. The air reeked of decay for weeks.

Three times the very first year Katya replanted her field. In the end she reaped so little that she could carry her meager harvest into the shade of her hut on her own tired back.

Yes, it was pitifully little that she had reaped, but it was a beginning. There were some beans left, at least, and some peanuts. She and Sara tore the plants from the soil until they were sure their backs would split along their spines. Lily Marlene was set to the task of shaking off the earth still clinging to the roots. Walter and Karin carried them to the house and hung them upside down on the rafters, shells to one side, leaves to the other. The kaffir was almost ripe enough to be cut. The fast-growing *manioc* stood healthy and fresh, two feet above the weeds. Next year, she would plant more kaffir, peanuts, manioc, beans, and watermelons. She would set aside one hour each evening to carry water from the depressions in the lower camps to drench the soil around her tiny citrus trees. She had heard of a fruit called *mango,* as big as a goose egg, full of delicious, stringy, fleshy juice, excellent for preserving. She would plant a row of them along the south side of her house.

One thing she had to admit: things grew in the tropical climate. Anything grew. Despite all misfortunes, some settlers reaped so many watermelons the first year that they started to feed them to the pigs. Fruits up to sixty pounds were no rarity. Many rotted in the fields, even though their juice could have been extracted and simmered to a golden syrup which would have been a welcome addition to their monotonous meals. But the entire colony had no kettle large enough, and so, regretfully, they had to see this richness rot.

By Easter time Katya could proudly count four dozen chickens as her own. The diligent creatures fed off the insects of the land, laying enough eggs to be traded in the store for some rice and salt and tea. Behind the window stood her corn patch, already yellowing and tasseling. There was enough sugar cane left to feed half a dozen pigs. She had replanted beans and

232

cucumbers; it remained to be seen what would come of such an effort next year. She would try to marinate the juicy watermelon rinds for variety. The cow gave enough milk for the children. A beginning was made; the rest was up to the Lord. She wiped her brow. She had done her part and more in putting the Mennonite farmer's seal onto the parched land of the Chaco.

"Our children are taught to live the life of the humble," she heard from the pulpit, and deep in her being she knew this to be right.

In the most unpromising of all of Paraguay's millions of unsettled acres, she thus became part of one of the quietest epics of colonization of all times. Undaunted courage in the face of unbelievable hardships kept her hands callused but her faith in her destiny unshaken. Through the direct intervention of her heavenly Father, the doors of Paraguay had opened. Anyone could now come to Paraguay with no more proof of worth than the ability to speak Low German to mark his kinship to the Mennonites. Katya remembered well how she had feared that war and flight might have erased that beautiful homely tongue, and how she had glowed with pride when Karin fell easily into the soft drawl that Mennonites had spoken for over a century on Russian soil.

She lived amid her kin. They had each other. She was not alone, and never would be again. She recalled her awakening the first morning when she had opened her eyes to a new life and had found beside her bed a pan with two beheaded chickens, plucked clean and ready for the pot. To this day she did not know which one of her neighbors had shown this kind of concern. A meat circle was started in which families took turns slaughtering cattle and pigs and sharing with the village twice a week. The sausages and smoked bacons one returned were always bigger than the ones received the week before. One's very honor was at stake in each cup of borrowed milk.

To be sure, there were so many human gaps. Two entire villages stood—house after whitewashed house—built by the hands of women and children, without a single man to head a home. There was not one family that had not been scarred for life by heartbreak that was untold and nowhere recorded. Katya would sometimes all but faint from the realization that out of every fifteen of her people, fourteen had perished in less than three decades. "Cut down like overripe grain under a merciless scythe," she would tell Karin, lest she forget. Why did it have to be? The wars had been for naught. The wars had choked truth and brutalized conscience and cut with deadly knives into living, quivering flesh. No one was left untouched. It would take decades to heal the wounds.

But then she always paused and asked herself: "Does it really matter, seen from the perspective of eternity?" For boys not yet twelve stepped into the places left empty by their fallen or exiled or executed fathers, and took the burdens of sustenance upon their young, suntanned shoulders, smiled with slow confidence, and did what had to be done. Youthful courage was in their midst, plentiful and to spare. There was optimism and confidence despite the hardships they had encountered almost as soon as they had taken on the wilderness with barely more than a jungle knife in their hands and raw will power throbbing in their veins.

This struggle was not in vain. To have a purpose in life meant being blessed abundantly. God's chapel stood squarely in the very middle of her village, waiting for the time to bury its roof beneath the dark citrus foliage, which grew thicker by the week. Sunday after Sunday Katya could go and listen to the message from the pulpit which was the center of her life, which sustained her easily for yet another week of sweat and toil and backbreaking work. She could sit and listen and never tire of what she was told. These were the values of her youth, affirmed and reaffirmed and passed on unstained and unbroken. She felt the very breath of heaven touch her soul when, with each sunset, she could watch her cattle slowly coming home.

Such were the circumstances surrounding Karin in her most impressionable years, and since she was young when

234

transplanted, she did not find them strange. She could have found life peaceful, had it not been for the fact that somehow, much to Katya's grief, Karin was out of step from the beginning.

10

Thunderstorms rumbled on the horizon. The rain monkeys howled.

For months, they had waited longingly for rain. Wave after wave of scorching heat had swept over the Chaco—hot, dry winds, blowing day in and day out. If rain did not come soon, the top soil would simply be blown away. Insects and bird pests continued to fall from the heavens. The children were hoarse from yelling all day to keep the screeching parakeets from raiding the crops, until the sunset would bring some relief. Their harsh screams grated on everyone's nerves. The sun had roasted the lush bitter orange trees to a brittle yellow-brown color. The juicy corn stalks of the spring had withered to shrunken tubes.

Vague lightning flickered along the horizon each night.

"On Sunday it will rain for sure," Jasch prophesied. "I feel it in my missing leg; it's sitting in my bones. Stiff and painful, they are! Hurting all night."

"You are getting old," said Katya, with little sympathy for his malingering.

"Not at all," he protested. "You still look good to me, Katyushka."

The hot, dry weather had brought a new plague: a skin infection that caused such tormenting itching that the girls would scratch themselves bloody in futile attempts for relief. Each night, Katya had to boil sheets and towels in vinegar water to wrap the children for the night—a treatment that caused Lily Marlene to sob in fright and Karin to fight her like a wildcat.

The Sunday passed. No rain was in sight. The next Sunday came, and the next, and the one after that.

But then the flickering on the horizon intensified. One afternoon, the firebrands soared sharply and quickly across the rapidly darkening sky. An ominous mountain pushed upward, so suddenly that the treetops stirred tremblingly in anticipation. A pitch-black cloud now pushed itself in front of the broiling disc. Karin almost choked on a massive, dust-laden current of air as the wind, with a sucking howl, shifted suddenly and started blowing ice cold air from a southerly direction.

The first stroke of lightning shook the air, loosening a handful of heavy raindrops from the clouds. They were quickly absorbed by the thick, thirsty dust, but more fell, and more. The wind, now furious, tore the palm leaves off their door. A gust of icy air took Katya's frying pan clear off the wall and hurled it across the yard. Boom after rumbling boom rolled across the tops of the trees. Chickens scurried for cover. And now the blessed wetness started to pour amid the lightning and thunder that proceeded to rip the sky apart from horizon to horizon. In minutes the village street had turned into a stream of dirty, whirling water.

Katya's skirts flew in the wind as she hurried to put buckets beneath her roof to catch each drop of precious liquid now falling in sheets from the skies. Lily Marlene stood outside, letting the raindrops wash her uplifted, enraptured face. Karin watched quietly from the window, listening to the howls of fury in the air, tasting on her lips the sensation of nature out of control. Ohm Hein had told her: "Watch what will happen. After the rain, the sun will practically pull the weeds out of the ground." The world smelled of wet hay and renewal. After a while, the sky's turmoil subsided. Steady raindrops began to hammer on the foliage.

It rained.

It rained all night.

It rained for three straight weeks, relentlessly.

The children sat, shivering with discomfort, wrapped in

236

blankets by the door. Outside, there was a dreary, murky blackness. Water dripped from the roof and dug ditches around their hut. The south wall had collapsed and buried Karin's bed beneath a soggy heap of mud. Millions of raindrops drenched the land and carried away in rivulets the sprouting winter beans they had planted the previous week. The soil was sodden. At night, the frogs croaked beneath the bushes. Sara almost fainted on a morning when, stepping out of bed, she set her bare foot upon a big, cold, hideous toad while searching for her wooden sandals.

Katya's stove outside had washed away. The cattle had disappeared into the bush. The road to Fernheim, it was said, was flooded. The air smelled strongly of mildew and decay.

Confinement was hardest on Sara. "I am sure," she complained to Katya, a tinge of hysteria in her voice, "that if I have to stay another day in this hut, locked up with the quarrelsome girls, I will for certain lose my mind!"

"Start a fire," said Katya. "Let's make some hot tea."

"How, in the name of humanity?"

"Take that pail over there. Here's some paper. Get some firewood from outside."

"It's soaking wet," cried Sara.

"Well, you could try," suggested Katya, sharply. "Instead of sitting there complaining about the rain you spent days praying for . . ."

"I overdid it for sure," said Sara ruefully.

"Most likely it wasn't you," replied Katya, in search of a different scapegoat. "I bet it was Ohm Jasch. No one prayed more fervently than he. He always meddles! He should have left it to the Lord to let it rain in His own good time. Now we are left to cope with the mess." She rose. "I am going to try to catch that misfit Don Bartolo has afflicted us with. Maybe I can persuade it to give us some milk."

To everyone's surprise, Don Bartolo had turned out to be a Christian of sorts despite his strange name and stranger looks. He had taken it upon himself to aid the hard-working settlers—a cow here, a pig there, some bare-necked chickens for families with hungry little children, a riding horse for the one-legged Ohm Jasch. One morning, his son Carlitos, home from the city, turned up with a heifer tied to his horse's saddle as a dubious present to Katya and the girls—a gift which turned out to be as lean and as shaggy as the land into which they had come. This creature was a monster of meanness and spite; it would lower its head and kick viciously and hold back the meager milk and fling its manure-coated tail at Katya's face.

Karin had watched the notorious youth with curiosity. Katya had frowned with concern. With strong misgivings, Katya had seen him smile seductively, and bow deeply, and speak soft words that sent, she could plainly observe, tingling currents into Karin's receptive ears. Karin had turned pink with pleasure. She, Katya, had had to send the girl in haste to the back of the house.

Remembering this incident did nothing to lift her spirits as she now hastened through darkness and fog along the village street. Mud stuck to her bare feet. The hem of her dress was heavy with wetness and dirt. Through sheets of rain she saw Ohm Jasch on the other side of the road, his hat low over his face. He hobbled over to her side and complained in a despondent voice:

"I searched the camp from fence to fence—our cattle are nowhere to be seen."

"Did you see our Whitehead?"

"No. I tried to keep track of directions, but sometimes the herd goes eastward, and then it turns and wanders north. I'll send Walter early tomorrow; he will find the cow for you."

She listened, grateful for his concern, feeling the rain trickle down the nape of her neck.

"Come with me," he said. "I have some sweet potatoes I saved to give to you."

Katya hesitated. She knew that the tiniest hint of gossip had started to stir in the village. Ohm Jasch was a widower, and men were hard to come by. Yet standing there in the rain, feeling chilled to the bones, she almost weakened.

238

"Come on," he urged again. "At least I have a roof that doesn't leak."

"At least there would be a man in the family," she thought. "There is the fence to be put up. The fields have to be plowed. The roots knock the plow clear out of my hands. Spring is to start in October. Maybe, before the new seedlings push against the sun . . ."

But no. She recoiled from the thought. He was alien to her inner being. She felt it most keenly each time he was near. She was harsh on herself for feeling like this, for she knew that the better part of his dual personality belonged to her in lifelong loyalty. He had helped to keep Gerhard from exile as long as he could, risking his own life many times in his futile efforts. He had brought David's body back to her through a fiery rain of shells. There was Walter, whom she loved as one of her own. She would have liked for Walter to belong to her completely. She derived comfort from just looking at the youth; he was so nice to have around. Sometimes he stayed overnight, not bothering to go home the short distance to his homestead. He would sleep on the bench in the kitchen. In the morning, before anyone else arose, she would ready the breakfast table for just herself and the boy, heating the water on the stove, unwrapping the buns, lovingly pouring a glass of precious milk. Then she would bend over his sleeping face and say gently: "Walter? Wake up. It's almost five o'clock." Sleepily, he would stretch, and she would watch him intently. He would rise and step outside for a moment, and over his shoulder, he would say:

"Another hot day, Aunt Katya."

"Yes. Another hot day."

"Maybe today luck will be on our side."

This was their ritual for starting the day's work.

"Come on out of the rain," Ohm Jasch now urged.

"I don't look very presentable, do I, Jasch, with my dress all wet and my feet cold to the bones?"

"Katya," he said again, his teeth chattering, "you always look good to me."

239

Karin would not like it at all! Karin and Ohm Jasch had turned into bitterest enemies, prompted by a mutual dislike so deep and fervent that it seemed that the hostile spark which had always smoldered had now surfaced with a roar. No, Karin would not like it at all if her foolish old grandmother . . . Katya gave herself an inward push.

"You can give me the potatoes," she said, "but I cannot stay."

"So what if the south wall has crumbled," she thought, pushing the blanket to the side in order to enter her hut. "We will manage. We always do!"

"Girls, it is cold!" she exclaimed. "Didn't you start a fire yet, Sara? In this wind we should be able to tolerate the smoke. I brought some sweet potatoes I will fry us for supper. Ohm Jasch gave them to me in return for some buns I promised to bake for him next Saturday night."

Sara said crossly:

"He takes advantage of you, and you know it, Mother. I think he still wants to marry you."

"That may well be," admitted Katya, flattered. "That is quite possible, daughter."

"Don't you dare!" yelled Karin, scandalized. "What a disaster that would be!"

"I was just teasing, child," said Katya, mildly. "I am too old to marry now. I leave that to the young."

Sara's face reddened. Life, Sara felt, was dissipating between her very fingertips. But what of that? When she walked by the village well, boys half her age would flush and shuffle their feet and greet her with low, shy voices.

"Karin and Walter will make a good match," she heard Katya say.

"Such talk is too early for the child," said Sara in haste. "Oma, what in the world . . . "

"Hurry up," said Katya. "I am so cold I am about to faint on the spot."

"Come on, Karin. Let's find some firewood outside."

240

"Oh, Mother! It's not my turn." Karin dreaded creeping out of her blankets and stepping into the wetness outside.

"Lily Marlene, you go help Mama!" Karin coaxed. "Be a good girl. I'm busy." Karin was leafing through an old Sears catalog that someone in Fernheim had brought along from Canada—when was it, fifteen, twenty years ago? Village women took turns borrowing it and designing their dresses from its pages. It was a much revered book, though loose-leafed by now and almost worn to shreds from use. Karin could sink into a trance looking at its pages, for of late she had begun to show some dangerous signs of vanity.

Lily Marlene ran up to Sara and snuggled in her lap. Karin watched closely. There were edges and corners to Karin's personality where there should have been softness and pliability. There was nothing but softness to Lily Marlene. She was as soft as a kitten, and just as noncommittal. Nevertheless, people would smile down upon her sweet, pink face and say: "She will be beautiful some day. Just like her mother." No one said such a thing of Karin.

"Karin," Sara repeated sharply. "Did you hear? You are to help me get firewood for Oma."

"It's not my turn," protested Karin. "I gathered wood for three days in a row. It's Lily turn. I want to finish the book. I have to return it tonight."

"I don't feel like it," said Lily Marlene amiably, and smiled her sweetest smile.

With one giant stride Karin jumped across the room, and gripped her sister around the shoulders. Lily Marlene, like a fierce hornet, expertly turned on Karin, grabbing her around the legs. Karin, who had misjudged her distance, crashed to the floor, bringing Lily Marlene down with her.

"That does it!" cried Sara, now in a real rage. "You are worse than boys, and at your age, Karin! You ought to be ashamed of yourself! You, too, Lily Marlene! Fighting like two wildcats, whoever heard of such a thing! Come with me, both of you. I feel like giving you both a good thrashing!"

She strode out of the room, dragging behind her the heavy axe. The girls started to laugh. They never took their mother very seriously, much to Katya's distress. Sara just did not know how to discipline her children. On rare occasions, Oma would punish severely. Her wrath could come down on them like the fiery sentence on Judgment Day. Those Were the Times to Close Your Eyes and Savor the Depth of Depravity, thought Karin, losing herself in poetic flair. That Was the Hour of Reckoning! But Mama? No. Mama could never hurt a fly.

The girls followed Sara, still nudging and pushing each other playfully. Sara had found a tree trunk and eyed it with suspicion. Most wood in the Chaco was so incredibly hard! The *quebracho* was so dense that it sank in water. Don Bartolo had advised them to build their fences with *quebracho* posts so they would last for fifty years or more. The village had followed that advice, for Don Bartolo, with all his faults, was known to be a man who knew these things.

The axe came crushing down. Sara groaned with the effort. The blade bit into the tree trunk and became wedged. The girls grinned at each other.

"Mama, I'll get you some softwood," offered Karin after a while, somewhat chastened. "It is much easier to split. Like this one here, see?" She pushed away some wet leaves and soggy grass and uncovered a half-buried trunk. "Let me split it for you, Mama."

"You know you are not permitted to use the axe, Karin."

"But you are so clumsy it's pitiful."

"Hush. Get out of my way, girls."

"Mama, honestly! I've split wood more than once. I know how to do it. I am almost as big as you are. And I am stronger already."

"Do you want an accident to happen?" asked Sara. "Get out of my way, girls, and stop making fun of your poor old mother." She swung the axe high over her head, letting it come down with all her might. The trunk split into two halves, in almost perfect symmetry. "There!" she cried, swinging the axe again,

242

triumphantly. She was never one to pass up an opportunity to dramatize.

How it happened, she could later never recall afterwards. To the end of her days, Karin would feel accused that she had pushed her sister. Lily Marlene could not remember anything. Sara, in later years, would sometimes recount these moments in a whispering voice, for the story never failed to bring tears to her listeners' eyes:

"The blade went into Lily's hand! She must have reached for the log just at the moment I . . . Oh, my God! It didn't even bleed right away! But then there was blood all over . . . Oh! I cannot talk about it even now!"

A neat slice of the child's hand, two fingers attached, lay on the log. Sara screamed and screamed. Karin stood paralyzed, holding her sister's quivering body, feeling blood seep between her bare toes. The whole universe reeled around her as she stared into Lily Marlene's face, which slowly crumbled from pain and shock.

There had been an unwritten law in the colonies that nobody—ever! was to go near anyone with an axe in his hands. The girls knew it. Everyone knew it. It was as if Sara's screams helped Sara fight the blackness that threatened to drown her on the spot. Katya came running, terror ripping her face. Across the field hastened Ohm Jasch, groaning with the effort of climbing the fallen trees in his way. He stumbled and puffed and almost wept in fright:

"What happened? Katya? What in the name of Christ... There comes Walter...Lily? Lily Marlene, please, please don't cry..."

Walter brought his horse to such a sudden stop that it slid several yards along a soggy path. "I'll take her," he said quietly. "Go into the house, Oma. Aunt Sara, for heaven's sake, stop whimpering." He held the child: "Lily, put your arm around my neck. Hold on tight, Lily. I'll take you to Don Bartolo. He has the best horses, he can get you to the doctor in no time at all . . . Hold on tight, Lilybee." His shirt was soaked with the child's blood, and his face, too, despite his efforts, slowly turned grey beneath the rain drops that ran out of his hair. "Aunt Katya, give me your apron. Tie it around her wrist so we can stop the blood. Hold on, my sweet." Cruelly he dug his heels into the horse's flanks, holding the girl tightly with one arm, leaving Katya mud-splattered, stumbling after him, doubling over with heaving moans.

Sara stood motionless, her face buried in Jasch Kovalsky's soft broad shoulder. His huge body almost enveloped her tiny figure. Then hysteria swept over her with such violence that she thought she would choke on her sobs. She groaned and moaned and shook like a leaf. Tears and soot and rain smeared her cheeks. Jasch gently wiped her face with the corner of his own wet shirt. She looked into his eyes, her own black with terror. He smiled carefully to give her comfort. She swallowed and went limp in his arms.

Gently he lowered himself onto the tree trunk. He rocked her in his lap and stroked her shoulders comfortingly, murmuring nonsense words. Sara discovered to her relief that she could stop shaking. There was a comfort in his body that reminded her of something pleasant that had happened to her long ago. What was it, now? Vaguely she thought of her father, and Franz—was that his name?—and Karl-Heinz, who had come and had gone and had left nothing but dust in her heart. She felt a man's shirt buttons press into her forehead, and there was comfort and reassurance in that feeling.

"You are so pretty," he whispered, and she nodded.

She did not open her eyes, vowing she would never open them again. Big hands stroked her shoulderblades, slid under her armpits, carefully encircled her left breast. There was now a murky softness in the world where there had been stark terror a moment before.

Karin stood like a wet, shivering chick in the middle of a rain puddle, feeling her heart jerk under the impact of what she saw happening to her mother. She was a very perceptive child, and she had seen and heard many things in her young and turbulent life. But she had been innocent up to this moment. With an effort she turned away.

Thus it happened that Jasch Kovalsky, in a roundabout way, came to live after all under Katya's widening roof. He and Sara were solemnly wed amid clouds of billowing smoke to drive away the swarms of mosquitoes that kept the wedding guests slapping and scratching and twitching despite Walter's efforts to feed the fire with arms full of weeds. Katya moved her bed to the back of the house to leave the most sheltered partition of her hut to Jasch and his giggling, flustered bride.

"He is your father now," Katya explained to Karin. "Like it or not. He is the head of our family. He has a right to deference."

Karin did not like it, to be sure. Once she told Sara, so outraged she could barely speak:

"He tried to pinch my . . . my . . . well, all right, my buttocks, Mama! He bothers me, Mama! He follows me everywhere. One day he almost . . . "

"Shhh," said Sara, in alarm. "Don't ever say a thing like that again. Ohm Jasch is now the village *Schult*. And your teacher. And a minister, at that."

Marriage agreed with Sara. On Sundays, when one could sit and be idle, she would rest for hours in the shade, a half-asleep look on her face, and Ohm Jasch would every now and then stride by her chair and never fail to give Katya conspiratory winks out of the corner of his left eye.

"It may be for the best," Katya would think with a mixture of discomfort, irritation, and considerable guilt. The latter caused her much distress. For she was sure she did him wrong. Ohm Jasch was thoroughly converted and now a pious, God-fearing man. He loved to preach; oh, how he loved to preach! Sunday morning seemed never long enough to reaffirm all that so badly needed reaffirming. He was jealous of the time the congregation set aside to sing their never-ending hymns. He

245

carefully laid out the groundwork for what was to consume the rest of his ambivalent life: a fervor and enthusiasm for tradition more sharp and uncompromising than the scoffing which for so long had kept him out of the *Gemeend*. All his life he had longed to be part of the Mennonites and their solemn way of life. He had been born a bastard through no fault of his own and had become a communist out of revenge. Then, God forgive him, he had briefly turned National Socialist by default. Now, finally, he could be pious by conviction. It was easy with a people drenched in sweat and toil. All he needed to do was to firmly plant his smooth, convincing voice right into the leaderless vacuum that sucked him willingly into their midst and elevated him to spiritual heights.

During mornings in school, at home in the afternoon and on Sunday from the pulpit he would announce:

"We have to find our way back to the simplicity of our forefathers' faith."

He eagerly kept an eye and an ear to the north from whence came steady guidance as well as monetary support. Such help, however, was not without a price. The brethren in the north, fortunate in having bypassed the European wars, were steadier in their faith and had preserved intact their inner substance as a people; or so, at least, they virtuously claimed. The Paraguayan refugees, in contrast, the *Voice of Peace* now hinted—and Jasch most heartily agreed—had had to deal with decades of disruptive worldly pressures. Was it not, therefore, right to think such influences had marred their souls? Did Chaco Mennonites not tap their feet in a most unseemly manner to some of their most revered songs? And did they not look about in ways that must offend the Lord? And were they not, off and on, greatly tempted to listen to the radio at high volume?

"In school we teach the Bible," Jasch would say. "Both the Old and and New Testament. The Catechism. And our old songs. The Confession of Faith. And the Ten Commandments. And some numberwork and spelling. But no more! Being farmers, why would we want to be of literary mind? Such wealth as we have is enough. We have our skills. And our varied experiences. And our deep faith. Why try to outdo the Holy Spirit and His illumination?"

It did not seem strange to them to set such austere limits for their children. Why waste one's time and cram one's head full of nonsense when a never-ending workload waited at home? When all one could do was to take a deep breath and grasp the machete once more to keep the ravenous green enemy at bay? When ignorance as to the nature of this land caused them to make mistakes that gnawed away at their confidence? There was no time, no money, no strength left to worry about good, sound, sustaining schooling for their young.

Not that they didn't try! They had built a school in their first year to keep the children safe and out of danger while tree after monstrous tree came crashing down upon their land. The school had earthen floors, to be sure, and no screens yet on windows or doors, The rains would come and wear away the adobe blocks, and the sun would continue to dry the roof and make rethatching necessary. A chicken would wander in every day and lay an egg behind the curtain and disrupt the instruction with half an hour of cackling. But this was an improvement over those early times when pupils had sat on sawed-off logs under the naked sky and had had to write on their knees.

The village was very proud of its school. The women took turns renewing the floor and raking the ground each morning. They cut away the underbrush around the place where the children, barefoot and mosquito-bitten, spent their days. And when the numerous tiny feet had trampled the school yard into a dusty bowl and sandfleas had multiplied as a result, a small patch of Bermuda grass was brought from Asuncion, separated, and then carefully replanted, root by tiny root.

Joyfully they saw it sprout, stretching a dozen tender fingers to all sides. They kept it moist for days and put little fences around it and cautioned the littlest ones to watch the precious velvety spot. In no time at all, the school yard turned into a

247

matted blanket of clean, short lawn; the children could roll on it for diversion and the sandfleas almost disappeared.

"That helps to cut down on sweeping," observed the settlers with satisfaction. Each village woman took pride in planting a similar patch in front of her house.

It was a mistake that they would live to regret. In a few short years, the Bermuda grass became one of their worst enemies. Where it grew, it choked the life out of every other plant. Whole acres of cleared land had to be abandoned to the weed, turned over to the jungle once more. If they had thought that clearing the jungle was hard, they now saw that clearing the land of Bermuda was impossible.

"That's our way of life," said Karin one evening in the sharply critical voice she had of late adopted. "The Bermuda is a symbol of our way of life. A thing that looks so good and innocent in the beginning will start to grow and spread and choke."

She was referring, Katya knew, to a spiritual matter that had started as a joke in the *Gemeend,* but had quickly developed a life of its own, causing the village people to split according to their loyalties and align themselves into opposing, hostile camps—like iron filings on a magnet, repelling each other by an invisible uncompromising force. And Karin's jesting was at fault! If only Karin had kept her tongue! If only she would leave Ohm Jasch be! Ohm Jasch, who in his childhood had never properly learned to use a polished High German, had in his new-found zeal and fervor tried to mimic its sounds during one of his sermons, and had finished the weekly lesson with the traditional, time-hallowed words:

"Fauther, into Thy haunds I commaund my spirit, Aumen."

Karin's unmistakable giggle had started an instant crusade. In his hands, this issue became a pious banner to be carried, a holy war against those who used the bookish and snobbish High German. "Aumen" rolled much more easily off his awkward tongue. From the pulpit he thundered that anything else was worldly pronunciation. The Lord in His wisdom looked with disfavor upon those whose vain tongues would lead them astray.

Karin, deeply stung—for she was very conscious of words and of sounds—had declared war on Ohm Jasch with a vengeance. She had spent an entire afternoon lecturing him self-righteously about the virtues of keeping High German clean and uncontaminated.

Ohm Jasch had smiled his most benevolent smile. More was at stake here than admitting to a slip of a bastardly tongue. He felt himself to be carrying a torch. Those who still used the heretical pronunciation he would yet bring to their knees!

Feelings ran high in the villages for weeks. Numerous church meetings were held in which the Proud Ones were blasted with Bible quotations and wholesale excommunication was discussed with much heat. There was loud talk about a split in the *Gemeend*. People were readying themselves to pack up once more and move to virgin land for conscience's sake.

There was no question that this girl of Sara's had turned out to be a most painful, poisonous thorn in Ohm Jasch's complacent existence. Her wit was sharp, and her body restless, and her eyes without a flicker of respect. He knew she had detested him ever since she had been a spidery child, straying around abandoned trains, with Walter trailing her in dogged devotion. She still disliked him intensely, but what of that? He could easily make her pay in more than full measure, for in school he had his thumb on her all morning:

"Karin!"

She would always jump a little when unexpectedly called upon—it was as if a spring gave way at the slightest touch. "Yes, Teacher Kovalsky?"

"Section two, the Creation of the Angels," he would announce threateningly. "Are there creatures that were created in heaven?"

"Yes, the angels, Hebrews one, verses six to seven, and Colossians one, verse sixteen," she replied, hastily taking a stab in the dark. "The foremost angel Gabriel, the guardian of the Pearly Gate."

He had hoped to catch her off guard. He knew of her ambition to be first in recitations. He exulted in her vulnerability. He moved closer, hot with the satisfaction of seeing her wince under his stare. "What are angels?" he asked darkly.

"They are ministering spirits, Hebrews one, verse seven and fifteen."

"Hebrews one, verse fourteen," he corrected, hovering over her.

"Fifteen," she repeated, her voice rising sharply, forcing herself not to back away.

He permitted himself to squint secretly at his notes. Had he made a mistake? Hurriedly he kept on:

"Why has God created the holy angels?"

"That they may praise the Lord and serve Him."

"Have any of the angels fallen?"

"Yes, some have left their position and were placed before the Great Judgment and are chained in eternal darkness, Ju-Jude six."

"What are they called?"

"Evil spirits of the Devil, Luke seven, verse twenty-one, Mark five, verse twelve."

He let go of his victim reluctantly. She obviously knew her lesson. Carefully he wiped his gleaming forehead. The heat was intolerable, even though it was only ten in the morning. His missing leg was itching most annoyingly.

"That was Hebrews one, verse fourteen," said Walter later. "You were wrong, and you knew it. Why did you persist? Aren't you ashamed of yourself? You bluffed your way from page fourteen all the way through twenty-eight. How could you?"

"Ha! So what?"

"No, honestly, Karin. Why did you persist?"

"Who knows?" she replied, brooding. "There are many things I do simply because I have to."

She turned away and walked off by herself. She spent much of her time alone so she could daydream to her heart's content. She like to think of herself as a tiny soap bubble. She had a hidden beauty. A beauty that could be seen only in a certain light, at a certain angle, in very special circumstances. "I am special," she thought, savoring vanity. "If anyone touches me, I shall burst." She was careful to let no one know of her fragility.

Of late, she had become acutely aware of her own lack of good looks. Had she been born into a different family, it would not have mattered so much, for symmetry of face was not a thing that counted a feather's weight in Mennonite teaching. She was straight of build, and her hands were firm and capable, and her eyes incapable of deceit. But with someone like Sara for a mother, so delicate that she could wear high-heeled shoes on the Lord's day and not be reprimanded, and with Lily Marlene growing up to be a tinted China doll, and with Oma having been a famous beauty in her times, her own strange looks were more than a passing concern for the girl. Secretly, she strove very hard to look like a Mennonite—like Katya, to be sure. She ached to be like Katya.

Katya, it was agreed, was the very epitome of a Mennonite matriarch—a stately woman indeed: tall, whitehaired, high-cheeked, with a face forbiddingly reflecting centuries of Mennonite inbreeding. When she knew she was alone, Karin would study herself in the mirror. She had her mother's heavy black hair. But it was far too unruly, not sleek and close to the head. Her cheeks were too wide. Her eyes were too dark. She had a far too stubborn mouth. No, she was not Mennonite, she decided on such occasions, feeling alienation in the pit of her stomach. She did not even possess a name that she could for certain call her own. A name was for life; it had to fit right and feel homely. Her name did not belong to her, for some strange, unexplained, troubling reason. No one, to her knowledge, had ever been cursed with a name as ill-fitting as her own. Liese, and Tina, and Annie, yes. But Karin? She scratched its letters into the dust of the road, frowning with uncertainty.

251

Quickly she then erased the traces of her differentness, a little guiltily.

She kept after Sara:

"Mama, what is the use, I ask you? I know the Catechism. I can memorize, you know that. When I recite it flawlessly, I am supposed to have understood. When I am 18, I will be called before the congregation, and they will judge my conversion by how well I can memorize. And why should I memorize? Just to placate dear Ohm Jasch?

"Hush," said Sara. "The saying of the catechism is a very important event."

"I don't see that at all," replied the stubborn girl. "All I can see is that I am being made a Mennonite by coercion. I want to belong freely. Willingly."

"Karin!" replied Katya, shocked. "Child, what ails you!"

"I want to know things, Oma," she said helplessly, tears filling her eyes.

Katya asked, more gently: "What things?"

"Oh, books and things," said Karin, avoiding her grandmother's eyes.

"What books?" Katya edged closer, sensing the world creeping in on her beloved grandchild. "What kinds of books are you talking about?"

Karin turned red in violent anger. "Books other than the Bible," she said, taking a deep breath. "Books that tell of people. How people feel. Books that are interesting."

"Isn't the Holy Bible interesting?"

"No," said the girl, bracing herself. "I read through Luke three times last week. And what in the world have I gained? And while we are speaking of it . . . " Her voice became a little shrill, "I have to say something else. It seems to me that our catechism and our baptism are tickets into the shelter of the church. People love to hear confessions of sin, so some of us dream up a sin just so we can repent and be admitted into the arms of the *Gemeend*. Our baptisms are emotional occasions, and people thrive on them. I tell you this: if I had committed a sin, a real sin, I would

252

not tell the congregation. I'd keep it all to myself. For spite!"

Katya put down her needlework and sternly peered at Karin over her eyeglasses: "You are very obstinate," she observed.

"Come to think of it, I might do worse." Karin found herself unable to stop. "Because this is what I think: the only reason some young people join is so they can get married. If I don't repent, I can't be baptized, and I cannot marry unbaptized. So I have to sin and tell the congregation. In order to marry. And that I don't like. I mean, first being made to sin in order to have something to tell."

"You have that all twisted," replied Katya, worriedly studying Karin's flaming face. "What kind of talk is that? Why mix marriage and baptism and reading all in one great big pot of dissatisfaction? What is it that is like a barb in your heart? Did you argue about the shape of letters when you were first taught to read? You believed. You did not question that an "A" was an "A" and a "B" was a "B". You took it on faith so you would have a tool that would help you see meaning and beauty. And once you had learned your letters by faith, books made beautiful sense."

"Why worry about marriage?" added Sara, angrily. "And you not yet baptized! Besides, you've picked your boy, and heaven help those who stand in your way."

Karin, on the warpath, would carry her feuds for weeks at a time, feverishly in search of victims. Not even Ohm Jasch was safe from her then; she would trail him for hours and jeer his peace to shreds.

"Your biggest problem," she would announce, always careful to keep a safe distance from his stubby hands, "is that you think of yourself as God's elect. You think that there are no other people on God's mind than the Mennonites. There must be others who are different, and who are still God's children. But you think that no matter what you do, and no matter what others do to you, it will all come out all right in the end because you carry the label 'Mennonite.'"

"And why not? It is dangerous to doubt. In fact, it is

253

undesirable to be concerned about this kind of question. You should read what you understand, and what you don't understand, you should leave alone."

"Just tell me this," replied the girl. "Where did you get this belief that God is your personal benefactor?"

He said suavely:

"He will take care of us as long as we are faithful to him. Thus it is written."

"You did not answer me," said Karin in frustration. "You pulled a Bible verse out of your shirtsleeve."

At such times, Katya would come hastily to Jasch's assistance:

"Our tradition serves us as a guide. It has stood the test of time ever since our forefathers adopted our beliefs. And since it has stood the test of time, it must be true. There is no point in continually re-evaluating our beliefs. It can become a source of tension."

"Tension. Ha!"

"Yes, tension," said Sara, a suffering look on her face. "Can you sit and listen for as little as five minutes without getting heaven and earth mixed up in the most senseless arguments?"

"Perhaps you could try a little harder?" Katya pleaded, too.

Perhaps she could. She would try. It was the least she could do. She spent two weeks in school, copying page after voluminous page from the Scriptures until her fingers cramped to a fist and her eyes started to spurt tears that fell onto the stiff and upright words she had so laboriously written. The words stared back at her accusingly as she sat motionless, enveloped by misery. She pushed them away from herself.

Ohm Jasch was such a fool! Every word he said slowly killed her a little more with choking boredom and pious slime and hideous monotony. And yet he was there, he tormented her, he could not be ignored. But she would get even with him yet! What could she do to bring him low? Were people blind to that which was so obvious to her? She had to help to make them see.

For an entire glorious morning she followed him around,

254

studying the horror-stricken faces of those who discovered her misdeed but did not have the heart to tell. Ohm Jasch, surmising nothing, haughtily marched along the village street, nodding benevolent Sunday greetings left and right.

Lily Marlene, spotting the impudence, fell into an urgent trot, searching the area for Sara.

"Well, and now he walks around with a pig's tail on his rear, and guess who did it?" she let her mother know.

Sara turned pink with anger.

"Where is your sister?"

"How should I know?" replied the child. "She goes her own way, as everyone well knows."

Just then Ohm Jasch appeared around the corner, puffing and panting in great distress, holding in a tight grip the girl, who had stiffened like a colt and let herself be dragged along.

"This does it, Sara," he cried. "Sara! Where are you, Sara? This does it, I tell you." He yelled until he was out of breath and had to be given a cool drink of water by his flustered wife.

Duty demanded that Sara talk sense into her daughter that night, but Karin gritted her teeth and did not say a single word in her own defense. Therefore, Sara was forced to say with a sigh:

"I guess if that's the way it is . . . I guess if that's what you want . . . I guess your school days are over."

11

Walter had insisted that a well be dug near Aunt Katya's kitchen so she would not have to walk to the end of the village to carry the water she needed for washing and cooking. Therefore Ohm Jasch, a man of many talents, had taken to water-divining on nights of a generous moon.

Karin, of course, had been skeptical of such an endeavor, forcing him to challenge her one evening at suppertime:

"If you walk with me tonight and hold my hand, I'll show you how it works."

While the village people watched seriously, Ohm Jasch and Karin stalked solemnly along the neighbor path, hand in hand, stiffly holding a forked twig in front of them. His hand felt damp and soft in hers; she felt it tremble slightly. Their shadows were long before them, distorted by a tropical moon so bright it almost turned night into day. She felt the hair on her nape all but bristle and goosebumps tighten her spine. This was nonsense, was it not?

"Don't speak," he whispered. "Keep your eyes on the twig."

Karin swallowed. The moonlight turned brighter still.

At the site of an old, moss-covered tree he stopped and shouted triumphantly:

"See? See?"

"Heaven help me," thought Karin, in the grip of icy superstition. "That twig swings downward by itself!" She clutched at it with all her might. She felt the bark turn in her hand. She almost fainted in terror.

"You made it bend," she said weakly. "How could it have moved by itself?"

"Dig here," said Ohm Jasch with authority. "About thirty feet, I would guess."

"You made it turn on purpose," she said, recovering. "I couldn't hold onto it because you twisted it in my hands. Let Walter try it; he has stronger hands. Let someone else try it."

"It doesn't work with just anyone," he said, drawing himself up to lofty heights. "It works only with certain people. You have to have faith."

Resolutely, she walked the stretch by herself several times, trying her best to concentrate. Nothing happened.

"It works only with certain people," repeated Ohm Jasch. "Those who believe in miracles. You want to walk with me once more?"

"No," she said, feeling repulsion.

To Walter she said later, still shaky:

"You know what? He just wanted to squeeze my hand, the old lecher."

"Karin," said Walter. "Girl, for heaven's sake!"

"Well, it's true."

"You should not always doubt," said Walter. "It's an obsession with you. It's not becoming."

The well was dug in its designated place. Hundreds of pails of dirt were hoisted to the surface by the girls. It took many a week before they came upon water, but Walter would not give up. Each day he insisted upon being lowered into the deepening hole. Once, to Katya's fright, he lost consciousness in the well, for the soil, sandy and moist beneath, gave way under its own weight. He was brought to the surface, bluish and limp and ill for days to come. But that very same night, a yellowish, mildewy liquid collected at the bottom of the pit. Katya strained it several times through an old pillowcase, and hung it for cooling in a container high in a tree. Sara, ignoring warnings, took a sip without first boiling it, and had thus brought down upon herself a case of dysentery. Now she lay moaning and mortified with shame behind a blanket, struggling against the knives that churned in her intestines and sent her, shaking with weakness and pain, intermittently into the bushes behind the hut.

The seasons pushed on mightily.

Walter said:

"We need money. We need cash above all else."

"That's right," sighed Katya. "I need to buy sugar. And some rice and salt. And soap. And a spool of thread, if possible, for mending."

"I could cut firewood for the river boats," he suggested. "I could borrow Ohm Hein's wagon, and take it to the harbor, and with the money obtained we could contract with the natives for the clearing of the land. You and the girls would no longer need to work in the fields."

But Katya was very opposed at first:

"I don't want Paraguayans lingering around my homestead. Aunt Lena has warned me that one should not tempt the *Hiesige*

257

with things that can be easily carried away. She says they conspire to set fire to one end of the village in order to rob the other."

"We could hire them from the *estancia.*"

"All of Don Bartolo's men are lazy," she objected. "And I don't speak Spanish to tell them what to do."

"We could pay them a fixed price per acre," offered Walter. "That way, their slowness need not bother us. They would be free to set their own pace."

"I don't like the idea."

"We need the money, Aunt Katya."

Reluctantly, she gave in. She felt a deep distrust of the natives' lackadaisical habits. She felt affronted every time she drove by the *estancia,* where half a dozen men would sit slothfully in the shade of a tree, sipping their disgusting greenish *yerba mate,* their prime excuse for idling time away.

"Why, even our dogs run faster than theirs," Katya had noted with grim satisfaction.

"Lazy, lazy, lazy!" Ohm Jasch would heartily agree.

With a crosswise cut of his knife, Walter marked the tree trunks to be chopped. He worked all week, perspiration pouring in rivulets off his deeply tanned shoulder blades. He earned a handsome amount of cash. At the end of the week he rode to the store with the list Katya had given him tucked away in his belt, and when he came back, his *maletas* hung heavy on both sides of the horse's flanks, and out of his shirt pocket he pulled a fiery red ribbon for Karin's long unruly braids.

Her face was set aflame by his present. She knew that she would marry him in time, but it was not this knowledge that made her heart beat like a hammer in her chest. For there was Carlitos.

She was then fourteen. She was convinced that Carlitos was the most romantic youth that she had ever seen. He wore wide fringed trousers, held firmly in place by a broad painted belt. His embroidered shirt was of such whiteness that it would sting her eyes and make her lower her lashes as he rode by. His dark, gleaming hair could make her mouth go dry. He always smiled a greeting. Once, in an impatient gesture, he had pushed his hat onto his neck, and for a moment she had seen his face grow tense with youthful passion. When she remembered this look on his face, she would forget to do her work and would fold her hands in her lap and smile a slow, tentative smile.

"What's with our Karin?" Sara would sometimes inquire. And Karin would jump up as if pricked by a needle and shoot by her with great haste and urgency, murmuring: "Never mind. Never mind."

Sara would shrug and exclaim with a sigh: "I wish I knew what's bothering her."

"It's that time of her life," said Katya gently.

Sara winced. "She's still a child," she said, almost in contempt. "When she walks, she's all hands and feet."

That was very true. Karin was awkward and edgy, and more difficult to manage by the day. One evening, seeing her stepfather approach against the sinking sun, she made a face at him and smirked. His skin turned purple at the provocation. She squared her shoulders and stepped into his path, daring him. His horse was wild, she knew. What would he do? What could he do but swing his horse around and—she hoped—land with his big fat bottom in the dust?

"You crazy fool," he whispered, barely managing to pull the horse out of her path. She turned on her heels and stared after him, her face fallen in misery.

By now, their feud had intensified. The entire village took notice of the rising tension. Despising her arrogance, ridiculing her moodiness, forcing her to suppress every trace of her flourishing imagination, he did his best to crush her spirit. Karin, in relentless retaliation, called him a hypocrite to his face and complained bitterly to Oma that Mama was a fool for having married him. But Sara, whose sweet voice carried the choir all by herself on Sundays, shot sidelong glances at his gleaming face and found him quite tolerable. And even Katya, always mildly irritated by Jasch's presence, thought guiltily:

"He cannot be as bad as Karin makes him out to be."

For almost as soon as they had built a roof over their heads, who else but Ohm Jasch had started worrying out loud about the immortal souls of the migrating Indians at their gates?

The Indian School was called to life shortly thereafter, and villagers had grumbled for months. The money that was sent by the brethren in the north could have been put to better use. The struggle for sheer survival was still rigorous. And looking back into the past, one could assert that Mennonites had never troubled themselves with gaining converts for their church. To be sure, in better times in Russia, they had sent their missionaries out into the world to aid the Lord in His endeavor. Yet those who came to accept salvation through Mennonite intervention were thought of as Christians but not Mennonites. One was born a Mennonite; there simply was no other way. Was that not like Ohm Jasch, thought Katya, not to perceive this simple, essential distinction, since he himself had never been one, no matter how hard and how long he had tried?

But the stark fact was, she had to admit, that heathen were sitting at their gates and somehow had to be saved.

It was only natural to let Ohm Jasch take charge of this pressing endeavor. For one thing, his missing leg made working the land a painful undertaking. Besides, large sums of money were involved, and Ohm Jasch could add columns with astonishing speed. He was a very busy man these days. Twice daily he could be seen limping to the office he was now occupying behind the central village store, where he spent his time writing detailed letters to the northern churches asking for funds and yet more funds to bring Christ to the poor, disease-ridden, nomadic tribes that would be lost for sure, were it not for his timely intervention and the dollars he needed for his work.

"Not so long ago," he would explain, "they were a dull and apathetic lot. Now look at them and marvel! They are beginning to shed the influences of evil spirits. For a watermelon or a slice of buttered bread, they are now willing to let themselves be photographed. Some of them now wash their faces in the morning, although when sick, they do not wash, for fear it will mean certain death . . . "

Not that his missionary zeal turned out to be appreciated! What was one to do with creatures that needed to be talked to with one's hands and one's feet? "What is this?" "What do you call that?" They shook their heads and grinned amiably. They nodded to everything, not understanding at all. He held up his stubby fingers in exasperation: "Five!" he said. "One, two, three, four, five . . . " They seized his right hand and shouted: "A great many . . . " Then they grabbed his left thumb and cried, " . . . and a great many more . . . " Through the window he could see half a dozen old ones sitting in the sizzling sun, blinking not a bit and moving less, threatening him from time to time in fragments of a glowering Low German:

"We stink. And we are very mean."

" . . . they have no word for faith, but they know a term for *lie,*" he wrote. "They are full of fleas and vermin, and they dance during nights which are too cold. But no longer do they take to their heels at the sounds of a sewing machine.

He had a way with words. He knew by instinct how to touch the sensitivities and pocketbooks of other people. " . . . How can we teach them manners?" he inquired of his North American benefactors, "if their language has no 'thank you' and no 'please'? Only if we feed them can we teach them certain things."

It was a most frustrating undertaking. He had tried to bring the Gospel to the Indian children, taking for granted their young pliability and willingness. Had he not spent hours luring the dirty little creatures away from their parents and into his hut, where they would sit, naked and mosquito-bitten, scratching their sandflea-swollen feet and staring indifferently at the man who talked to them in words and signs they did not understand? And just when it seemed to him that he had finally succeeded in making a dent in their stubborn heathen souls, there would appear a hostile relative and walk straight through his palm

261

screen, snatch away the little ones, and disappear back into heresy on soundless feet.

"Persistence is what counts," he told Sara time and again.

Anyone could see that he loved his work with a passion, for its power as well as its built-in prestige. Now, when highly esteemed visitors arrived from Vancouver, they always stopped at his house. He could always count on Katya to have ready for his guests a huge plate of ham and eggs, and coffee water boiling before they had time to wash the dust off their feet. Yes, he was important indeed! He was a man of very many obligations. Weddings, baptisms, and funerals kept him in his Sunday suit deep into the work week when others had long since changed into their everyday, sweat-drenched clothes. For good measure, he appointed himself guardian of the young people's virtue as well, spending many a night sneaking up on lovers hiding behind the bushes or in the moonshade of huge barns. And his name, before too many years, appeared in bold print on the front page of a worldly influential paper telling of the miraculous progress taking place in the dry, dusty colonies of the diligent, undaunted Mennonites.

The hazards of jungle life began to take their toll. Many of the young children were chronically weakened by dysentery.

"It's the Chaco," the settlers would moan in exasperation. "It's the air. It's this Godforsaken land. Why, even our feet take on the flatness of this land. No one was flat-footed in Russia."

It was a blessing, many thought, that it took very little effort to raise pigs on their land. All one needed were some baskets full of sweet potato climbers, plenty of watermelons, some corn and *kaffir*. The colonists were accustomed to eating pork; back home lard and bacon and ham had been some of their most prized commodities. Pork had fortified them against the raging winter storms. Who could have told them that harm would come of ignorance and by adherence to outdated customs and habits?

Karin would sometimes protest:

262

"Will you please not pour so much straight lard over my food, Oma? It makes me so sick! I can't eat grease in this heat. It makes me throw up, Oma."

"It's good for you," urged Katya firmly. "We always ate *Griebenschmalz* in Russia. It makes the *manioc* go down."

"Manioc and pork! Pork and manioc!" cried Karin. "Day in, day out!"

"Don't slander *manioc!*" was Katya's severe reply.

The patch of *manioc* that flourished behind the house now stood six feet above the ground, and provided Katya with a reliable supply of tasty, nourishing roots. She was very grateful to the Lord for this plentiful provision. Lena had explained to her that such a patch would last for several years if she could manage to keep the weeds at bay.

"Crack an egg or two into your frying pan for variation," Lena had suggested. "You won't even know you are eating the roots of a tropical plant. You will come to appreciate the *manioc* yet, for it has a hundred uses in this land. You can feed it to chickens and horses and pigs. You can grind up the roots, mix them with water, and strain out the starch for your laundry. With the liquid that's left, you can smooth your floor free of cracks. You can cook a variety of soups with them, and you can bake buns and cooies and pies. It's our staple food here in the Chaco—we serve *manioc* to our families morning, noon, and night."

There was an ever-present craving for some tartness on Karin's tongue. She was hungry for something that had no name, though Oma had identified it as a craving for Russian fruit. In Waldheim, she told her grandchild often, there had always been available a wide assortment of fruit for the asking: apples, pears, cherries, plums, and apricots, inky mulberries and purple raspberries and clusters of grass-green, sour boysenberries that grew along the neighbor path.

"What did those fruits taste like?" Karin would ask, just to be told.

"They were not as sharp and bitter as the fruits here in the

Chaco. They had a firm, fleshy texture, and one would never tire of their taste. We had rows and rows of cherry trees which separated one homestead from the next." Then, invariably!

". . . Every farmer had his well-cared-for orchard behind his house . . . "

" . . . and we had to prop supports beneath the branches so heavy from fruit that one summer the gypsies . . . "

" . . . and the jams and jellies we made . . . "

" . . . and the special way we dried our apples for the winter so that during Christmastime . . . "

Here in the Chaco, they had to content themselves with the prickly, teeth-dulling *rosella.* This cotton-related plant grew abundantly along one side of the Bartolo corral, where the village children would sit for diversion, watching Carlitos and his men break into obedience the young, untamed horses. The hedge came to hold an enormous attraction, for its branches hung heavy with purple-red richness. One could put bud after bud into one's mouth, sucking its tartness with pleasure while watching Carlitos' magnificent riding skills and catching a teasing smile here and there.

Karin was convinced there was no horse, dancing and prancing with grace, straining against the reins with fervor, that would not calm down the moment the flamboyant native youth put his foot in the stirrups to force his strength upon the untamed beast. He would make it jump at will, and he would calm it with the slightest motion of his wrist. It would throw its forelegs in the air, and his body would be flush with the animal's spine. She never tired of watching him. Enthralled by the spectacular display of skill and daring, she barely noticed that the buds she was sucking were so acid they drew tears into her eyes and puckered her lips and tongue. This was exactly the kind of taste her rapidly growing body needed. Thus, in Karin's mind, the sight of Carlitos came to stand for a feeling of craving fulfilled.

She knew, of course, that Carlitos could never be trusted. Everyone in Neuland understood that not for one moment could a native be trusted with a Mennonite girl. Ever since she had come to the colony as a ten-year-old child, she had avoided the Paraguayan men. Terrible instincts lurked beneath their smooth and pleasant appearance, ready to jump the racial barrier at the slightest provocation. She knew that not even a little thing like taking his firm brown hand into her own would be permitted by her family. A proper Mennonite girl aware of her worth would not return a smile given by someone of foreign descent. Even young children were taught to hide behind the bushes at the sight of a native *peon* on a horse.

When Carlitos rode through Neuland, he was greeted cordially, yet with thinly concealed reservation. He was, after all, Don Bartolo's son, and Don Bartolo had helped them generously during their neediest, most difficult years. Yet they never quite learned to be at ease with this youth—what with his richly embroidered pantaloons and his wide-rimmed hat pushed brazenly back on his neck and a carved riding whip held loosely in his hands and a knife in clear view behind his belt!

Karin could only surmise the nature of Carlitos' power over her, but she knew, fully and instinctively, its utter inescapability. Under his sidelong glances, she trembled in distress. He was part and parcel of that nameless tormenting ghost that had taken hold of her spirit of late and would not let go. He was part of the endless green wilderness that was the Gran Chaco, and somehow, in his presence, there seemed to be the promise of release. Karin was drawn to him with a constant, steady pull, the way she was drawn periodically to the sour taste of the discovered hedge.

One day, driven by boredom and restlessness, she mounted her horse and took to the backroads of the village. She had to duck low in order to keep the branches from scratching her face. Out of breath and quite shaky, she had tied her horse to the palm tree in front of the *estancia* gate and had resolutely clapped her hands.

At the sound, half a dozen dogs roared to life beneath the trees. Frightened, she backed away. Carlitos disentangled himself from his hammock and put a reassuring arm around her back.

"I meant to ask you . . . I was just going this way by chance
. . . I saw some magazines you were reading . . . "

"Magazines?" he teased.

"Magazines," she replied, close to tears.

There were stacks of papers piled around him on the porch.
These magazines had come from the city. They contained
pictures of the world. And there were books, and stacks of loose-
leafed binders, and rolled-up sheets of drawings and maps, all
piled around his hammock in a most careless, disorderly fashion,
while he stood there languidly, taking such riches for granted,
laughing at her and her silly confusion, mocking her craving
with his dark, taunting eyes.

How she hungered for printer's ink different from that of the
Mennonites! The sight of these treasures and Carlitos' nearness
sent bolts of lightning through her veins. She trembled as his eyes
caressed her face. She was hot and cold with anticipation. An
abyss was there before her feet. All it took was a little step.

"Take whatever you want," he said with unconcern, loading
her arms with treasures. "I won't need them back until I return
to my studies at the end of the month."

Not long thereafter, he came to the village at dusk and
quietly motioned to the girl. She hurried with the milking. Oma,
she knew, would not watch her closely tonight. Lily Marlene had
turned weepy from a rash that had developed between her
shoulderblades; and Katya was preoccupied with giving her
relief. Walter was gone with a load of firewood for the boats.
Sara was off for choir practice, and Ohm Jasch had retired early
with a towel soaked in vinegar pressed against his neck where a
painful malady had settled from a toothache.

No one saw Karin slip out of the house. With her pulse
beating in her throat, she met Carlitos by the gate.

"I want to show you a miracle," he said. "Have you ever
seen the Queen of the Night in full bloom?"

The cool winds swept the grasses of the camp flush with the
scented earth. She felt as if she were in a church, alone, shaken
by wonderment. His flashlight, from time to time, made visible

the exquisite transparency of petals opening to a brief, luminous glow in the dark. Silently they watched as bud after bud unfolded to full beauty.

"They will be limp before dawn," he said. "They are most delicate. They last only part of the night, at most." His voice was thick. His hands lay on her bony shoulders. She felt it natural that they trembled. With an effort she said:

"Take me home. Please."

He lifted her onto his horse. They rode through the night, her face now pressed against his chest. At the village gate, he set her on her feet.

"Good night," she said uncertainly.

He did not answer. His horse stood motionless. Softly, she closed the gate. Her bones felt hollow. She felt as if she had been sucked dry of all emotions. She never told anyone of this night.

But how she waited for Carlitos' nearness afterwards, with a craving deep within her, with a longing close to madness, she was sure!

She tried to guess the hour he would ride by. When she heard his horse's hoofs, she would snatch up her water pails and rush to the well and would linger, trying her best to look aloof, shifting her yoke from shoulder to shoulder. At times he would lean deeply out of his saddle and unlatch for her the bolt at her gate, and she would feel his glance on her nape. She could see his dogs hanging in clusters at his silver-spurred heels. Once, while riding by after a brief, violent rain, he had sent a shower of mud all over her dress. She did not mind, however, she did not mind at all! It gave her an excuse to walk into the house and say loudly:

"Now look what Carlitos Bartolo has done to me." For his very name felt like honey on her lips.

This secret, forbidden attraction lasted throughout all of Karin's awakening, formative years. It made her bring home one day, wrapped in a worldly newspaper, a little *paraiso* seedling she had found behind Carlitos' corral. Lovingly, she planted it beside her gate and watered it each morning and built a little fence around it to keep the chickens away. The tiny tree shot up

267

toward the sky and in no time at all grew straight and tall. The very first year it spread around its stem a solid patch of shade.

"There are hundreds of seedlings like that on the *estancia*," she explained to Katya with pride, as if by mere gesture she could hand out treasures for the asking.

In time, the entire colony sank into the foliage of the *paraiso* trees. The hottest summer day became endurable. One could walk to church bareheaded, no longer feeling like a heathen with a straw hat on one's neck to keep from fainting from the rays. Perhaps a tiny bit of adaptation did not hurt as long as people were on guard against the encroachment of alien temptation? For no one forgot for even one second that there remained a clear, most distinct, concise division. There was the world of the Mennonites and the world of other people like Don Bartolo and his son. On guard they were, and remained so. And pity the one who tried to forget for even one moment why such a distance had to be!

This was the reason why a malicious rumor—how had it ever started?—so quickly crept from fence to fence, was passed along to neighbors at the village well, was picked up in passing and taken to the central store, from where it spread to the outskirts of the settlement. By night, it had reached the very edges of Neuland and beyond. The story ignited the homes like wildfire. It was strange how gossip could travel that fast, how it was possible that all should know except Katya, who—as the victim to be pitied greatly—was the last one to be told:

"Each night, your grandchild sits with a native on a stump behind the well."

Katya nearly died of mortification.

"*Ein Hiesiger!*" she cried, more sharply than she had ever spoken to anyone before in her life. "Child, have you lost your senses completely?"

"So what?" said Karin.

"So what? We are to keep to ourselves, as you well know."

"He is helpful and friendly and I like him a lot. He has never done anyone harm."

"Just last week, he cut through Janzen's fence and drove his cattle across his sugar cane patch."

"His peons did. It wasn't Carlitos. And do you know why? Because some of our boys rode at great speed through a herd of cattle which his men were driving along the road. It took hours to get the herd together again."

"Those boys were punished," replied Katya, "as well they should be! But what has that to do with your sitting with a native by the well? Don't ever cause us such embarrassment again!"

For weeks, she felt forced to atone. No one would let her forget her transgression, least of all Jasch. Each time she believed that the emotional waves had finally settled, he would lean back and grin maliciously and bare her disgrace anew.

"Ein Hiesiger," he would say, and snicker.

"A Paraguayan," she would reply.

"Natives know nothing about providing for the future. Do they know how to take advantage of opportunities that lie in their path? Lazy, lazy, lazy; that's all I can say."

"Not so long ago," Karin pointed out, cheeks flaming, "Paraguayans used the big two-wheeled *carretas* to haul everything from tree trunks to their sick people. And now one seldom sees those oxen wagons any more. They have been replaced by the four-wheeled wagons and pretty buggies that we are using here."

"Exactly," said he. "They learn from us, not we from them."

"Ha! And don't you spit in the sand, just like *ein Hiesiger?"* She was glad to win her point by exposing the habit she so loathed. He had become adept at spitting at the Wednesday night services—was it for emphasis or out of nervousness? She had come to judge the zeal of his speeches by the force with which he turned around and let go of his energy. "And don't you drink *terere* from morning till night even though you know it makes your teeth decay? And have you not learned to work only at the tail end of the day and take a *siesta* at noon, just like *ein Hiesiger?"*

269

He drew himself up to meet the challenge: "Compare our well-laid-out central town, our villages, our pretty homes in the midst of trees and orchards, our flower gardens, our fields heavy with good crops, our pastures fenced in and cared for, with their shabby huts and their lazy way of life! Don't we have reason to be proud?"

"We have done nothing more," said Karin, forced against her will to the wall, "than white-washed our homes. They are the same mud walls, and we drink the same muddy water, and we are just as poor, if not poorer, than the natives of this land. The only difference is our vanity."

At that, Katya laid down her work and looked at her sharply and said: "To dirty one's hands is no disgrace. To tolerate dirt, however is. We have separate rooms for sleeping, eating, and cooking, and we sweep our floors twice a day. You can walk the Chaco from end to end, and you will not find one native who thinks himself superior to the Mennonites. Nor will you find a Mennonite who thinks less of himself in comparison to a Paraguayan."

"Lazy, lazy, lazy!" Ohm Jasch would add for good measure.

Karin groped for substance. She, too, was justly proud of her colony. On both sides of a wide street that now stretched for miles into the bush, there was a double string of homes—one like the other, with gleaming windows and painted shutters and red geraniums back and front. Their citrus orchards were a pride and a joy to behold. Their fields stretched into far distances—clean, weedfree each spring, enclosed with barbed wire fencing to keep the cattle out. The hot, searing north winds would still do considerable damage, and would dry out the soil and take their toll from the ranks of the young, tender calves. But the harshest beginnings were now in the past. One could ride for days on end and still find cattle bearing the ear-cut of the Mennonites.

"And we did it alone," said Katya. "We did it with our own hands and with nothing but our willpower and the help of our God. We have important government visitors flown out to us into this wilderness who stand in awe before such feats as were

270

accomplished in this most lonely and barren place of all. We have been successful by any standard by which success can be measured, and we have done it in a few short years, while *Hiesige* have lived here all along and have never done anything else except lie in their hammocks and sing songs to the silvery moon."

What could one reply? Carlitos, as Karin found out shortly thereafter to her silent distress, had left once again for the city.

"To finish his studies," she would bravely explain, and stare people down.

But inwardly, she was deeply, irrevocably wounded. He was gone, and he had not bothered to tell her good-bye. To Katya's enormous relief, there was talk that his father had sent him away to woo and marry a rich native girl—a dark-eyed, skinny beauty, it was said, the daughter of a city friend.

Karin would have been hard pressed to tell just when she fully realized the gulf between herself and those who were her kind. At night, she would lie on her bed, hands folded behind her head, staring up into the darkness, acutely aware of a turbulence within her, a longing so dark and deep and pervasive that no words sufficed to even tell of its existence—this ever-present, incomprehensible, all-encompassing hunger that would not let her be. There was in her a constant searching, a restlessness that nibbled away at her strength, an impatience without purpose or clear goal or even well-defined boundaries.

Beneath her window, the people of the village would congregate night after night to visit with Ohm Jasch, who was steadily becoming more revered. By the flicker of the dim kerosene lamp swinging outside on the bitter orange tree, they would sit and listen to him talk. Ohm Jasch, it was now understood by all, was so truly full of wisdom from the past. He could spin threads that connected continents and oceans and past and present and future. There was such utter comfort in those evenings, when one could sit and stretch to all sides and feel in

271

one's bones a day's work well done. The land, having sucked in the heat of the day, kept pouring it back long after sundown in gulps of somewhat stale but comforting warmth. Every once in a while, the lower door would swing back, and Sara would move noiselessly between the guests, savoring the knowledge that her beauty could still stop the flow of words for a moment. She moved swiftly and with grace as she hospitably refilled the plates and cups. Katya could be heard humming softly and contentedly in the kitchen just beyond. One could sit at leisure and take one's time before talking.

Talk, though it was slow to start, had always been plentiful among Mennonites. The same predictable talk would swing back and forth like a pendulum, all night long, over weeks, over months, sometimes over very many years:

" . . . and then I went down to the waterhole to fetch my brothers Hans and Fetja, who were later slain by the anarchists, and I remember to this day how cool the grass was on my feet, how soft the water on my ankles . . . "

" . . . when the Whites retreated with the Red Army on their heels . . . "

" . . . We passed the Red Gate and left Hammer and Sickle behind . . . "

" . . . Our houses were roofed with durable red tiles. . . . Even the fences along the villages were made of brick or stone, with giant double entrance gates . . . "

" . . . towering acorn trees. They shaded the sidewalk and the fence behind. During Czarist times . . . "

" . . . That night we confiscated the black flag of Nestor Razin's army . . . "

This was the cue that now the legendary bandit would rise to life once again. Katya, as one who had witnessed his cruelty, would be called upon to testify so that the young ones would be told and stand revolted. Katya, at such times, would say quietly:

"He was an evil man such as the world had never seen. I believe my father whipped him once for using foul language in his presence. Many years later he killed my father and my

272

mother, and my twin brothers Peter and Paul. He killed our neighbor's three young children, and the baby he threw into the fire alive. He wiped out whole villages. He walked knee-deep in human blood, and he laughed as our people were dying . . . "

Karin's imagination ignited itself on these tales, when the Russian past took an overwhelming hold on the minds of the settlers.

"Oma, was that God's will?"

"No, child. It was not God's will. It was simply that the Devil proves stronger than our Lord once in a while. Those were very frightening times. The Red Army was fighting the White Army, and both were fighting the partisans. And everyone was fighting Nestor Razin. God in His wisdom saw fit to teach us humility through suffering." The old Mennonite woman studied Karin's face for a while, and then she said with a sigh:

"I wish I knew how to teach you humility in the Lord."

"What happened to Razin?" asked Karin.

"I don't know," said Katya. "He disappeared after his army dissolved. He was never heard of again. I am sure he died a very lonely death somewhere."

"Oma, where is God's justice?"

"It is not for us to question our heavenly Father's ways, Karin."

Karin's heart mutinied. Things were as they were meant to be. Somewhere, they had a meaning. Or did they? Her rebellion gave Karin a surge of power whose source she could not understand and was too young to question. With sobered concentration she gazed into her grandmother's eyes. Then she shrugged:

"I may be a lot of things," she said, and her face whitened a little from intensity. "But stupid, Oma, I am not!"

"Nobody thinks you are, Karin," replied Katya, mildly. "Who says you are?"

Memories lingered like the fire outside in Oma's oven, glimmering and smoking, flaring into beauty now and then. Those were the good, the valiant, the volatile days! They had

273

been part of two ferocious wars that had transformed the face of the world, that had reduced to dust and ashes institutions meant to last forever, that had extinguished kings and emperors meant to rule by the grace of God. They had been witnesses to the forces that had doomed these rulers to the bloody pages of a history that now became more myth than truth, more saga than reality, that was—they came to feel with clear-cut conviction— no more and no less than a mysteriously designed and meticulously executed plan to test the steadfastness of the last, mortally beleaguered and persecuted Russian Mennonites.

Karin listened with a keen ear for the epic flavor inherent in these tales, feeling bitterly the irony that never again would all this pain and sorrow be weighed and counted by someone capable of spelling out just why it had to end this way! She tried to grasp its essence: Homeland. Mother tongue. Folkish unity. Kinship. Customs and traditions tinged with reverence. God. His Bible. We as Mennonites. We the Chosen. Our impeccable virtues against the disintegration of 'the sinful world. A certain glamour, a keen excitement, could be had by simply reaching into one's storage of assorted memories—by taking broken bits and pieces, half-forgotten, distorted by time, shopworn yet still glistening, by stringing them and re-stringing them into colorful chains which would be gently passed back and forth for further adornment. Remember when . . . ?

No longer did she have the urge to join the people on the porch. She would bury her face beneath the pillow to shut out the ever-present voice of the past. She for one could never live up to such heroism as those people outside remembered with such obvious relish. She tossed in discomfort. She felt an unarticulated obligation edging in on her, enveloping her, suffocating her, draining her strength, sapping her spirit, making her mean and furious with an anger she could not understand, empty with a hollowness that ate at her day after day.

What did a world of excitement and disorder look like—she wondered dully. What could those times have meant to her, had she then been alive? How could it be that those bland,

274

simplehearted people beneath her window who now derived such pleasure from stories that had no beginning and no end and no texture in between were the same kind of people who had valiantly coped with chaos and lawlessness and anarchy and war and death and the repeated threat of total physical and spiritual annihilation? Where had such strength come from? How could they have emerged triumphantly? There was now such order and predictability to life. A rosebush planted sideways, she was sure, could turn into a cause for shunning.

Walter now held her left hand firmly in his right when they walked along the village street, each of them in a separate deeply-cut, rainwashed wagon track.

"We will never meet if we keep walking like this," she said, teasing him lightly, knowing that Walter took badly to teasing. "If we walk to the end of our life, we will never meet."

He replied, after thinking it over:

"We can't walk together on one track. That would be foolish. You stay on your side, and I'll stay on mine." People looked out of their windows, and shook their heads and said:

"Just what does Walter see in her, I would like to know?"

Sometimes she wondered herself. He had grown up with her. He owned her and loved her in his own quiet sensible way. Yes, of that she could be very sure! She felt his love all too clearly. At times she felt it like a chain around her legs, restricting her movements, making her trip and fall, or spring alive with incomprehensible, dissatisfied fury. But most of the time, she took him for granted. His strength was so different from her own. He knew how to absorb her searing emotions with a smile and a shrug.

"Imagine," she would challenge him, highly agitated, "if all the people in the world would suddenly turn into Mennonites. What would become of us? Aren't we the ones who must separate ourselves from the world? Would we then not create a different order?" Her eyes danced. "Is this perhaps how we started in the beginning? *Wanting* to be different? Holier than thou? Do you know what I mean?"

275

Walter found himself hard pressed under such searching questions. Karin would corner him constantly with problems no sane man would ever want to solve. He saw no point in questioning the reason for his existence. It did not lead anywhere. He was at a loss as to what to do with her—she was closer to him than anyone else in the world, but she certainly gave him no peace.

"You assume your father uses the Scriptures correctly," she would accuse him fervently. "You think that beliefs long embraced must therefore be valid. Why, just the other day he said, 'Dear brethren! Thinking comes from thanking ...'"

"I don't see anything wrong with that," replied Walter solemnly. "That sounds perfectly sensible to me."

She knew that she was quicker of mind and quicker of words than he. She had an unfailing ear for the finest shades of meaning, and she loved what she could do with language. He was helpless before her then, for he was trapped in mortal combat with High German grammar. And Low German would stretch only so far for handling twisted thoughts. It agonized him greatly and often made him tongue-tied and sullen. He seldom used High German. But Low German—homely, plain, gently affectionate—rolled off his lips and covered her like a comforting blanket. She loved to listen to him, for the sheer sensuous bliss of his low-keyed diphthonged speech. But when she answered, her words were sharp and precise, and she strove hard to keep her diphthongs out.

"I am trying to make a point," she told him as they rode the range. "I am talking about consistency. I am trying to see whether there is only a "yes" and a "no" to every word in the Bible, or whether there is some leeway. I have to test that. I have to find out. I have to come to a conclusion."

"See that calf over there? It has no earcut. I bet that's ours. That's Whitehead's calf. I haven't seen it for weeks. My, it has grown."

"If God's word is without fault, I see reason for submission. If, however, there is a double . . ."

"I should take it in for the night. I bet it has screw worms. Hold my stirrups, Karin, I'll try to lasso it."

The leather swirled through the air. The horses danced. She held onto the reins with all her might. The lasso cut into her hands. She took the horse around a tree to break the force of the struggling animal.

"For if God's rule is unshakable . . . " she yelled. The calf fell. Walter knelt at its throat. "Didn't I tell you?" he yelled back. "They have eaten away at the flanks to the very bones! Throw me the creosote jar, Karin."

12

It was about that time that there appeared in the villages a man of dubious intentions. Many suspected him of wanting to undermine the Chaco Mennonite way of life, because he went around the homesteads with a pencil stuck behind his ear. It was openly speculated that he had been sent from Canada to check on church life in the south, for there was strong consensus that of late the richer brethren were trying to lord it over the Chaco just a tiny bit too blatantly. Undoubtedly, there was tension now between the brethren here and those in the north. Did it not happen more and more often that those who were strong by worldly measure would give meagerly with one hand and write harsh rules and regulations with the other?

Times of need had always removed Mennonite barriers and borders, had always seen a tightening of brotherly love. But peaceful, uneventful times caused bitter strife to surface out of nowhere—strife as old as their history. Disputes and disagreements that were known to have echoed through generations—that were known to have split families and villages and often an entire *Gemeend*—now flourished unhindered in the heat of the Chaco. For was it not a matter of personal pride to be short-fused when it came to the purity of one's religious beliefs?

277

Was it not crucial to scrutinize with jealous zeal a brother's way of life and demand that it not deviate from the Scriptures by one iota?

It always puzzled Karin to learn about the forms such zeal could take. Some northern Mennonites had grown a beard, out of concern that otherwise the Lord might never recognize His own. Others in Canada felt strongly that their churches were adorned with far too many purple windows. A *Gemeend* in Pennsylvania was very fond of dark clothing, wearing white only twice in a lifetime: to be wed and to the grave. Most felt contempt for rings and ornaments. Some Mennonites in Mexico felt deep disdain for rubber tractor tires. Still others had coined a proverb in order to frighten their children into submission with the following threat:

> *Die mit Haken und Oesen*
> *Wird der Heiland erloesen*
> *Die mit Knoepfen und Taschen*
> *Wird der Teufel erhaschen.**

And some outlying villages in the Chaco colonies became fervently convinced with time that there was mortal sin inherent in baptismal sprinkling and insisted on dunking their young ones twice into a muddy waterhole behind the camp for true salvation's sake. So much confusion was there now in the *Gemeend* that those who had greatly suffered together took to warring with each other with spiritual zeal.

"What is wrong with the Chaco?" the *Voice of Peace* inquired with thinly disguised disdain. "Why is it that these people now lack a certain gratefulness? And why is their Indian mission still so slow in getting off the ground? Have they perhaps—made lazy by the sun—now abdicated their proverbial diligence?"

Such needling always brought an angry reply from Ohm Jasch:

---

*The ones with hooks and eyelets are going to be saved, while the ones with buttons and pockets are going to be snared by the Devil.

"Fly in with a suitcase full of film and take pictures of what Mennonite determination can do!" he would fume. "Slides tell nothing of the heat that can kill and the vermin that eats into one's flesh and the slime of locust clouds that devour in minutes weeks of back-breaking work."

It was the fallacy of the righteous North, no less, to think the Chaco struggle had now ceased. It was intolerable to read their patronizing letters; one could not help setting one's jaws and saying uncaring, hurtful words in response to such ignorance of the true dimensions of what was happening beneath the scourge of the merciless equatorial sun.

It was therefore natural to be suspicious of a stranger who came to live in their midst. Did he not brazenly—in broadest daylight, at that!—walk right along the village street, a smoking pipe between his teeth? Karin, smitten with awe at such daring, watched him intently. Would he let the pipe disappear into his pocket at the ominous sight of Ohm Jasch? But no, he kept it most casually in his hands and let the bluish smoke curl gently around Ohm Jasch's offended nostrils, talking to him in precise, strong, hard-clipped sentences while smiling at her now and then with friendly ease.

She had made Kurt Hartmann's acquaintance the previous week. During services she had glanced at him in curiosity and had observed that in the middle of a powerful Biblical passage, delivered with special aplomb by a very perturbed Ohm Jasch, he had casually pulled out his leatherbound notebook and had written with a fine and even hand:

"Linguistically, these people reflect a dichotomy. Theirs is a Sunday religion, dressed in a formal, stilted High German that is alien to the essence of this sect. A very anemic Low German, instead, serves as their awkward means of daily communication."

All throughout the sermon she had turned this passage over in her mind. She had never heard words of such weight. What did such language mean? She felt strangely stirred. She knew, did she not, that Mennonite life was holy and God-ordained? Her

279

complex nature was susceptible to the emotional tenor prevalent in their church: the spirit of solemnity, the utter respect for the Supreme Being, the total submission to His will and Word in hours of grief and sorrow. But she longed to test the sources of that solemnity, of that total reverence and awe. A part of her stood back and watched, and that part of her she knew to be her own.

As they walked out of the church, she stayed near the stranger's side. Struggling to hide her shyness, she asked him, softly, tugging at his sleeve:

"Are you a writer, sir?"

Surprised, he looked down upon the girl. "In a way," he said, kindly. "I am a semanticist, from Germany, temporarily located in the city. I try to understand the drive behind your people's faith."

She edged closer, eagerly. Mustering her courage, she asked: "What did you mean by dichotomy?"

"A gap between two poles," explained the stranger. "Or better, two mutually exclusive points."

"Sir?"

"I speak of faith versus reason," he said casually. "A question that is as old as the world. I, too, would like to know why faith and reason have to be arch enemies since the day God is supposed to have created the Garden of Eden."

"We have a saying in Low German," she said, struggling to understand, '*Je jeleada, je vetjeada.*' Which means the more you study, the more twisted your soul will become."

He looked at her in surprise.

"You are most perceptive," he observed. "How old are you?"

"Sixteen," she said, blushing with pleasure. Her blood felt heavy in her veins. She had no idea what he was talking about, nor did it really matter. This man used language with a purpose. This man did not need parables and Bible verses and allegories and fables to illustrate what he would say. It was a moment of searing recognition. Right here and now, she resolved, she would

280

attach herself to Kurt Hartmann with all the questions burning beneath her skin. She would hang onto him much like the *Lustjekrut* that grew in the camp and with a thousand tiny barbs stuck to one's clothes and did not let go. Indeed and double yes, she had a million questions at her fingertips right here and now with which she could cling to this rare find.

In the weeks to come, she discovered with an awesome feeling in her heart that she could simply dip into this chaos of confusion and pull out a question at random and ask without fear:

"Why arguments regarding pouring, or dipping, or dunking, or sprinkling? Aren't we all trying to get into the one and only heaven? For that matter, why baptize at all?"

"I have no idea," admitted her friend. "But I would guess it might be worry that imperfect knowledge of God's strict law might interfere with one's chances on Judgment Day."

She knew about Judgment Day, of course, the Solemn Day of Reckoning when the wheat would be sorted from the chaff. She had often been puzzled as to just how—by what measure—this screening of worth was to occur. Ohm Jasch was convinced of a sifting *en masse* on the final resurrection day, always insinuating she might be among those to be found sadly wanting. But Oma had been reassuring:

"It will be the Lord's decision on individual merit at the very moment of death," she had said. Karin found this thought comforting. Someone such as she might easily be cast aside in a massive sorting shuffle.

"How would the angel Gabriel know?" she asked her new-found friend.

"The angel—who?"

"The angel Gabriel. The guardian at the Pearly Gate."

"Oh. You mean St. Peter? I don't know. I guess there is a spiritual criterion of sorts."

"St. Peter?" she asked alarmed. "Peter the doubter, the restless disciple of Christ? Why would he, of all people, be given the task of sorting the sheep from the goats?"

281

"It's just a legend, Karin," said Kurt Hartmann. "Don't take it literally. Legends take different forms among different people to account for man's different ambivalences and fears."

"But how?" she insisted. "Why would we believe as we do in just a certain way?"

"I wish I knew," said he. "That is the fascination that binds me to your kind." He looked closely into her eyes, wondering from where such independent thinking could have sprung.

Karin would say:

"Oma insists that I run about as if to escape eternity."

"Do you?"

"Well, no," she replied, shocked. "It is just that I want so many different things." Her face colored a little at this confession. "I don't feel the way I am supposed to feel," she admitted, leaning closer.

She remembered with what passion, for example, she hated the sound of the milk as it streamed against the sides of the milking pail. She hated milking. Oh yes, she did, even though hate was a sinful emotion, to be suppressed in all circumstances. She, for one, hated the ugly creatures she had to milk. She shook with revulsion when a manure-stiff tail would fling into her face. She could not laugh and say, "Now . . . now!" the way a proper farm girl would.

Once she said, shyly: "I don't hear music. I can't sing. I can't paint. I look at a landscape and feel an ache where joy should be."

"You know that you are missing it," he said, looking along the monotonous street. "Where could you have learned? Where there's no nurture, there's no growth." He added, after a while: "Where talent is the greatest, Karin, frustration may be the greatest, too."

"Oma says I talk a lot of senseless, angry words. She says I talk beauty and certainty right into the ground. 'Talk less, and pray more,' says Oma, 'and see what will happen.' 'Your tongue is small,' she says, 'but it can start a fire that could consume your very soul.' She says: 'God has given you two ears but only one tongue. That means that you should listen twice as much as you speak.' She says: 'It is better to slip with your foot than with your tongue.'" And Karin would take a deep breath and say to her friend:

"It is hard to stand tall under such a siege." And she could be certain that he would understand.

"I know," he would say kindly.

With the right words at the right time, a pain could be chipped away, a darkness could be illuminated, a freedom of sorts replace force and constriction.

"I'll tell you something else," she said one day, taking a deep breath. "I lack true hunger for the Word of God."

Lightning did not strike. The day was young and cool. Her friend walked closely by her side.

"That is surprising," said he. "From where do you get your notions?"

"My notions get me," replied Karin, dimpling, flinging her braids to her back.

One day, sick with longing for Carlitos, she asked:

"Why can't I learn to speak Spanish? And go to the city to work?"

"Your German would be crushed by the sounds of the Latin language." He put an arm around her shoulder. "The ties to one's homeland are strong. Your German heritage is an astonishingly strong source for cultural unity on foreign soil."

She stood in awe before such revelations. An interpretation for everything was now at one's fingertips if one had eyes to see and ears to listen and a tongue to ask the right questions. It was just a peek into a different world that she was granted that year, but it was more than enough to sear her soul forever. It was a miracle how well Kurt Hartmann understood. His very voice brought order to her thoughts and calmness to her heart. He gave her such courage! He gave her the assurance to say to Sara at suppertime:

"The sun is not going to last forever, the way it says in the Book. It is a cooling body, believe it or not!"

To Oma she could say:

"Someone in the city has now invented a piece of machinery that blows hot air when it is cold, and cold air when it's hot, and all it takes is an electric cable to the house."

Walter could be taunted:

"In the city they now sell boxes that show talking pictures, right in one's living room, drawn out by an apparatus that hums like a bee."

She could even muster her courage and needle Ohm Jasch:

"And man has descended from the apes. Yes, sir!"

"From there it's but one single step to condoning animal desires," declared Ohm Jasch. "Your talk reminds me of a Chinese braid. It's in the way. It's useless. And it's vain. The sooner it falls, the better!"

There were times when Karin woke up in the middle of the night, bathed in perspiration, shaking with fear that in the morning her friend would be gone. She would gulp down her breakfast, watching the minutes tick by. When, finally, the front gate fell shut, the tremendous tension gave way; her face would turn white with relief. She lived in anticipation of his firm, strong handshake—a gesture that made her feel weak with gratitude. He would ask seriously: "Is my young lady ready?" opening the door wide for her to step through.

To Oma he would say: "Her sense of language is astonishing."

Sara would be informed:

"I may need her for three or four hours today. I will bring her back safely at noon."

And Ohm Jasch would be told, in passing: "I could never untangle Low German without her help."

He once said casually: "I have a friend in Asuncion who has heard of the diligence of the Mennonites. This man is looking for a place to build a sugar refinery."

"Hmmmm," said Ohm Jasch, cautiously.

"He is very rich. He could change the face of this colony, for he could give work to all. He is willing to wait for a profit, if the colony is willing to gamble on a new crop of sugar cane."

Ohm Jasch made a hasty mental calculation: "It grows faster than the weeds. It grows and grows and grows. It needs no care at all. You chop it up, you stick it in the ground, and you need never worry for twenty years or so."

"In five years," said Kurt Hartmann, "you could buy machinery for your land. Then you could do without horses. Your women could stay in the kitchen, and your children would not run barefoot any more. You could send them to school in the city. If you give me a note to the effect that . . ."

A note? Why would he ask for a note? Did he think Mennonites were natives who could not be trusted? Wasn't one's word good enough any more? And what about the North and its ever-present watchfulness? For as sure as the sun hung in the sky, if he as the elder were to entangle himself with a worldly enterprise, the ready money for his Indian mission would dry up.

For right from the start, Jasch had seen to it that private profit in the colony was vehemently denounced and sharply suppressed. There was this one and that one who might have been tempted to open a little store and make it his business to buy eggs and milk and fruit from the farmers and sell these commodities for a profit to Don Bartolo's *peons*. Hein Epp, to spite him, had once tried. But on Sunday he found himself sitting all by himself on his bench during services, with ears that were purple with shame.

Ohm Jasch, torn strongly between his pious loyalties and greed, felt compelled to call a meeting to bring this offer properly before the eyes of the *Gemeend*. It was gratifying to see that the settlers did not feel enticed at all. There was something wicked about a contract set in Spanish words. It turned friends into enemies; it would make them lose their sleep. They shook their heads and whispered. They became irritated with each other without knowing why. All were relieved when Jasch stepped forward and settled this matter with just a single question:

"Can we stand upright before our children, knowing that sugar is used to make alcohol? Are we to lend our hands to the Devil's work?"

Thus Kurt Hartmann's offer was firmly rejected. With a choking lump in her throat, Karin heard him come up the sidewalk, and by the way the front gate fell shut, she could tell that a weighty matter would now be decided. She held her breath in anticipation. Sara, very flustered, dropped the pot of *manioc* she held in her hands so that the pieces rolled all over the kitchen floor. Lily Marlene faded quietly into the darkness beyond. Oma squared her chin, readying herself for battle. Ohm Jasch, however, not a man to be intimidated easily by anyone of late, put a perspiring but jovial hand on Kurt Hartmann's shoulder and cried in heartfelt hospitality:

"Come in. Come in, dear friend. Sit down. Sit down. Bring another plate for our guest, Karin. Walter, give him your chair and go sit on the log over there."

"Thank you," said Kurt Hartmann politely, standing in the middle of the steaming water on the floor.

"I have come," he explained, "to talk to you about my dear friend Karin." He drew the girl to his side and held her lightly encircled in his arm. "I would like to do something for her future. She is a very gifted child."

Karin felt the blood rush to her cheeks.

"Yes," said Katya, guardedly. "God has endowed her with greatest gifts than most. Now it is up to her to use her blessings to the glory of the Lord."

"Why pay her a compliment for something that comes easy?" said Ohm Jasch in thinly disguised reproach. "Why tempt her with conceit when her humility is shaky anyway?"

"With your permission," said Kurt Hartmann, as if he hadn't heard, "I would like to take her along with me to the city. I have three girls of my own. She could stay with me and my wife and help with the household chores. In return, she could go to school with our daughters."

"Schooling," trumpeted Ohm Jasch, "is fine as long as it does not interfere with one's duty in the *Gemeend.* If she goes to the city, she will never come back! Some have gone and have not come back and have been lost to the world. We want our people to live among us."

Karin's heart pounded so hard against her ribs that she could barely breathe.

"Oh Oma! Please?"

"You crave excitement," worried Katya. "All kinds of curious questions grab hold of you, and all you need is a false prophet to come and take hold of your soul and hook your attention and give food to your sinful longing."

"There are services in Asuncion, too," she pleaded. "Carlitos told me once that one can hear a sermon on the radio on Sunday night."

"On the radio," proclaimed Ohm Jasch, scornfully. "And how do you know a man who hides behind a radio? He might be an Adventist, or a Baptist, or even a Jehovah's Witness, and all he might have in mind is to snare an unsuspecting soul."

And Katya could not help pointing out:

"If God had meant us to listen to a radio, it would have been mentioned in the Prophets." One could not trust Karin with a radio, and Karin not yet baptized! With her tendencies for rapture, at the mercy of a devilish instrument! She turned to the stranger politely:

"Books would make Karin lose interest in farming. People who read are always dissatisfied."

It was a well-known fact that too much reading softened the brain. It was so much safer to listen to a sermon that one had heard before, to build on that which had already been tried and found worthy by previous generations. And deepest truths, she knew with unshakable conviction, were better left unspoken anyway. One did not reach out with mortal hands to that which was eternal. Everything that was needed to guide fallible human

287

beings could be found between the pages of the Holy Book. It was more than a puzzle to her that Karin, who soaked up knowledge like a sponge, could somehow not absorb the Holy Scriptures. The good words washed over her and around her and colored her cheeks but did not make the slightest dent in her resistant soul.

"There would be no point," said Sara, quaintly. "She will marry Walter in two or three years, so there would be no purpose in stirring up her mind. She is too big, and too unruly, anyway, to be put behind a student's desk. But thank you for thinking of her, dear friend."

That visit had clearly harmed Karin, for in the days to come a strange contortion would rip across her face from time to time—a brief convulsion of such violence that Katya, all but frozen by a lurking terror barely kept at bay throughout the years, finally made this concession with a heart as heavy as lead:

"I might give you permission to go to the city to visit—for a week or two at the most."

Karin sucked into her nostrils the unfamiliar smell of hot asphalt, feeling faintly motionsick from her long voyage on the little river boat. Her bare toes curled in unaccustomed sandals. In her hand she held a crumpled envelope with Paraguayan coins. Cars flew by. A streetcar rattled around the corner. Overhead, a plane roared so low she ducked in fright. Her ears had never been assaulted by such noise! To her relief, she saw a cat swish by that did not look a bit different from the cats at home in the village. What an impressive, flamboyant, boisterous place! For the first time it dawned on her what human knowledge could accomplish, what human rigidity could prevent.

She looked about in curiosity.

The women promenading along the pier wore braids—long heavy tresses, wrapped tightly around their heads, or worn loosely with a flashing tortoise shell comb fastened to their necks. Long golden earrings were all but touching their shoulders. Young girls, not older than she herself, walked quickly about, with light, feathery steps, their small high-heeled feet squarely upon the ground, their eyes lustrous from sun and youth. Karin turned to Kurt Hartmann with breathless admiration, exclaiming loudly:

"My, but aren't non-Mennonites an elegant creation!"

Her friend took her by the arm, depositing her gently amid the soft cushions of a cab he had brought to a stop by a mere slight motion of his head. It purred with swiftness beneath her now, over street after pillared street, past roof after red-tiled roof, past courtyard after fragrant courtyard to the outskirts of this miracle of a vibrant, throbbing city. It came to a smooth halt in front of a wide lofty doorway which opened, she saw in passing, into a splendidly secluded yard.

Strange faces surrounded her; arms eager with welcome and warmth. A grey-haired, elegant woman held her to her bosom in a fragrant embrace.

"My wife," said Kurt Hartmann, smiling.

"How do you do?" whispered Karin, overwhelmed, shifting from foot to foot.

Above all else, insisted her gracious hostess, she was now to rest from her strenuous voyage of more than a week. Had it been only a week? Or had an eternity passed since she had come down the stream which divided the Mennonites to the west and the rest of the universe to the east?

She let herself be taken to a windowless bedroom, with walls more than three feet thick, superbly designed to keep out the heat and the noise. She slept a sound, dreamless sleep for a long stretch of time. She was awakened for a meal which was served beneath a roof all but buried in long twisted ivy clusters hanging richly to the ground. There was an earthen fireplace in front of which a very old woman—a Paraguayan servant, no doubt—busily stirred a pot of spicy food. The floor beneath her feet was tiled. Karin could see with sudden tightness around her chest that it was black with the smoke and dirt of many years, for Paraguayans, Oma had stressed many times, were blind to

289

the virtue of cleanliness, as some are regretfully blind to the splendid spectrum of colors. Here was stark evidence of Oma's belief! But the *chipa* she was now handed were as tasty as anything she had ever tried, white and tender as a dream, served with tiny curls of butter swimming in a bowl on top of chunks of crushed ice.

She ate carefully, hesitatingly but with pleasure. Those long, cylindrical rolls, Frau Hartmann explained smilingly, giving her a reassuring hug, were kneaded from starchy chunks of lard, lots of melted fat, salt, *manioc,* melted cheese, and drops of ice-cold water, then baked in earthen ovens to scented perfection. Would she like to have some more?

The sharp sound of a bell on the wall made her jump in fright. Through this black instrument one could speak into a distance, she was told. She stiffened. The conversation around the table ceased. Everyone was watching her.

"Fine . . . " she whispered, awestruck. Yes, she was rested. No, she was not tired any more. No. Yes. Oh, yes! Yes, Carlitos. To her horror, she caught herself giggling. She was close to tears from exultation, confusion, and fright. Kurt Hartmann gently replaced the receiver she left dangling to the floor. Frau Hartmann patted her hand.

"Carlitos will call for me," she explained loudly, blushing to the roots of her hair. She could not understand why everyone was laughing.

"I know," said Kurt Hartmann. "I called him and told him you were here."

She had not seen Carlitos for more than three years. She barely recognized his face. He was a stranger now, a man of the city, suave, self-assured, yet very handsome still. She kept glancing at him, trying to recall the graceful youth she had remembered in her dreams. The silver-spurred Carlitos of the *estancia* was not this man of the world.

They must have walked for hours along lanes framed with *cedras* and bitter orange trees. They walked past courtyard after courtyard, heavy with the summer scent of abundance in full bloom. Orchids hung in clusters from the wayside trees. Fireflies tumbled about the air, flashing mysteriously in the foliage that covered the borders of both sides of the road. The night was very warm and still, save for the gentle sound of guitars somewhere in the darkness just beyond.

Her shoulders ached from the weight of Carlitos' arm. Her heart ached from the weight of unarticulated feelings.

"There's dancing," she said timidly.

Several couples moved to the sweet wailing of some faraway guitars. They watched them awhile from behind the iron-grated wall.

"Would you like to dance?" Carlitos asked.

She shook her head regretfully. "I wouldn't know how," she confessed. "Dancing is forbidden in our life. It leads to evil longings."

"Does it now?" he said, pushing her gently against the wall, smiling down at her excited, flushed face.

She pulled hastily away from such temptation. But then, in sudden resolution, she turned swiftly and put her arms around his neck, having to reach up to his impressive height; and thus, on tiptoes, close to his face, she asked in great urgency:

"Can we, perhaps, Carlitos dear, one day be married—you and I?"

He smiled, bending closer. Any moment he would kiss her now. She closed her eyes in anticipation, as she was sure one needed to do to taste the utter sweetness of such a strategic moment.

He said:

"I am already married, you tempting little fool. As if you didn't know."

No, she had not known.

Walter was waiting for her at the pier, his face alight with relief. She climbed onto the buggy. She sat very close to his side as they rode along, in silent concentration, watching him swing the whip most artfully across the horses' backs. They reached

291

their village just in time to unfasten the gate for the cattle waiting patiently along the barbed wire fence, noses to the ground. As the latch behind them swung shut and the horses fell into an urgent trot, sensing that they were near home, Walter's arm was squarely around her back although it was not yet quite dark. From then on, whenever they walked together, they walked in step so as to serve notice to all that now they were openly promised to each other.

And as the coming years' seasons flowed into each other more swiftly and uneventfully than any previous years that people could remember, it was observed by even the most skeptical ones in the *Gemeend* that finally Karin was changing most surely from a defiant, willful, hard-headed child into a proper, demure young maiden. Even her sorely-tried stepfather could come to certain terms of peace with her—no small feat, it was agreed, given their preceding bitter feuding.

Ohm Jasch was now firmly entrenched in the life of the *Gemeend*. He was very gratified, therefore, to find that Karin no longer disagreed with him in matters pertaining to her needy soul's salvation. She sat quietly during services now, her embroidered handkerchief properly in her hands, her eyes in her lap, listening intently for hours to what he had to say.

"Two decades of ungodly communist teachings," he would thunder from the pulpit, mixing once more the well-tried Mennonite ingredients of politics and pious conviction, "did not destroy our deep faith in the promise of God's word. Did it? Did it, I ask you? And are we to slacken now in our zeal, now that we have liberty and freedom from persecution?" He leaned forward, peering fiercely at the congregation.

"No, it did not," said Karin to herself. "But neither does more than a decade of immaculate Chaco life make saints out of sinners." Such thoughts, though hidden now, would sear her still, the way a chronic fever would flare up on provocation and burrow into one's bones.

In unguarded moments, she would look shyly about her. Her peers grew up more silently now—a generation, she was convinced, of look-alikes, feel-alikes. All of them content, to be sure, complacent and happy. All of them, save herself, already in the possession of the Lord. And why should it be different with her? With a bitter taste in her mouth she remembered the story of an arrogant braggart who had once declared: "Give me a place to stand and I will lift the world out of its hinges." Had such outrageous insolence made even one iota of difference, as far as she could see? The earth still remained where it had always been, and let the sun, moon, and stars rotate around it. Such teaching, she herself could now see, was certainly useless baggage.

Did she come closer in those years to being purged for good of her persistent worldly longing? Even Katya, always cognizant of a strangely disturbing, low-keyed worry that would not let her be, could not be sure of that. When questioning herself in such moments—for it was up to her alone, she knew, to make her grandchild see the light—it seemed to her·that she had wasted her time calling Karin's attention to the well-fitting but trifling pieces that made up the mosaic of Mennonite life, that were the sum and summary of the sacred and beautiful patterns of esteemed, austere Mennonite living. For certainly there was a continuity to their existence once again, as births and weddings and deaths continued to draw them together, to bind them to each other more tightly still, as cups were filled with scented coffee in sorrow as well as in happiness, as stories were told and retold, as German songs were sung and German poems were recited and Ohm Jasch's sermons grew more convincing by the year. But pieces alone, if ever so pretty, had never made sense to Karin. Karin lacked the years and the patience and the distance to stand back and comprehend.

There was no mistaking the message when Ohm Jasch leaned forward, shouting: "We were in the throes of the Devil! Let us pause and give thanks. This is occasion for serious contemplation, for is there even one family in our midst which has not paid with precious blood for leaving the Narrow but Promising Path?"

293

The following years, made ever more confident by Karin's apparent surrender, the ingredients of his sermons became spiced with hints and warnings to spare. Like a sledgehammer he would let God's fist fall upon the hushed congregation. Even young children, the smell of brimstone in their nostrils, would rise and give sobbing testimony of angels that had visited them in their sleep. The church was all but filled with the mighty thunder of damnation. Night after night he shook the listeners' consciences, night after night he saw to it that people came forward, crushed into tearful remorse by their guilt, humbly asking his forgiveness and his guidance. At times he would weep along for good measure, frustrated by the resistance of certain members in the *Gemeend* who laxly held that one conversion was enough, who would shrug off the renewed salvation which he promoted with such sweat.

"Once saved, always saved?" he would shout, accusingly. "That's what you think! It's a must to have an up-to-date understanding with the Lord. We are sinners. Indeed we are! Indeed! Indeed! We have to be reborn again and again, John seven, verse twenty-two." He would spread his stubby fingers and count out the congregation's many sins: Selfishness. Irritability in the heat. Habitual complaining about God's weather. Gossip that did not stop before a neighbor's bed. Grudges against a brother more diligent than oneself. Jealousy toward the North. Lack of gratitude. Bickering. Harshness with the Indians. At strategic points he would circulate the collection plate, hovering near to make sure that enough was given for his mission. He would count out how much had been collected, how much was missing still. "Giving is better than taking," he would assure the congregation, walking away with the offerings. Returning, he would startle Sara out of a little dozing twilight dream with an unexpected roar:

"Aren't we all stingy, miserable louts? Aren't we? Eh? Eh? Aren't we? Aren't we all?"

Sara would nod vigorously and daintily rearrange her skirts about her legs. Jasch, reassured, would draw himself up to his

294

full pudgy height, fix a glowering eye on this sinner and that, and point out—stabbing the Bible with his forefinger for emphasis—that God was a God of revenge as well as a God of eternal patience. He took great care to alternate harsh and wounding words with verses that were soothing. Sara, sensing the end of the sermon, would start to sing softly: "Jesus is all that we need," pleasing the congregation with her pure, silken voice. She was very proud of her singing; she would look about coyly, and Karin would bite her lower lip and keep her eyes averted. Then, overcome by humility and shame at her own daring, Sara would bend her head and shade her eyes behind her hand, and Ohm Jasch, with proud satisfaction, would wipe his forehead with a handkerchief embroidered by the Indians, who now sold such useful items at the village store.

For the last half hour, Karin knew, Ohm Jasch would shut his book and rely on memory and zeal. Lily Marlene smiled sweetly in Walter's direction, openly glad that the final "amen" was drawing near. Karin stifled a sigh. She tried to concentrate. Another fifteen minutes. Outside, the midday rays were blazing. Please, God, forgive Ohm Jasch his many useless words. Oh, please, just make it short today.

At Ohm Jasch's insistence, Karin had seriously taken to studying the Book of John. This book, she discovered to her surprise, was of a complicated nature, full of puzzles and teasing hints. Why had she never seen its artfulness before? There were treasures to be found, she realized with a sudden surge of eagerness. It would come into focus, surely, if only she could hold herself humble enough for the illuminating light. But the beauty she thought she had found became leaden-footed as soon as Ohm Jasch laid claim to it for one of his sermons each week.

She came to perceive an astonishing truth: that Ohm Jasch could meticulously interpret the Bible to the last detail and at the same time be perfectly tedious and odious. His vague, blatant fumbling enraged her to tears. He plowed away doggedly through the staleness of his imagery. He perspired from lack of precision. Did he have a kernel of truth somewhere that he did not know how to bring to light? Or was he totally indifferent as to whether his message meant anything at all? Did he just like to hear himself talk and watch the congregation listen attentively to what he had to say? Just what was at the roots of his muddled confusion?

No one could point a finger and claim she didn't try. She did her best. Now when she walked along the village road, she did so with lowered lashes, careful not to offend, inwardly cringing. But when she was spoken to, she could still spring to life. She would reply feverishly, spilling disjointed words, dart-like with hurt and despair. People did not like her ways. But less often than in the past was it now said of her: "She has been out of step from the beginning."

"What are you waiting for?" Katya would ask sadly. "What is it you want?" For even to her patient mind the Holy Spirit was far too slow in enlightening Karin.

But Karin would only shake her head.

"You could marry, you know."

"Oh, Oma!"

Katya felt helpless before such agony. How could she, a simple woman, put profound thoughts and feelings into frail mortal words? She looked at Karin and saw in her the white-hot intelligence that had driven . . . Resolutely she quenched her forbidden thoughts. But could she help that every once in a while her heart would painfully constrict with fear that the evil that had once laid claim to her youth would now destroy this child? What could she do? She felt a lump in her chest every time she saw Karin lift her chin in defiance.

Most frequently, she had observed of late, Karin was thrown into a mood of serious contemplation by the fervor of their songs. These songs—handed down from many previous generations—had clearly retained a spiritual life of their own. The tunes, to be sure, had become dragging with use; somewhere along the way, the content had been partially lost. Verses, truncated beyond recognition, had had to be patched and repaired so often that strangers like Kurt Hartmann might wince, not understanding the comfort that came with familiarity. For centuries, Mennonites had sung the songs from their noteless and meterless songbooks. There was a reason, moreover, why hymns were dragged out to unbearable lengths. They had to help fill out a four-hour service. Those gifted with musical talent had found a way of preserving the hymns by translating the tunes into numbers which even the unmusical ones could grasp—"four, seven, seven, six, five-four-three..." —until the words could be safely hitched to the melody and the song leader could call out next Sunday with a loud and confident voice:

"Oh, That I Had a Thousand Voices ... "

Katya's faith had solidified firmly. She had carefully sorted out of her life those truths that truly mattered, and the rest she had put out of her mind and forgotten. This was as it should be. The pioneer years had shortened her breath, had twisted her spine, had weakened her knees. But she was part and parcel of a people content within themselves, convinced that everything in this world had its order and its certainty, if only one had the insight and the patience and the humility to wait out God's inscrutable plans. What more was there to ask?

Katya most dearly loved her life the way it was now. By worldly standards, she and her kind were still poor, compared to the way they had been in her youth. But there was a vast comfort in the demure, still pleasures of life. It was a luxury to open doors and windows without fearing the evils of a wicked world. It was exhilarating at night to hear the winds move across the prairie and bring with them the shrill sounds of crickets at mating time. The odors of the Chaco spring would mingle with the scent of freshly plowed land. The days were still hot, but her windows were shaded thickly by the foliage of the *paraiso* trees, and if she remembered to close the shutters each morning, the inside of her house remained dark and cool quite far into the day. A glance could reaffirm the perfect order she had helped to create: the beautifully cared-for flowers outside on her window sill, the curtains starched to perfection, the floors swept free of ants, the whitewashed gigantic *lapacho* outside on which the little monkeys still swung on certain days before a rain, yelling and marauding, or sitting motionless for hours, watching the people inside with beady curious eyes. She was very fond of the funny creatures, although most settlers saw them as a nuisance—howling for weeks at a time, for spite, they were sure!—when rain was on the horizon but could not push up far enough to drench their thirsty land.

Where had the years gone so swiftly? Spring had been but a dream, now barely remembered. Summer was past now; a fall had come upon her filled with work, as autumn days should be. There were times now when she was weary with old-age giddiness. She would sit for hours, hands folded in her lap. Her body moved slowly under the weight of her years. She had shrunk a little in size. Her heavy frame was now bent, her hair as white as snow. Into her face were deeply carved the painful struggles of her life, but her eyes were clear and calm and full of a mellow, subdued wonder.

The end, she knew, was at her elbow now.

She would say wistfully: "Most of my loved ones are waiting on the other side of the river Jordan. Death, where is thy sting?"

She would take Karin's arm for support:

"Let's go. Ohm Jasch has left already. And don't forget to sit straight today. Please, dear! Your posture weakens your concentration."

"Yes, Oma."

"We are late," Katya would urge her on with great impatience. "Let's hurry up, child."

"There is plenty of time, Oma. More than enough time!"

"I don't like to walk in in the middle of the sermon. People stare."

"Don't worry. They have only now begun to sing."

Karin could hear the singing voices from afar, loud and unmelodious but lusty and straight from the heart. Singing was a lawful means for, giving vent to pent-up emotions. The palm screens shook and the chickens scurried into the bushes. The song, Karin knew, was the warming-up prelude for the thunder of damnation that was picking up momentum just as they entered the church.

Walter handed her the songbook, frowning at the interruption. Karin swallowed. She tried to find her place, but the pages were suddenly blurred by tears that came unprovoked, out of nowhere. She moved her lips silently. What was the matter with her ears? She could not make out a single solitary word. She heard some sounds but the words did not make sense. The Tower of Babel became a reality.

" . . . has our life been fruitful up to now, or barren . . . Search my ways, O Lord, and decide who I am. . . . on an evil path . . . Psalm 139, twenty-three, twenty-four . . . We are in debt in God's ledger . . . "

Oh, the horrid barrenness of contentment where a pulse should have been! She would have to pull herself together! Ohm Jasch, she could see, was edging closer to the German proverbs, of which he kept a generous supply so that they would haunt her throughout the week with their stern admonitions. After the proverbs, she knew, he would pick away for a while on a concrete example of sinful behavior. If she wasn't the target, perhaps she could tune out his voice for an hour. Yes, here he was now, blasting full force the despicable vice of card playing among the youth in the *Gemeend,* a habit that had become rampant of late.

" . . . You may say that games are games and that there is no difference between a game of dominoes and a game of cards. Or a game of hop-scotch, for that matter! Oh, but there is! There is, dear brethren in Christ! Our legends depict Satan with cards in his hands. Therefore, card games are clearly the Devil's invention. Our grandparents knew there was a curse upon cards. Didn't many of our Russian workers gamble away in one night what took them a summer to earn? . . . "

Another half hour, and Ohm Jasch would have safely arrived at the promise of deliverance from sinful worldly longings. She could see that the congregation had already begun to show signs of a mollified transformation. The scolding was almost over for the week. People leaned back and breathed a sigh of relief. If she could only sit through the citations!

" . . . Romans three, verse nineteen and Romans one, verse fourteen. . . . even though our sins are redder than blood. . . . fullest absolution. . . . thank God, Micah seven, verse nine, and first John one, seven to nine . . . seven times seven . . . times seven... times seven... There Shall Be Showers of Blessings..."

The song, she was sure, was designed to strangle her on the spot. She glanced at Walter under her eyelashes, astonished that such tedium could be endured so blandly. He sat stiffly, his knees pressed against each other. Perspiration, she could see, had trickled down to his collar. But surely he must understand! She reached across the aisle and tapped his shoulder. He turned his head unwillingly. Hastily she withdrew her hand.

Ohm Jasch now took up with eagerness the countdown of her many sins: "Conceit," she heard him say. "Dissatisfaction. Grumbling. Jealousy. Lusting for the world." She tried to arouse herself to a prayer. But there was the devil now in her neck, locking her jaws so that no word came out. She tried to use her fingers to atone for what she had done—all her sins which were supposed to crush her now. But why? Why should she ask for forgiveness when God knew perfectly well the thing she had or had not done? When He was the One who should really be held accountable for the way she had turned out, with all of her virtues and vices?

With a strangled sob, she threw the songbook to the floor.

"I don't feel well," she whispered, struggling past Katya, stumbling blindly past the startled congregation, swaying in the sunlight as it struck her full force the moment she stepped outside.

"I must calm myself," she thought in panic.

She must keep her tears in check; she must find a way to control that helpless, choking, twisting, raging feeling that had no focus and no purpose and no beginning and no end! She walked more slowly now along the village street, feeling

300

sticky with perspiration, bloated with millions of unwept tears, feeling ugly, deserted, misunderstood, utterly alone in the universe, a pitchblack mutiny in her heart. She sat down on the tree stump opposite Ohm Wiebe's house and put a trembling hand to her face. And there she took the balance of her life, and this is what she said:

"By God, I am cheated."

She listened closely. Would she be stricken from above? She kept on: "I am cheated. I feel nothing. I feel absolutely nothing that has any meaning for me at all. Am I crazy? I must be out of my mind. I must be losing my sanity. Is that what it is? Oh, God Almighty! Listen to me! I am at my wit's end; that's all I can say."

Walter had cut away the lowest branches of the citrus trees to make room for the seating arrangements beneath. From where Katya stood by the window, she could therefore easily see that the first rows of the benches had already filled with wedding guests important enough to come early. Late yesterday, Sara had sent eight girls to go from door to door with flower-decorated baskets in order to collect the many dishes and utensils that would be needed for the extended celebration—cups and saucers, spoons and forks and knives, salad bowls and cake server, half a dozen coffee pots. Lily had made it her task to oversee that everything was perfectly arranged, for the dishes were to be marked, the silverware polished, the three dozen tablecloths washed and ironed to perfection so that no shame would fall upon the bride. Katya had laid claim to the village *grapen* for an entire week—that huge, cast-iron pot-bellied monster of a container which served the village for so many uses throughout the year: to simmer the sugar cane syrup to yellowy luster, to fry out the lard during hog-killing days, to hold, on festive occasions, the main course of the elaborate meal. Forty gallons of the tastiest Ukrainian *borscht* now bubbled aromatically beneath the old *lapacho* tree.

At the back of the house, five women were up to their

301

elbows in huge basins filled with ground meat, kneading onions, salt, and pepper into the pinkish, sweet-smelling mixture. Seventy of Katya's finest chickens had had to lose their heads the previous night. The *manioc* salad was ready, decorated to perfection under Sara's watchful eye. There were *rosella* pies and desserts in the pantry—enough to satisfy an army, Ohm Jasch had proudly observed. Katya, by the window, could see Lily Marlene take out a basket heaped with buns to offer to the village men, who had already started digging the hole that was to hold the grid for the barbecued meat.

For days, Neuland had hummed like a beehive with expectation. At this very moment, Katya could see a ripple of anticipation run through the wedding guests as little children, here and there, rushed to the street at the sound of rolling wheels:

"They are coming! They are coming!"

"There are the Ensens now."

"And the Wiebes."

"And there are the Janzens from village Number Four."

Buggy after buggy lined up along the street, packed to the brim with fodder to last at least three days. "Mennonite hospitality is truly taxed to its limits on occasions such as this," thought Katya with proud satisfaction. "And who would have had it any other way? A happy, well-planned wedding is truly the highest point of earthly joy."

She was dizzy with contentment and the strain of days of frenzied work. This was her day as much as Karin's—perhaps even more! Very early this morning, she had counted out bowl after bowl of whitest flour from her pantry, to be mixed with the boiled and cooled milk that the village women had brought to her home late last night. The dough had been carefully stirred, then covered with a clean towel to rise to twice its size, then kneaded and punched to springy elasticity, then covered again to rest and ferment. Around noon, it was ready to be held between the palms of her hands. For over an hour, with a much-practiced, artful little twist, round sweet-smelling balls of dough had been placed on buttered baking sheets. Three of her neighbors had helped. Walter had been put in charge of keeping the ovens hot; and though she trusted his skills and his conscientiousness, she felt she had to make doubly sure the heat would be just right. So she had pushed him aside time and again with impatience to put her own hand into the earthen oven and quickly count to ten. But it had all been worth her worry! The *zwieback* now piled nearly to the ceiling on a bleached sheet across her bed were as white and as tender as any wedding *zwieback* she herself had ever tried.

Countless times this past week, she had hurried from the kitchen to the house, back to the barn, along the neighbor path, and back home again, worrying and fretting:

"Is everything all right? What if the coffee runs out . . . ?"

Early this morning, a quick glance had reassured Katya that the neighbors had done their work. The yards and streets had been swept clean of the week's leaves. The church pews had been dusted. Fresh flowers had been put on the altar. But in between all that commotion—how had she managed to keep her head?—she had squeezed out a silent minute here and there for a brief prayerful moment alone: "Thank God she has finally come to her senses!"

She took a deep, satisfied breath, watching with pleasure the steady stream of wedding guests that now began to pour in droves through the rose-decorated gate. One could already hear the shouts of the village youths announcing their arrival to the giggling girls along the benches. Any moment now, the bride and groom would arrive.

Ohm Jasch flung open the gate. Yes, here they were, her two dearest worrisome children! The horses, alive with the excitement in the air, shaking their heads and swishing their carefully brushed long tails, shot through the opening and came to a gliding stop in the middle of the yard. The bride, swinging fold after fold of her wedding dress over her arm, tried to peel herself out of the seat and step down from the ornamented buggy. And Karin was most certainly a beautiful sight to behold!

Anyone who had ever felt any misgivings at all must now be silenced by such elegance! Her skirt was wider than any thus far worn by Neuland brides, faced by a ribbon as wide as the palm of Katya's hand. The stitches along her hem were invisible, as well they should be. Her collar was starched to perfection. She now lowered herself from the buggy, holding onto Walter's arm. Katya put a final trembling hand to her hair, as she readied herself to walk forward to put her arms around her grandchild and the serious, sensible youth she had long ago come to count as her own. And as she stepped out of her door, she saw Carlitos Bartolo leaning languidly against a tree.

Karin, too, had seen Carlitos' horse tied to the gate, and her heart had started a slow, painful beat of its own. During these last five, six, seven resentful, mutinous years, she had gone out of her way to violate many an unwritten code of meticulous living, but this much she knew: One did not invite into one's midst on a day such as this a native of this land! *Ein Hiesiger* at her wedding! She had nothing to do with his being here. She had not seen Carlitos nor heard a solitary word from him since her fateful visit to the city more than three years ago, and she was sure she did not care if she never laid eyes on him again! Yet everyone would think that she had written to him and had invited him here, to wound Walter and put grief into her grandmother's heart.

Raw fear made her stumble a little. She saw the village girls sitting in the front rows, eyes downcast in embarrassment and shame. She saw that Neuland's young men had retreated to the barn, where they stood hovering in ominous clusters. She knew that any moment now a fury would whip loose such as the colony had never seen. Village boys were very protective of their girls; it had always been accepted custom for village youths to beat up their rivals from other colonies. The ministers had been busy admonishing the hotheads to give up such a childish practice since love should be permitted to fall where it may. But this was no simple jealousy; this was vastly different indeed. Carlitos Bartolo had come to defile an unwritten sacred

304

tradition; and to add insult to injury, he had not come alone, he had brought along a dozen of his men.

Carlitos, not sensing that the air was crackling with tension, smiled warmly and raised a hand to greet the bride and the groom. Karin saw him reach backwards and fetch out a hidden guitar. It was a beautiful instrument. She could not help being touched by the very grace with which he held it in his narrow hands. The double metallic strings gleamed in the light. His fingers now gently called to life a tune that was tender, yet tinged with longing, a poignant Spanish love song rising and falling fitfully, rejoicing and teasing, yet imperceptibly sad. His *peons* were about him; they moved their bodies to the rhythm of the melody, they snapped their fingers and smiled at her with the whitest teeth and stomped the dust with their feet. Karin's hand went to her throat. Between her fingers she felt the little twisted bunch of paper flowers she was given to wear tonight as the last meager concession to the vanity of youth before she would be married tomorrow and put out of sight and dead and forgotten forever.

"Let's dance," said Karin blindly, putting both arms around the bridegroom's neck. "Just once, dear. Just once. Please. Just once?"

Walter put an uncertain hand to her back. She tried to move to the melody, never having danced before, yet feeling in her very blood that she could dance as well as any girl if only her heart were not so leaden in her chest. Half-turning, she caught sight of Ohm Jasch, whose cheeks had discolored to purple with anger and zeal. She saw him come forward limping, she felt him put onto her satiny wedding sleeve a hand hard with self-righteousness, she felt him look her straight into the eyes and say loudly and for the farthest wedding guest to hear: "And didn't John the Baptist lose his head because of dancing?" She could see now that Katya, by the door, was weeping. "Have you forgotten the punishment that was visited on the Israelites for dancing around the Golden Calf? How dare you have a wedding according to worldly customs! Are you going to behave like a heathen on this important day of yours?"

Karin yanked free of his hand, turned on her heels, and ran. She reached the gate, feeling her wedding dress catch on the barbed wire and rip along her thigh from seam to seam. The feel and the sound of the tearing material gave her a piercing satisfaction. She ran along, blinded by tears, stumbling, weeping, convulsed by fury and pain. She heard herself sob in the grip of a hurt such as she had never before felt in her life. And yet, in between sobs that all but strangled her, between curses and muttered words of blasphemy and wails of rage and grief, in the midst of all her confusion, she could not help thinking: "If exit I must, I might as well exit in style!" She should tear off her veil and stomp on it, grind it in the mud, yes sir! She was in such agony that she was hot with revenge. She heard a horse behind her and ran faster. She was forced to stop when it blocked her way, but she could still grip its reins and yank at them and say under her breath:

"Let go of me, Walter! You fool! Let go of me, let go of me, let go!"

She felt herself held tightly against a man's broad chest. She felt the smell of tobacco and wine; she felt a heartbeat that was strong and commanding through an embroidered Paraguayan shirt. "Carlitos?" she asked. "Carlitos. Carlitos. Carlitos." Her wet lashes stuck to his cheek. She whispered his name, over and over; there was no way to stop. He carefully wrapped his poncho around her shaking, heaving, trembling body. He stood, tall and silent, holding her without the slightest hesitation until her voice died away. There was such comfort in a native's poncho. It served so many uses. One could wear it as an overcoat on wet and rainy days. One could roll it into a pillow for a glorious night beneath the stars. One could hang it in front of a door to keep the nosy chickens out. One could spread it over the grass on an early Sunday morning to read a worldly magazine if one felt so inclined . . .

"Let's go," said Carlitos, softly.

One could even wipe one's nose with a poncho! Karin took the fringed edge and demonstratively wiped away her tears. This was romance, was it not? With great determination she lifted her face to be kissed.

_____

On the horizon, the outline of the bush vibrated in the sun. The chickens in the *estancia* yard moved dizzily, with widespread wings, beaks gaping, giving way now and then to croaking, drunken sounds.

"A killer sun," observed Carlitos, swinging in the hammock. "A dangerous day. Too dangerous to walk a single step. The Indians will complain of scorched soles tonight. A day good for nothing. Good for nothing, my heart, but slow, sweet love." He reached backwards for Karin's hand without looking at her fully. "Are you all right? Are you hungry? You haven't eaten anything since last night."

"It is too hot to eat," said Karin.

Preoccupied, she stroked the back of his head. It was natural to blame the heat outside, but it was not the heat alone that took her appetite away. At breakfast today, she had matter-of-factly folded her hands, as she had done at the sight of food on a plate ever since she was large enough to rest her arms on Oma's knees. It was a habitual gesture. But just as she had bent her head, she had caught the look of amazement on her lover's handsome face. It had been enough to make her push her plate away.

She bit her lip in vexation. She felt uncertain as to how she was now to go about swallowing her food without the time-hallowed ritual of thanksgiving to the Lord and Provider. This was an unexpected complication. It did not seem right, somehow, to take advantage of certain privileges that had been hers for the asking before. Grace had meant precious little as long as access to ritual was within easy reach. She knew full well that on thoughtless days it sufficed to mutter a few vague words of appreciation into one's lap, without much concern as to whether such mumbling was duly registered in heavenly regions. On special occasions, to be sure, she had savored the prayers that

307

were audibly spoken, slowly and weightily, in deepest heartfelt reverence for the miracle of plentiful provision. The point was, she was now forced to admit, that a guiding principle had to be acknowledged in some way. It had to be done somehow, that much was clear. But how?

"Preciosa," Carlitos whispered, pulling her down into his arms.

He was shirtless; she could feel his shoulderblades beneath the palms of her hands. It was an odd sensation, evoking a feeling strangely drowsy, yet keenly familiar now and exquisitely sharp. His skin was brown and warm. She pressed her lips to his collarbone, feeling wave after pulsating wave surge through her veins.

"It is too hot to eat," she repeated, swallowing hard.

He began to kiss her, and through her body surged a sweet glowing current. He kissed her expertly, his lips bruising hers, his teeth biting her lightly, his strong, demanding tongue pushed against her lips. There was a blissful feeling within her now that reached into the very tips of her fingers and toes. Over his shoulder she saw that the orange trees outside, usually resistant to the tropical heat, had been curled to almost half their size by gust after gust of a searing north wind that suddenly began to blow.

She knew of no one who made love in broad daylight. She must surely have taken leave of her senses! She felt sucked along a powerful river, drawn by a potent, irresistible force. Dimly she was aware of a sacrifice that went beyond her body, beyond this man, beyond her own entire life. Carlitos, as a matter of fact, had precious little to do with what was happening to her now. She looked into his tense face, hoping for something to steady her. But it held nothing beyond the urgency of the moment.

"Do you love me?" she asked, desperately.

"Of course." His voice was very suave.

"What about your wife?"

"What about her?" asked he. "Need she ever know?"

She thought this over carefully. After a while, she said:

"I would like to go home now, Carlitos, to get my

belongings." She would ride through the village with her head held high, past every single house, past every closed shutter. She would walk into the kitchen where her family would be, and she would look straight into their eyes and would say with as much casual assurance and calm as she could muster:

"I need to take my clothes and my shoes. And a towel or two to last me until I go to the city to live with my man." She would ride out of the village at his side, and she would never once look back.

Carlitos brushed the hair out of her eyes.

"You need a comb."

"I know," she smiled. "Where can I find one?"

"You can't," he said.

"Why not?"

"I have no comb."

"You can't be serious."

"Oh, but I am." There was a tiny hint of malice in his voice. "Go home the way you are, *mi corazon*. Go tell them."

She looked about in panic. How could she go back, with her hair in tangles, with her nails unscrubbed and her teeth unbrushed and sin written all across her flushed face?

The hounds roared to life beneath the trees.

"Go see who it is, Carlitos," she said. "Who would come to visit at this time of the day?" Only a stranger, ignorant of the cruelty of the midday sun now glaring outside, would take such foolish risk.

"It's your grandmother," called Carlitos from behind the screen. "It's Dona Catalina."

"Oma!" Karin exclaimed, jumping up.

Katya's face was livid despite the heat. She stood and looked about and did not say a word. Her eyes took in the room with all its careless disorder—the blankets on the floor, the dishes in the corner with bits of food from last night, the mud-crusted fringes of the poncho which hung on the post by the door, the tipped-over cow-horn filled with stale *terere*. Katya was trembling from the impact of an insult to her meticulous Mennonite sense of

309

order that went beyond all the words she could have mustered. Her hands hung by her sides. She stood and stared until Karin could stand it no longer and stammered:

"Would you like to co . . . come in? And sit down?"

Katya said with an effort:

"What I came here to say, I can say standing."

Her lids were swollen from the tears of last night. She said with difficulty:

"Karin! Karin, my dear child. When two rivers, each having its own predestined path, unite with each other contrary to God's will, destruction will follow for many years to come, for the course of their current will change forever." She breathed in shallow gasps: "There may be people who will say: 'I don't know, and I don't care.' But you are not one of them, Karin, and you know it, and I know it, and our God Almighty knows it, too." She wiped the perspiration off her forehead. "I never told you before, but the time has come to tell you now why there's this turbulence in you that causes you to go astray . . . If you come back with me, I will tell you the story you should have heard long ago, the story that will make you understand that you have sprung from two worlds, and that forever two worlds will try to tempt you. For there's a depth to the root of your life that will put an obligation on you and will not permit you to say: 'I want my happiness and nothing else.' For happiness cannot be had at your price, Karin."

"I don't want to hear the story about Russia," said Karin.

"You and I," continued Katya, as if she hadn't heard, "come from a people whose history is covered with the blood of the martyrs. We have been eternal wanderers upon this earth for conscience's sake, and we have gone from country to country searching for a place where we could worship and teach as our conscience dictated."

"That's hardly news to me," cried Karin, now giving way fully to her own pain. "I have heard you say that before. Many, many times, Oma! I don't feel these goods to be my own. How could they be my own? Who has ever taught me in ways that I

310

could understand? Where are the teachers that could have taught me right? Your story means nothing to me. Russia means nothing to me. Germany means nothing to me, for that matter, except hunger and cold and death and some other memories I would just as soon forget. Listen to me carefully, Oma dear! I have chosen my own life, for I am now of age."

"Do you really have the heart to violate the principles for which so many suffered and died?" Where were the words to tell of this chain of painful destinies, one after another, interwoven through decades, and stretching to the boundaries of this earth? She searched for words of greatest impact, and she did what Mennonite generations before her had done. She groped for an awkward High German: "Is it not clearly written in Matthew five, verse . . . " and had to fall silent before the icy resentment in Karin's young face.

Karin said harshly:

"I have my own life to live. You may have sought escape and isolation from the world as a means of preserving that which has value to you. But Oma! It has no value for me at all! You and your people have founded islands in the middle of a country that is different, and among customs that are different, and among other people who are very, very different indeed. And there you sit and . . . "

"We are to have no fellowship with the world."

" . . . there you sit and remember the old homes that you left and the life that you left and you turn your face away and think that only that is good which is old and proven and tried. Maybe it is, Oma, but I cannot be sure." She swallowed. "Your faith looks all but dead to me. Can't you feel the internal wrestlings and endless quarrels and never-ending gossip and petty splits and conflicts over less than nothing at all? There is a need in me for ideals and ideas worth living! A need so compelling it all but chokes me to death! Did you ever see how much I have suffered, and how bored I have become, and how lonely I have been, and how meaningless and senseless all your values seem to me? Can you understand at all?"

311

Katya replied quietly:

"Your words offend me to the quick. We learned from our elders, whom we respected and never would have dared to criticize. Deluded and foolish we may be, according to your modern notions, but we are an honest, devout, and sincere people who never wanted anything but to do our best for God. And by living in a colony, living with others of like mind, we draw strength from one another. Time and suffering have made customs a sacred and valuable possession . . . "

"Sacred and valuable?" cried Karin. "Sacred, how? By what authority? Mennonites lean on one another because they know they can no longer stand alone. People live in a past where there's no longer a future. You came as refugees . . . displaced people with no other choice. No other country would have you in groups and permit you to settle in closed communities. There were forces pulling you out of Europe and pushing you into the Chaco that had nothing to do with... "Where were the words to talk of the pressure of circumstances? The effort brought tears to her eyes. "Are we allowed to sing the songs that are in our hearts? Are we allowed to play the most innocent games or wear a flower in our hair or dance at our very own wedding? Are we allowed as much as an open greeting to the man we have chosen to love? What in the name of common sense *are* we allowed to do to keep from choking alive?"

Katya said slowly:

"How can it be wrong to have stood for that which is decent and right? Look at what happens if we don't! You went to the city but once, for less than a week. And look at what heartbreak has come of such yielding. When two people meet who are so alien to each other as you and this native are, there's nothing but fleshly desire . . . "

"It is more than that," said Karin, helplessly. "If only you could understand."

"No, it is not. As sure as the sun stands in the sky. Karin, child! Don't you see your precious heritage? Would this . . . this Paraguayan here ever respond to the invitation of a disciplined

312

life? Strong families cannot be built where there is no common language, no common religion, no common God, no common interest in anything . . . We cannot help offending each other."

"In time, Oma," cried Karin, now very embittered, "we will have to . . . We cannot forever and ever cling to ways of doing things and believing things just because they have had meaning in Russia! There is more to life than that. I am only now beginning to realize how much more there is to life than what I have known. Carlitos says life should be leisure. Carlitos believes that occasional work is justified only in order to make leisure possible. But he says we glorify the virtues of work while life passes us by."

"Life is for work," said Katya. "Child, will you please open your eyes? How dare you live like this? In an unswept room, with unmade beds, with your wedding dress soiled and ripped?"

How could one be steadfast before such grief as that in her grandmother's eyes? Oma was right, of course. Oma had always been right. As far as she, Karin, could remember, Oma had been right with a saintliness before which no other will could have even a timid, humble, prudent existence of its own. But there was a flaw in such righteousness, if only she, Karin, could put her finger on the flaw and stand proud and declare: "It is here, Oma, where a wrong has been done." She looked for help to Carlitos, wondering if he knew enough Low German to have understood, and she saw him smile at her with a waiting, tentative smile. It made her wonder, in sudden sharp pain, how loneliness could still have such a hold on her when she had so clearly chosen her own independent direction.

"Sit down, Oma," she said, suddenly utterly spent. "There must be reconciliation." Surely if one took time, if one chose words to say most carefully those things in need of careful explaining, there would be found a resolution of some sort. "Rest a little, dear. I will get you a cup of coffee, and we will both calm down. All right?"

"Well, no," said Katya. "But thank you just the same."

Karin saw her shoulders heave and hardened her heart. But

an issue too compelling to be compromised was at stake here, and so she only said:

"In that case, Oma dear, Carlitos will harness the horses and take you home through the camp."

"*Ein Hiesiger* to ride with me?" cried Katya, scornfully. "Whatever would my people think!"

Carlitos rose smoothly, reaching up past Katya's back to take from the wall a gaudy straw hat such as the heathen wear when frolicking in gluttony. With a half-teasing, half-taunting smile, he placed it firmly on top of her head.

"It is very hot outside, Dona Catalina. You should not walk without a hat."

Katya took the offensive object from her hair with both of her hands and flung it in a corner, turning her back to him without a further word. It was a gesture of utter contempt that sent the heat to Karin's face. Only once did Katya have to grope for support. As she reached the gate, the camp before her eyes—trees, bushes, grasses, and all—was spinning wildly as if on a giant disc. But she steadied herself with firm resolution and walked on doggedly, her bent shadow but a shrunken blotch beneath her feet.

13

Many would think it symbolic that Katya's life, having proceeded so slowly through darkness untold, should end rather swiftly and sharply amid the blaze of the hottest hour of a Chaco January afternoon. The Lord's cogent seal, it could be seen once again, was set firmly at the end of a fragile existence. Karin was later informed that Oma had come home in somewhat of a daze, staggering a little as she reached for the door, asking in passing that voices be kept low and window shutters be closed, since the merciless bolts from the sky were painfully stinging her eyes. She had let herself be eased onto the bed to rest—"for just a little

314

while," she had explained apologetically, since the food for the day was not yet prepared. Lily Marlene had hurriedly pushed a pillow beneath her head, and Sara had run to soak a towel in vinegar and cool water. Ohm Jasch, eager for salient specifics of her morning encounter, had lingered by her bed for a while, but Katya had been impatient and had motioned him away with her hand. Only Walter had been permitted to stay with her in the darkened room.

She had talked to Walter at length—in a long, slowly weakening monologue. All that a faithful soul could do, she had explained in a whisper, was to lay down firm rules of conduct for one's brief life, and then follow these rules accordingly. Every bit and tinsel of her life, she told him, eyes closed, had been planned and executed toward this end—to follow the unerring voice of her conscience.

He had nodded reassuringly, glad to see the tension leave her face. He had listened patiently to the familiar, impeccable theme and had held her hand, feeling in his very fingertips the days' minutes diminish. Then, when he had thought her asleep and tried to leave, she had turned to him fiercely and had asked for Ohm Jasch in sudden distress, to give him the urgent instruction:

"Go get the foolish child. Right now! And hurry!"

But when Karin arrived—shaken for once—it was for Walter to meet her by the gate, put his arms around her back, and put his head to her shoulder.

"Called Home by Our Lord," the *Voice of Peace* would proclaim the following fall, for it still took more than a season for sorrowful news to reach the Canadian brethren and return to the Chaco in print. The familiar story of old Oma Katya would briefly rekindle for a few weeks the speculations about the details that had put a stop to her persevering, unfaltering heart. Some would insist that the blame must clearly be laid on the sight of a native's insolent hand on a Mennonite girl. Others would be convinced that Katya had succumbed to the aftershocks of the ill-fated wedding. Still others, more kindly

315

perhaps, would recall the grievous burdens of Katya's long life, the weight of which must have borne down on her age-weary mind. But most would agree that it was Karin—this strange, intense, dissatisfied soul—who should now stand accused forever.

All this Karin knew, and more. Ohm Jasch had said as much when he reminded the mourning *Gemeend*—tears of true grief streaming down his own old withered face—that by the death of loved ones, the living should be warned.

Afterwards, Karin was overheard to say to Ohm Jasch in a voice constricted from isolation that if one valued the search for the truth for once in one's life, one would have to decide that Oma had died from a lack of a sensible protection against God's very own murderous sun, and that therefore . . .

"Shut up, Karin," Ohm Jasch had replied curtly, no longer seeing any need for mincing words.

"She wouldn't listen," Karin had cried, choked, grasping the mourning Ohm Jasch by his sleeve. "You know how stubborn she could be! She knew better than to walk back through the camp at noontime, all by herself, without a cover on her head . . . I asked her to wait! But she wouldn't . . . wouldn't even sit down for a minute in a Paraguayan's home. You know how she felt about *Hiesige* . . . "

"She's dead, the elder Jasch Kovalsky was heard to reply. "Now leave her in peace, Karin. Just for once in your life, hold your tongue."

Thus, Karin was muted for good, it was noted with grim satisfaction.

All this, somehow, now had to be put into focus. Karin struggled valiantly to get a sane grip on this latest of life's incomprehensible riddles. She and Walter had been in the saddle since early dawn, absorbed by the enormity of what had happened in less than three days' time when finally, for all to see, the Devil had won over Karin. The last riverboat was due to leave in a few days; they would have to hurry to reach it in time. The river was said to be shrinking rapidly. The water level, dependent upon the torrents of Brazil, was the lowest in a century. The horses' hoofs were hard on the ground. The water holes in the camp had virtually disappeared; the cattle, they saw, were rampant with thirst.

"She's dead," said Walter, too, as if by wounding her he could somehow ease his own grief.

His young, stern face was grey despite the last, softening light, hardened by a relentless bitterness. She could not bear to look into his face. She stared at the hands which held the reins— were those the hands of a friend who had been part of her life as far back as she could remember? Those were the hands of a man adhering firmly to a straight-laced, virtuous cruelty—knotty hands, big hands, with ugly hard nails, full of knuckles, quite capable of causing hurt. She kept staring at those hands, trying in vain to recall that once she had felt them in her own and had thought the sensation pleasant. How could she have been so mistaken as to think these hands could give her comfort in times when comfort was needed?

But Karin, being Karin, tried to put her feelings into words. Anything was bearable, she knew from past experience, if there were words to go with searing feelings. The day had been unbearably hot. Her tongue was parched against the roof of her mouth, her eyes bloodshot from the glare of the sun, her lips cracked as if from a violent fever now broken. But now the sun had departed; there was some relief from the sky.

"Walter," she pleaded, moving her horse in his path.

"What is it that drives you?" he asked. "If only I understood that much."

She shook her head. In her ears she felt the pressure mounting. How could she express in an hour the hurt that had taken a lifetime to grow, that had crept up on her and eaten away at her and had burrowed its barbs into her innermost being? The dust rose under the horses' hoofs. The wind bent the grasses. Words were too feeble at a time like this. A hand had come over her life and had silenced her before she could speak, and she had struggled against that hand. That was all she had

317

done. No less, it was true, but no more! She tried to tell him how she had fought against having what was best in her branded as inherently unworthy, how she had longed to touch the heartbeat of life with passionate, sensitive fingers so as to be allured and intrigued, and how, almost accidentally, there had been, within her reach, the warm, brown skin of Carlitos. But she had no words to express her feelings concisely, and so she told him shyly, thus expressing as best she could her craving for a life hugely lived:

"I wanted to balance a water jar on my head, the way the Paraguayan women do, and feel myself capable of walking freely and gracefully."

She searched his eyes intently. Did he understand? But how could he understand, this serious, taciturn, unimaginative Mennonite youth, who had never understood her even in their closest moments, who groped with that which was concrete, and who now told her sadly, as she had known he would do:

"It is a sin to think of one's heritage as a bondage to be shaken off at will."

She stammered out incoherent bits and pieces of her hurt:

" . . . On our wedding day when . . . when I tried to shed the chains I didn't even understand, when I thought that perhaps with you . . . this thing within me snapped. And your father . . . " She swallowed hard, taking her courage in both of her hands. "...Why, just tell me this, why should everyone knuckle under his rule, just because he is an elder of the church, without protest, without the slightest hesitation, without a flicker of resentment, without for one moment even realizing the preposterousness of it all! Just tell me! I don't understand! Why did it not occur to anyone—Ohm Jasch could just . . . "

"Yes," said Walter. "That was quite a show you put on, and what grief and shame your conduct brought to us all."

" . . . And then I ran away believing . . . But it didn't help. Carlitos did not help. Carlitos only made it worse, even though looking back now, I know that I could not have helped myself. It was beyond my control."

"What are you talking about?"

"I don't know. Isn't that . . . isn't that ironic? I only know that I have reached the limits of what I can bear. I am drowning, Walter. I think schools could help. Good teachers could help. Books could help. If I count generously, perhaps in my entire life I have read some twenty books. That's less than a book per year of my life . . ."

"There is such a thing as disagreeable knowledge," said Walter quietly.

" . . . Listen to me! Less than a book per year! I have had to live with an inner poverty so devastating that I doubt I can ever truly recover. I don't know if I can find the answer for myself. Once, I think, I came close. Once, my dearest friend Kurt Hartmann spoke to me of . . . he said something to the effect that one too base to read a book would be too weak and stagnant to guard man's most precious possession." Recklessly she reached into the innermost niches of her soul, struggling for words to label the compromises, the self-deceptions, the meaningless daily complacencies, the horrid choking trifles, the many unnamable despairs that had marred so much of her vulnerable youth, telling Walter—no, telling herself!—of her fight against the surrender of independent, joyous, fruitful living:

"It surely must be better for a soul," she cried emphatically, "to see things clearly as they are than to be ignorant of truth and mistakenly think oneself blessed!"

She bent over to him; she took his reins away from him so that he had no choice but look her full in the face: "How could it have been wrong for me to long for that pulse beat at my fingertips?"

Walter said wearily:

"Aunt Katya, though she never finished a book in her life, was one of the sturdiest people that lived on this earth. She had more than her share of storms. But did that make her rootless? The more she was shaken by outward winds, the tighter her roots were forced to cling to the soil of her deep inner faith. The currents of her life, though turbulent, carried her into the harbor which is Jesus Christ. She but needed to keep her sails straight and to keep her eyes on her goal. Her teachings, though simple, served her well."

"You speak in parables," she said, angrily. "In Bible quotes. Have you no words of your own?"

He leaned back haughtily, feeling quite spent. He was not a man of many words. Why should he care, at this point, about another one of Karin's impassioned accusations? He did not in the least feel hampered. He missed no language. He, for one, had long ago come to appreciate the merits of efficient, timely silence. It was the most expedient weapon that he knew of to keep abreast of Karin's fervor—this crazy, insatiable girl who had more words at her command than he would ever want to master. What theatrical, upsetting nonsense she would always speak! She had never learned how to be silent, when to leave well enough alone, how to let go. And nothing but heartbreak had come of such pushing. Even now, even at this very minute while he was straining to compose himself for the very painful hour of departure, she had to keep on:

" . . . there was a richness within Oma put there by times of plenty in her youth. But there's a hunger left in me that she could never see or comprehend . . . " She had to block his path; she had to hold onto his horse, forcing him thus into an emotional quicksand most repulsive to a man striving hard for inner constancy: " . . . Look at me! My grandmother, dear woman that she was, would close her eyes and ears and heart to any inner torment not her own!"

"I hope you find your peace," said Walter, not knowing what else to say.

She let go of the reins.

He said, after a long pause:

"What will you do?"

"There is Kurt Hartmann," said Karin, very softly now. "He will help me find the German Embassy, where I will say if anyone will listen: 'I was born in Russia, but so help me, I am

320

German, after all. A birthright has been sold for a mess of pottage. I want it back, for it is mine.'"

"You speak in Bible quotes, too," said Walter with a tight, weary smile.

"I know." Delayed tears, suddenly, welled up in her eyes and took away some of the burning sensation. "That's what I struggled to say all along."

"I almost forgot," said Walter, digging awkwardly in his pockets. "There is a letter here. From Russia. It came today, addressed to your . . . to Aunt Katya."

"From Russia?" she asked, incredulously.

Never in her entire life had she known of anyone receiving a letter from Russia. Russia was unreal; a ghost from the past good for nothing but to haunt and torment. And as far as she was concerned, Russia was now done with, put out of sight, forgotten already! The letter felt alien in her hand; she recoiled from it as if it had the power to reach out for her again, to drag her into imprisonment once more.

"Who sent it?"

"A non-Mennonite," said Walter, indifferently. "Someone by the name of Kamarov."

"I have no idea who that could be."

What did it truly matter? She ripped the letter in half, fiercely, crumbling the pieces into a ball, flinging them far away into the darkness. Who cared about what someone in Russia had written? Now that it was totally dark, could she not permit herself to weep? She bent over her horse's neck. She wept in utter exhaustion, but with a definite sense of relief. She, too, had loved Oma, but Oma was gone, and a sorrowful freedom had come with the parting. The searing emotions of the past days had had a purging effect, leaving a vacuum in her mind, ready to be flooded with the soothing balm of new perceptions. Already she could feel it happening, this inner resurrection. Already it was possible for her to call once more to life her dearest, dearest Oma—the quiet, high-cheeked face, the soft white hair, the wrinkled hands that held the Bible securely. Karin was not surprised at all that the thought of Katya, now as before, carried considerable consolation. Oma's deep faith, she began to comprehend at this very precious minute, was like air—a necessary condition to maintain life once begun, but not sufficient in itself to call forth a new, fertile, bountiful life such as she, Katya's grandchild, was craving. A new ingredient was needed. She had always believed it enough to understand the compelling mysteries woven in from the past, still so forcefully controlling the present and dictating the future. But now, propelled forward by the shock of what had occurred, she realized that in addition to understanding, there was a clear duty to act. But Oma certainly would not have agreed that one should want an earthly life thus fashioned by one's own purposeful, intelligent ambition. Oma, of course, would have frowned.

However, there was no need, not really, to grieve about Oma, who was now safe and secure in the hands of her Lord. Oma Katya, whose ancestors had claimed more than their share of this earth, would assuredly lay claim to the heavens as well. Karin wept harder, glad for the darkness, shaken by sheer, blessed relief at this comforting thought. There was regret, to be sure, sharp, piercing regret, for the harsh, hurtful words she had spoken. But there was also this clear, lucid knowledge, deep down in her heart, that Katya was now at peace, put to respectful repose beneath the shade of the dark *paraiso* trees that Karin and Walter had lovingly planted as children, in a most proper, revered, most cherished location. Karin saw vividly God's very own Acre, well fenced, meticulously maintained, flooded seasonally with the scents and the sounds of the receding Chaco bush. There, to the right of the wide, clean-raked road that cut with dart-like precision straight into the heart of a wilderness now tamed, Katya's solemn journey had come to an end, in the very midst of a huge tract of dry, fissured land she herself had helped christen Neuland. New land it was, Mennonite farmland, the staunch weed-free cornerstone of a determined triangle on Paraguay's vacant map, there for everyone to see: southeast of Fernheim, faraway home,

322

southwest of Menno, first pioneer settlement named in reverence after a zealous Netherland monk whose fervor, four centuries ago, had paled the fires of the German Reformation.

THE END